I0831684

SENSING DECOLONIAL AESTHETICS IN LATIN AMERICAN ARTS

SENSING DECOLONIAL AESTHETICS IN LATIN AMERICAN ARTS

JUAN G. RAMOS

University of Florida Press
Gainesville

Printed in the United States of America on acid-free paper

This book may be available in an electronic edition.

23 22 21 20 19 18 6 5 4 3 2 1

Library of Congress Cataloging-in-Publication Data
Names: Ramos, Juan G., author.
Title: Sensing decolonial aesthetics in Latin American arts / Juan G. Ramos.
Description: Gainesville : University of Florida Press, 2018. | Includes bibliographical references and index.
Identifiers: LCCN 2017032198 | ISBN 9781683400240 (cloth : alk. paper)
Subjects: LCSH: Counterculture—Latin America. | Decolonization in art. | Decolonization in literature. | Aesthetics, Latin American.
Classification: LCC HM647 .R36 2017 | DDC 306/.1—dc23
LC record available at https://lccn.loc.gov/2017032198

UF PRESS
UNIVERSITY OF FLORIDA

University of Florida Press
15 Northwest 15th Street
Gainesville, FL 32611-2079
http://upress.ufl.edu

To Ruth, Virginia, Tito, Azu, and J.S.

CONTENTS

ACKNOWLEDGMENTS

Completing this book would not have been possible without the initial support and motivation of David Lenson, Edwin Gentzler, Jose N. Ornelas, and Angel Rivera. As the manuscript took on new directions, I was extremely fortunate to have the intellectual and moral support of Antonia Carcelén-Estrada, Tara Daly, and Sara Ceroni. Thank you for your encouraging words and patience along the way. At the College of the Holy Cross, my colleagues in the Department of Spanish have been very supportive throughout the entire publication process, particularly Isabel Álvarez-Borland, Cynthia Stone, John Cull, and my two department chairs, Estrella Cibreiro-Couce and Daniel Frost. Working on revisions of the manuscript would not have been possible without the institutional support of the Robert L. Ardizzone ('63) Fund for Junior Faculty Excellence and the Research and Publication Award, both from the College of the Holy Cross. I would also like to express my gratitude to Margaret Freije, Provost and Dean of the College, for her constant support.

At the University of Florida Press, I would like to thank my editors Stephanye Hunter and Erika Stevens for believing in this project and for guiding me through the entire publication process. I also would like to extend my words of gratitude to the rest of the production and marketing staff at the University of Florida Press. Without the advice and recommendations of my two anonymous reviewers, this manuscript would not be in its current form. Thank you for your insightful comments.

Sections of chapter 2 appeared in a very different form in the article "Utopian Thinking in Verse: Temporality and Poetic Imaginary in the Poetry of Nicanor Parra, Mario Benedetti, and Roque Dalton," published in

Hispanófila: Ensayos de literatura 178 (2016): 185–203. I would like to express my gratitude to Juan Carlos González-Espitia, editor of *Hispanófila*, for granting me permission to reprint sections of the article. Likewise, I would like to extend my gratitude to the editors and licensing personnel who granted me permission to reprint verses, lyrics, and translations as they appear in chapters 2 and 3. I would also like to thank Juan Sebastián Kingman and Avelina Kingman for granting me permission to make use of Eduardo Kingman's painting "Músico callejero" (1956) for the book cover.

Finally, I would like to thank my family in Guayaquil, Ecuador, for their support and encouragement throughout these years of research, writing, and revising. Muchísimas gracias tía, papi y ñaños por todo su cariño incondicional y motivación. Sin esto creo que el proyecto hubiera sido más difícil de completar.

Introduction

As two key authors deeply engaged in the production, exchange, and circulation of literature produced in the context of post-1959 Latin America, Roberto Fernández Retamar and Mario Benedetti agree upon the centrality, originality, and truly unprecedented global reach of Latin American letters of this period, albeit from slightly different perspectives. Even by acknowledging the undeniable importance and contributions of authors such as José Martí, Rubén Darío, César Vallejo, Gabriela Mistral, Jorge Luis Borges, and Alejo Carpentier, among others, Fernández Retamar argued that "solo a partir de la década del sesenta puede hablarse realmente de una entrada de la literatura latinoamericana en el mundo, de su articulación orgánica con la literatura universal" [only starting in the 1960s one can really talk about Latin American literature's entry into the world, and of its organic articulation with universal literature] ("La contribución de las literaturas" 25). This might seem like an overstatement, and one might even disagree with such a claim. One ought to keep in mind, however, the context of such a rotund assertion, since Fernández Retamar read this essay at the 8th International Comparative Literature Association (ICLA) conference held in Budapest in 1976. Fernández Retamar does not make his claim lightly regarding the innovative and profound reach of the 1960s generation. In fact, he touches on the canonical names one might expect, ranging from colonial authors to the boom writers, and places them in context in Latin American letters. His point is that by the late 1950s and 1960s, there had been significant historical progression and maturity in Latin American letters that enabled a generation of writers to collaborate, exchange ideas, and shape each other's works. This generation of the 1960s also happened to be one that has been widely translated and thus widely disseminated. Fernández Retamar's argument about Latin American literature's "organic articulation" with universal or world literature is one that certainly resonates today in academic circles.[1]

Benedetti made a similar argument about the context of the 1960s in Latin American letters as one that enabled artists to develop their own voice and reach an unparalleled level of creativity. Even if there were instances in Latin American literature in which there was some measure of originality, such as in the case of *modernismo,* Benedetti makes the claim that Latin American literature before the 1960s was almost always lagging behind, imitating the fashions, techniques, and models coming primarily from Europe. It is in this context that Benedetti writes: "El escritor de América Latina ya no imita fielmente; tiene la necesaria libertad para crear, sea a partir de variaciones ajenas, sea a través de descubrimientos propios, un lenguaje afortunadamente original" [A Latin American writer no longer dutifully imitates; she/he has the necessary freedom to create a fortunately original language, whether based upon variations of foreign influences or upon his or her own discoveries] ("Subdesarrollo y letras de osadía" 32). Written in 1968, Benedetti's claim has specific resonances in the political and cultural landscape that enabled writers of this generation to produce "original" works, many of which have become landmarks of Latin American literatures.[2]

Beyond concurring upon the centrality of the 1960s generation of writers and artists in creating truly distinct works of literature emerging from various locations throughout Latin American on an unprecedented scale, perhaps a more subtle point of encounter between Fernández Retamar's and Benedetti's respective positions is their emphasis on literature as only one dimension of art. This emphasis on the divisibility or separation of the arts in the Latin American context of the 1960s is one that has always struck me as particular and assumed as the norm. Part of what *Sensing Decolonial Aesthetics in Latin American Arts* seeks to do is to bring the arts into a dialogue, rather than treating them as entirely divorced from each other. If one accepts Fernández Retamar's and Benedetti's singling out of Latin American literary and poetic production of the 1960s as that of a generation of authors that truly had a global, unprecedented reach and impact, one can also argue for the contribution of Latin American films to third-world cinema or *nueva canción* songs to the widespread appeal of folk, socially committed, and countercultural music. And yet these art forms are treated and studied in isolation, as though each form reached its worldly potential in a silo or on an island. Instead, this book aims to recast attention to these art forms as an archipelagic network of artistic contributions that collectively marked a temporal division in Latin American arts by producing artworks that sought to engage larger sections of the population, rather than just elite circles. It is this investment in seeking transparent, democratic, colloquial means of aesthetic and affective expressions that allows me to focus on just some of the most salient figures of this generation of the 1960s and their representative artworks. Certainly, there were important films before this decade, for instance, in Mexican cinema's so-called Golden Age (1930s–early 1960s). But the development of film techniques truly distinct from those of Hollywood or European cinema, and their lack of political and social engagement, are what make this cinema so different from what emerged in the 1960s. This is just one example, dealing with film. One can think of other such examples in reference to poetry or music.

My focus in this book on the generation of the 1960s and its distinctive contribution to a redefinition of the arts echoes the positions stated earlier by Fernández Retamar and Benedetti, but also those of more recent studies such as Jean Franco's *The Decline and Fall of the Lettered City* (2002), Diana Sorensen's *A Turbulent Decade Remembered* (2007), Samuel Steinberg's *Photopoetics at Tlatelolco* (2016), or Juan J. Rojo's *Revisiting the Mexican Student Movement of 1968* (2016). Where my contribution and study differ is that I will not focus on the novels from the Latin American boom or a single country, but rather on the productive intersections that might ensue if we emphasize the relations among poetry, music, and film as connected art forms. This, in short, is one of the points I make about the need to sense otherwise. Later in this introduction I will briefly engage with some key positions that have informed my framing of this project as one that focuses on the possible unity of arts by tracing threads, networks, relations among artworks, and emphasizing what Daniel Albright has called "comparative arts."

But what is the sense we give to "art"? How do we sense artworks as seemingly diverse or distinct as poetry, music, or films? A partial answer emerges when we situate these questions in the context of a thought-experiment or a hypothetical scenario that may not, in fact, be so hypothetical after all. How do our undergraduate students sense a song such as Violeta Parra's "Volver a los 17," or a poem such as Roque Dalton's "América Latina," or a film such as Tomás Gutiérrez Alea's *Memories of Underdevelopment* (1968)? What is their aesthetic and affective response to such works either in isolation (on their own) or when they are studied alongside each other in a comparative framing? At best, even if the instructor situates these works within their historical contexts and in relation to relevant secondary sources, students more often than not will see these examples as art strictly belonging to Latin America's post-Cuban Revolution era and, by extension, as tinted by the artists' socialist or communist ideologies, which infuse their artistic and aesthetic propositions. This is why there is a need to sense otherwise, particularly when confronted with works from the past that have been read or critiqued in a reductive historical, political, and ideological context. The key to recovering alternative readings of such artworks is twofold: to read such works as producers of their own aesthetic propositions (related to Badiou's concept of inaesthetics), and to bring them into dialogue with contemporary aesthetic thought. In his *Handbook of Inaesthetics,* Badiou suggests ways to redefine the relationship between philosophical aesthetics and the arts. Rather than assuming that philosophy must make art its object of study, Badiou suggests that the arts are their own producers of truths and can thus be independent and on equal ground with philosophical discourse. In my understanding of my chosen corpus of artworks, I treat them as producers of their aesthetic propositions, which collectively are foundational to an archive of what is now called decolonial aesthetics. As such, decolonial aesthetics simply names a process of undoing the hierarchical relationship between philosophy and art, as well as Eurocentric conceptions of art in relation to those artworks produced elsewhere in the world. What follows is only an option, one alternative among various possible aesthetic models seeking to resituate the importance or validity of works from the past not simply as artistic artifacts retrieved from the archive, but as things that reveal important keys to understanding contemporary cultural and artistic productions.[3]

On the Decolonial Turn toward *Aisthesis* and Sensing

As a critical project emerging from various disciplines, fields, and practices, including painting, film, philosophy, and art criticism, the notion of the decolonial has gradually appeared and gained prominence in academic scholarship, art exhibits, and installations, as well as conferences and alternative art biennials.[4] A prime example of this line of thinking comes from the introduction to an online *Social Text* Periscope issue from 2013 titled "Decolonial AestheSis: Colonial Wounds/Decolonial Healings." In this introduction, Walter Mignolo and Rolando Vázquez provide a brief account of how decolonial challenges to aesthetic thinking and practices have been gestating since 2003 in South America and the United States, and how such lines of thinking have now traveled to other parts of the world, including Asia and Central and Eastern Europe, as well as the Caucasus. As part of this intervention, Mignolo and Vázquez articulate how the decolonial emerges as an option for undoing and revealing the embedded legacies and the totalizing and normative forces that modernity/coloniality have come to mean. As is now well-known, coloniality describes the perpetuity of colonial and imperial forces and phenomena that emerged with modernity and continue today. Coloniality also references the occluded side of modernity by positioning itself as constitutive of modernity, rather than merely a derivative effect of Western Europe's global expansion since 1492. Furthermore, coloniality helps us to understand the complex grid of subjugation and domination that intersects race, gender, knowledge, being, various forms of capital, and aesthetics. In Mignolo and Vásquez's own words, "Decolonial aestheSis starts from the consciousness that the modern/colonial project has implied not only a control of the economy, the political, and knowledge, but also the control over the senses and perception" ("Decolonial AestheSis," n.p.). In this attempt to question the modes in which the senses, perception, and aesthetics have been controlled by the rhetoric of modernity and Eurocentric understanding of philosophy, a group of scholars has activated decolonial aestheSis as an alternative to dominant or normative aesthetics. On the one hand, scholars working in South America, such as Adolfo Albán Achinte or Zulma Palermo, have worked toward the "re-valuation" of popular culture and popular arts, which have been rendered "invisible or devalued by the modern-colonial order" ("Decolonial AestheSis," n.p.). A second and interrelated trajectory of decolonial aesthetics focuses on the types of arts related to contemporary artistic practices appearing in art exhibits, biennials, and other related curatorial projects that seek to give prominence to alternative artistic practices that at once deploy and articulate how the decolonial might serve to question aesthetics by becoming "a radical critique to modern, postmodern, and altermodern aestheTics" ("Decolonial AestheSis," n.p.). As Mignolo and Vázquez point out, the activation of decolonial aesthetics has the possibility of illuminating artworks, including theater, music, literature, visual arts, that would perhaps otherwise be invisible or neglected under dominant aesthetic categories.

At this juncture, it becomes important to discuss briefly and connect the decolonial turn of aesthetics in relation to some key rearticulations of aesthesis/*aisthesis* and sensing that become instrumental to *Sensing Decolonial Aesthetics*. As articulated by Mignolo, Vázquez, and others, decolonial aesthesis distinguishes and distances itself from Western European thinking as part of its own articulation, and also for its own expansion as an operation or concept that can be easily adapted and deployed in a multiplicity of geographical and cultural coordinates. And yet, in the work of Jean-Luc Nancy and Jacques Rancière, for instance, it is possible to detect engagements with a re-valorization and reconceptualization of *aisthesis*, precisely in order to update what has become an imperative for contemporary aesthetic thought, namely a direct confrontation with history and politics. Already in the 1990s, Nancy had presented in "Art, a Fragment" a reformulation of *aisthesis* in relation to fragmentary art and what he perceived to be a fragmentary and even fragmented world, despite the world's totalizing gesture under the practices and rhetoric of globalization. In this particular piece, Nancy frames *aisthesis* as implying neither "transcendence nor immanence," by which he means to zoom-in on the entangled "heterogeneous entelechy of the sensing/sensed" (128). An engagement with *aisthesis* dwells, out of necessity, on this double operation of sensing and being sensed, given their duality and entanglement as two faces of the same coin.

Aisthesis for Nancy allows for the possibility of engaging with a work of art as a thing that simultaneously senses and can be sensed. This duality or complementarity of Nancy's notion of *aisthesis* finds a useful expression for *Sensing Decolonial Aesthetics* in the following statement: "What art does is to *please*: and so it is neither a *poiesis* nor a *praxis*, but another kind of 'doing' altogether that mixes together with both of the other kinds an *aisthesis* and its double entelechy" (134). For a work of art to sense and to be sensed—and let us think of Nicanor Parra's *Poemas y antipoemas* (1954) as an example—it means that an artist is attuned to the intended audience's sensibilities and how best to connect with them, to affect them politically and sensorially. In this sense, the emergence of Parra's quintessential poetic collection is attuned to the need to update not only poetic language in Chilean and Latin American contexts alike, but also the role that poetry plays in connecting to audiences so as to shock them and produce laughter and discontent when reading rather unconventional poems and verses for the time in which they were published. Following this invitation, a discussion of Parra's poetic proposition needs to engage with other contemporary propositions so as to understand its way of connecting with and differentiating itself from what Benedetti, Roque Dalton, or Ernesto Cardenal was seeking to do, and this is discussed in chapter 2, "The Poetics of Sensing." To return to Nancy, I take his emphasis on the fragmentary nature of art as an invitation to reflect upon the possible sites of relation, the connective threads that generate new modes of sensing relations, themes, ideas, responses, and dialogues among works of art, but also between the works and their audiences without necessarily reducing or dwelling on reception as one of the predominant parameters of aesthetics. Ultimately, what we find is an invitation to think comparatively, to think relationally, rather than dwelling on the absolute singularity of the artwork and the marked divisibility of the arts.

This possibility of rethinking aesthetics as a relational or comparative practice finds its roots in Rancière's key concept of the distribution of the sensible, which he defines as "the system of self-evident facts of sense perception that simultaneously discloses the existence of something in common and the delimitations that define the respective parts and positions within it" (*Politics of Aesthetics* 7). By calling attention to the sets of operations that categorize the arts and the senses, Rancière is also drawing our attention to the sometimes subtle and unrecognizable modes in which certain sectors of the population or social actors are grouped and divided for social purposes, which have political and aesthetic repercussions. This same Rancierian system of the distribution of the sensible describes the processes by which we participate in the set of operations that allow for the clustering or grouping of certain things (art objects/works of art), while other things are kept apart. One mode in which this divisibility or distribution of the sensible becomes prevalent, for instance, is thinking of genres as categories that enable grouping, separation, and categorization. In allowing such operations of distribution to happen (grouping/separation/categorizations), what are our responsibilities and our roles as viewers, readers, consumers, and spectators in allowing such uneven distribution of the sensible? Rancière's distribution of the sensible is in itself a political gesture that creates a common ground for aesthetics and politics. But which type of aesthetics is created? And what are the ends of such politics—the aestheticization of the political or the politicization of the aesthetic?

As much as it might seem that the decolonial project of rethinking aesthetics is completely at odds with a rethinking of aesthetics from the perspective of European thought (such as Nancy or Rancière), there are some detectable common points in their respective gestures of retracing how aesthetic categories and ways of thinking about aesthetics have come to us. Mignolo, Vázquez, Achinte, and Pedro Pablo Gómez, among other Latin American decolonial scholars working to rethink alternative models to Eurocentric aesthetics, could argue that Nancy's and Rancière's respective philosophical projects only serve to instantiate a Eurocentric view of aesthetics. Indeed, one detects a lack of engagement in Nancy or Rancière with artworks that are not from Western European or North American traditions. Yet, what is useful in their respective works is exactly the implicit and subtle gestures of self-criticism wrapped up in pointing to the need to rethink Western European aesthetics to allow for engagement with art's role and effects in contemporary times. That lack of engagement with what is beyond the purview of Western Europe is an undeniable characteristic of both Nancy's and Rancière's work. Nonetheless, it is also undeniable that one could extrapolate from their examples and think of ways in which the "distribution of the sensible" or Nancy's emphasis on the separation and fragmentation of the arts can be applied to Latin America's artistic legacies. These concepts also have something to contribute to the rich and productive conversations taking place among decolonial circles of scholarship. The key distinctions between these seemingly oppositional sides of aesthetic thinking are the sites of enunciation and positionality.

In Mignolo's work, for instance, the locus of enunciation becomes a way to circumvent dealing with the rhetoric and language of representation, which is so prevalent when dealing with art.[5] By this Mignolo means that an artist can simply be an observer and someone who perpetuates the very same mechanisms and modes of rendering visible or sensible those bodies that are merely objects (as represented or representable) and not as subjects of art. As Mignolo put it in an interview, "enunciation is constituted by certain actors, languages, and categories of thoughts, beliefs, and sensing" (Gaztambide-Fernández 199). The locus of enunciation demarcates specific sites and positions in geographical, ideological, and experiential terms from which a decolonial subject, as one who engages in decolonial thinking and doing (which involves border thinking, dwelling, and other series of operations), can enunciate and render her- or himself sensible (as sensing others and being sensed). This double move that enunciation affords is relatable to the "heterogeneous entelechy of the sensing/sensed," as discussed above in relation to Nancy's rethinking of aesthetics. By focusing on this locus of enunciation, which allows the individual to find modalities of self-positioning and self-articulation, the possibility emerges for that person to find relatable, sensible bodies, other humans who have been categorized and segregated under the double-sided rhetoric of modernity/coloniality. An undoing of such categories, borders, and other forms of divisions and fragmentation connects with Rancière's notion of the distribution of the sensible. The conjoining factor among these three reframings of aesthetics is an attempt to open art beyond its narrow definitions, so that it becomes reactivated and reclaimed as one way of thinking the political in contemporary times. Another common factor is the way in which individual social actors coalesce as a community to reach a common social and political goal.

In this vein, in *Sensing Decolonial Aesthetics,* I treat artists as diverse as Roque Dalton, Mercedes Sosa, and Humberto Solás as forming a community or a generation of artists that, from the vantage point of the long decade of the 1960s, shared a number of common features in their respective attempts to challenge and undo what we now call coloniality or the distribution of the sensible. Rather than simply dismissing continental philosophy's engagement with aesthetics, I seek to bring into conversation what I am here calling decolonial aesthetics with certain strands of

European or continental aesthetics. My move is to activate continental aesthetics and confront it with a certain type of non-philosophical thinking and doing that emerges from a wide set of artists. In other words, I am interested in testing out some of the insights and limitations of continental aesthetics. I do so not with the intention of evaluating European artworks, which is more often than not the Eurocentric blind spot of authors like Rancière, Nancy, Badiou, or Agamben, but rather to bring onto equal ground the contributions that artists and philosophers can make to undoing aesthetics from a distinct Latin American perspective that intervenes and responds to Eurocentric interventions that have often sought to silence Latin American, non-philosophical ideas on aesthetics. Such a dialogue is one of the meanings I give to decolonial aesthetics.

Returning to aesthesis, as a dual mode of making and sensing artworks, it must also be related to the idea of the inseparability of the arts, which helps to frame the case studies present in *Sensing Decolonial Aesthetics*. In Daniel Albright's *Panaesthetics* (2014), he argues for the need to pursue a type of comparative arts by which he means to trace some of the legacies that have reached contemporary audiences in our fixation on separating the arts. This emphasis on the disunity of the arts is one that appears in Jean-Luc Nancy's *The Muses* (1996), which is one of the philosophical works informing Albright's approach. What I find intriguing and inviting in Albright's articulation of comparative arts, or panaesthetics, is precisely what might emerge from the interaction between a poem and a musical composition. In treating the arts not in isolation, but rather by focusing on the possible points of contact, Albright's model is one that informs the framing and elaboration of chapters 2, 3, and 4.

While this book takes as its premise the simultaneity of the senses in relation to art, any discussion of artworks enters the realm of language, and by extension, the means of conveying such a discussion is writing.[6] For instance, while a discussion of one of Violeta Parra's songs could be done entirely in terms of musical composition by employing technical musical language (notes, keys, pitch, timbres, etc.), my interest in her songs rests precisely on the sensorial interplay between her musical arrangements and lyrics, though more often than not my emphasis will be on the latter (which are primarily meant to be written and heard). A song's lyrics can be adapted to a different musical arrangement, as was the case when Francisca Valenzuela arranged Violeta's song "Run Run se fue pa'l norte," in which Valenzuela played a piano, instead of Violeta's traditional guitar accompaniment.[7] Such types of connections are part of an extended discussion in chapter 3 and this work's conclusion. This simple example becomes important to underscoring three points. First, while I emphasize a discussion of the written word over musical composition, I do so with the intention of highlighting a decolonial gesture on the part of *nueva canción* musicians. I contend that one can hear, understand, memorize, repeat, and make sense of a song's lyrics, even if one is not fully able to read or write. But to understand the formal intricacies of meter, rhyme, and versification or the intricacies of musical composition is an altogether different matter, which detracts from what I perceive to be the primary goal of *nueva canción* musicians: to reach a wide audience first and foremost through lyrics. Second, let us remember that many of the *nueva canción* musicians, including Violeta Parra, were not formally trained in music theory or composition. Instead, in Violeta's case, she was an autodidact musician who learned music through an extensive but informal (she had no academic training) ethnographic compilation of popular music, and who taught herself to play a variety of stringed and wind instruments. Third, perhaps because of my own academic training, I frame my analysis of musical compositions as accompaniments to the lyrics in which the former layer the latter with affective resonances. Furthermore, an imposition of an academic musicological study would further reiterate the coloniality of academic discourses, which displaces popular Latin American music to the reductive terrain of ethnomusicology, folklore, or world music.[8]

The primary reason for turning to this period for case studies and examples that help to illustrate decolonial aesthetics in this book project as an instance of what it might mean to sense otherwise is because literary or cultural scholarship in English focusing on the 1960s in Latin America has often neglected a comparative analysis of key figures in poetry, music, and film. Instead, Latin American literary and cultural studies scholarship has placed heavy emphasis on and given renewed attention to the Latin American boom authors, key examples of New Latin American Cinema, and other genres of artistic production of the decade, but almost always focusing on the disunity of the arts. Such studies, more often than not, still privilege the treatment of artworks in isolation (the separation of the arts for Nancy or the distribution of the sensible for Rancière) or continue to place an emphasis on the boom novels as the highlight of this period of the lettered, cosmopolitan city.[9] By focusing on key poets, filmmakers, and musicians of this period, and reading them as contributors to what I am calling decolonial aesthetics, I do not mean to claim that no artists before the 1960s engaged in decolonial gestures, albeit somewhat *avant la lettre*. After all, it is only in the last two decades that coloniality as a critical concept has gained currency and that decolonial interventions as such (in academic and non-academic contexts) have emerged as responses to various modalities of coloniality.[10] What I am seeking to do is to add possible contributors to the genealogy of what we understand as decolonial thinking today, via a type of thinking and doing that emerges from the arts. Suffice it to say that authors and artists going back to Inca Garcilaso and Guamán Poma de Ayala through to Gamaliel Churata and the recent architectural interventions of Freddy Mamani are part of a multi-art archive of decolonial interventions seeking to disrupt, undo, and challenge the coloniality of aesthetics or the coloniality of sensing.[11]

Sensing Poetry, Music, and Film Otherwise

This book's original emphasis on the 1960s had to do with looking at other modes of artistic production beyond the critical attention the novel in Latin America has had and continues to receive. Much of the research around the 1960s and early 1970s in Latin America has focused on what is known as the "boom," or on the study of antipoetry, *nueva canción*, and third cinema (sometimes placed under the broader category of New Latin American Cinema) in isolation, as though they were independent of each other. I should emphasize here that I chose not to focus on the narrative "boom," since much of the scholarship of the period and even today continues to privilege a literary approach to understanding the culture of the period. There has also been some relatively recent scholarship that has studied how the atmosphere of the Cold War shaped literature and culture in Latin America. This book could have easily been expanded so that each of the chapters on poetry, music, and film became a book in its own right. Such a move, however, would betray the perspective that *Sensing Decolonial Aesthetics* seeks to offer, which is to underscore how some poets, musicians, and filmmakers individually, relationally, and collectively contributed to new aesthetic configurations and other ways of thinking about aesthetics.

Throughout this introduction and the rest of the book, the term "decolonial" appears in a number of ways. A few words are necessary to clarify from the outset how this term differs from, while building upon, postcolonial discourses. The term *decolonial*, as I am employing it, comes from recent scholarship by Walter Mignolo, Ramón Grosfoguel, Nelson Maldonado-Torres, María Lugones, Rita Segato, and a number of other scholars working in the United States, across Latin America, and in other parts of the world.[12] In the introduction to *Globalization and the Decolonial Option* (2010), Walter Mignolo asserts that "de-coloniality names critical thoughts emerging in the colonies and ex-colonies, Jewish critical traditions in Europe, since the nineteenth century, materialized as the internal response to European formation of imperial nation-states" (1). Elsewhere in the introduction, Mignolo adds that decolonial thinking is a "particular kind of critical theory" and that the decolonial option is "a specific orientation of doing" (1). Thus, my use of the term "decolonial" follows Mignolo's lead, particularly by focusing on critical thought in theory and in the arts that has emerged from Latin America. In fact, even if at times it is implicit, my approach to writing the subsequent chapters has been informed by a decolonial way of thinking and doing.

One may wonder why there is a need to employ a decolonial critical strategy in relation to aesthetics. Part of the response comes from Rodolfo Kusch—a recently rediscovered Argentine philosopher—who argued the following: "In América [Latin America] we treat philosophy in one of two ways, an official way and a private way. From the university we learn of [the] European problematic translated philosophically. The other is an implicit way of thinking lived every day in the street or in the countryside" (1). This is to say that we should not readily dismiss European philosophical traditions simply because it is how we are trained to think academically. Instead, we need to think of alternative ways of conceptualizing and imagining how aesthetics plays itself out in relation to and also beyond Eurocentric philosophical discourses, especially in everyday scenarios and the arts. Following the work of Mignolo, Kusch, and other Latin American thinkers, I seek to draw a distinction between Eurocentric and elitist ways of thinking about aesthetics and how aesthetics can be connected to decolonial work. If decolonial thinking is preoccupied with an "undoing" and rethinking of dominant discourses and traditions, then decolonial aesthetics is my approach to reframing conventional assumptions and articulations about aesthetics.

As a continuation of some of the concepts presented in this introduction, in chapter 1, "Sensing Otherwise," I elaborate further on the return to aesthesis as it has appeared recently in both decolonial scholarship and continental philosophy. The chapter begins with a brief exploration of what it means to sense works from Latin America's cultural past, particularly from the 1960s. This exploration is then a distinction between *aisthesis* as related to some concepts that appear in the works of Rancière and Badiou and the meaning that Mignolo has given to aesthesis in line with decolonial thinking. This exploration allows me to engage with what it might mean to think about sensing in terms of relations and assemblage.

Following the theoretical possibilities that sensing otherwise and decolonial aesthetics might proffer, in chapter 2, "The Poetics of Sensing: Decolonial Verses in Antipoetry and Conversational Poetry," I focus on exploring how poetry can be used to challenge its own terms of production, reception, and consumption. I extend the category of antipoetry beyond a Chilean model, as proposed by Nicanor Parra, so that it includes alternative voices and ways of writing poetry. In doing so, one finds different gradations of antipoetry, which is to say, different levels of social critique that have as much to do with the place where such poetry is written as they do with the subjects of critiques, the conjugation of leftist political ideologies, and the procurement of a distinct poetic voice. Antipoetry, then, refers to a mode of writing poetry that goes against poetic conventions, challenges canonical poets, and seeks to make poetry more accessible to the everyday reader, but also takes an interest in addressing more urgent social concerns. To use Mario Benedetti's concept of the poet as communicator, such poets are guerilla fighters, engage with liberation theology and various strands of Marxism, and work as journalists, editors, and professors; some are persecuted into exile, assassinated, or ostracized by canonical poets and critics. In this chapter, decolonial readings of select poetry by Nicanor Parra, Mario Benedetti, Ernesto Cardenal, and Roque Dalton allow me to explore how these poets moved toward colloquial and accessible poetry intended for a wide readership and underrepresented voices in the historical narratives of the region. While paying close attention to examples of their respective poetry, I also illustrate their different approaches to writing antipoetry or poetry that seeks direct communication with readers.

The relationship between Nicanor Parra and his sister, Violeta Parra, bridges chapter 2 and chapter 3, "Decolonial Sounds: Redolent Echoes of *Nueva Canción*." This chapter centers on *nueva canción* and some of the musicians in Latin America who sought to converge an interest in folklore, socially committed lyricism, and the use of autochthonous instruments and musical styles. Sometimes known as *nueva trova* (the new troubadour music), such a term is nowadays restricted to Cuban troubadours after the Cuban Revolution. Other times, such music is referred to as *canción de protesta* (song of protest), which denotes the sociopolitical dimension of certain songs, but it does not embrace other artists who were not as overtly political in their lyrics. Likewise, *la nueva canción* (new song) is often used to refer to Chilean music of this period, though the principles of the musical movement spread and had a profound impact across Latin America. The potential of the term *nueva canción* offers the possibility of including under one umbrella new troubadours, folklorists, and those who were protesting against injustices through their music. Much like the previous chapter, because of the wealth of material that can fit into this category, the music analyzed in this chapter is also highly selective. Nonetheless, this chapter presents the major voices in this movement by studying select songs by Violeta Parra, Víctor Jara, Mercedes Sosa, and Silvio Rodríguez as salient voices of a committed generation that sought radical societal changes, and whose music continues to have an appeal with newer social struggles. By exploring select examples of their songs, I argue for the relationship that sensing and decolonial aesthetics can have in our reevaluation of the work of these musicians.

The relationship between musicians of *nueva canción* and New Latin American Cinema can be seen in the early participation of Silvio Rodríguez in a group that created scores for Cuban films or Chilean musicians, such as composer Patricio Manns, who left Chile due to Pinochet's dictatorship. Violeta Parra's work also marks a transition between these two chapters by showcasing her artistic versatility in creating *arpilleras*, weavings that were once displayed at the Musée du Louvre. In chapter 4, "Decolonial Visuality and New Latin American Cinema," I situate some distinct cinematic expressions that emerged in the region around the principles of third cinema or New Latin American Cinema, which served as an umbrella term for *cinema novo*, peasant cinema, militant cinema, revolutionary cinema, and imperfect cinema, among other approaches to filmmaking in Latin America. For this chapter, I decided to discuss some of the most representative films of the period, while also underscoring aesthetic choices in the work of Fernando Solanas and Octavio Getino in their seminal film *La hora de los hornos* (1966–1968), Tomás Gutiérrez Alea's *Memorias del subdesarrollo* (1968), Humberto Solás's *Lucía* (1968) and *Cantata de Chile* (1975), and Raymundo Gleyzer's *México, la revolución congelada* (1971). In choosing these films, I wanted to present examples from fiction films and documentaries, some of which are well-known and others that have been less-studied. In this chapter, I examine the specificities of each film, while also paying close attention to each director's aesthetic propositions. The chosen films are essential in my study of national and regional preoccupations with developing new cinematic languages and depicting histories of colonialism, racialization, failed revolutions, the oppression of women, and tensions among the bourgeoisie and various labor movements.

As a way to connect the various readings deployed in the preceding chapters, in chapter 5, "Decolonial Aesthetics in Latin America," I make the case for the importance of decolonial aesthetics as a way in which to understand Latin America's relationship to aesthetic discourses, while also serving as a tool to analyze examples of antipoetry, *nueva canción*, and New Latin American Cinema. Although a decolonial approach serves as a point of departure, I provide a brief account of anticolonial and anti-imperialist discourses from intellectuals to ground the use of this approach, precisely because I seek to make a critical distinction between an anticolonial stance and a decolonial critical position. In a different section of this chapter, I lay out the connections and differences between decolonial aesthetics and the philosophy of liberation as articulated by Enrique Dussel. Of particular interest for my project is Dussel's emphasis on the need to rethink aesthetics in non-European and non-elitist terms. In a different section, I underscore the theoretical foundations and debt that decolonial aesthetics owes to Aníbal Quijano's concept of coloniality, and its connection with select thinkers from the 1950s and 1960s. Because the concept of coloniality is broken up into axes along which access to power is enacted, in the next section of chapter 5, I connect decolonial aesthetics with one of these axes, namely coloniality of knowledge. Coloniality of knowledge describes the mechanisms through which some people have access to knowledge, while others do not, as well as the types of knowledge that are deemed valid. Related to coloniality of knowledge is coloniality of being. In the next section of the chapter, I underscore the importance of thinking about the ontological problem of who can produce "valid" forms of knowledge, particularly because popular and indigenous forms of knowledge and culture have often been undervalued or dismissed in Latin America. In the last section of the chapter, I argue for decolonial aesthetics as an approach to discern the specific ways in which antipoetry, *nueva canción*, and third cinema challenged dominant ways of doing art, as well as ways of interpreting and evaluating them.

In the conclusion to this book, "Sensing the Irresolute Past in the Present," I trace the importance and relevance of some of these artists today, particularly when contemporary musicians such as Francisca Valenzuela or Los Bunkers are doing covers of Violeta Parra or Silvio Rodríguez songs, when biopics about Mercedes Sosa and Violeta Parra are appearing, or when poets like Nicanor Parra or Mario Benedetti are awarded prizes or have university buildings named after them. Technology's role is also explored as tools such as the Internet and television afford renewed attention to the works of some of these musicians, poets, and filmmakers. As I argued in the earlier chapters, antipoetry, *nueva canción*, and New Latin American Cinema were invested in seeking new and socially committed means of expression. These movements were concerned with changing the way language (in poetry, music, and film) was used and, by extension, the way in which aesthetic practices could be modified and adapted to suit the specific needs of Latin America. In other words, the main concern with all three artistic movements was the aesthetic power of language in poetry, song, and film, and seeking new directions in which to transform it, make it more accessible, give it political meaning, and define a different intended audience for it. My concluding argument here is that, contrary to what some critics may like to think, the work of these artists still holds an aesthetic and political significance for today's generation of Latin Americans and global audiences. Differently put, the past is not entirely closed down and still has a bearing in our contemporary (decolonial) aesthetic sensibilities and thus offers cross-disciplinary ways in which to sense these artworks otherwise.

Keeping in mind what each chapter sets out to do, I define four main objectives for *Sensing Decolonial Aesthetics in Latin American Arts*. The first is to rethink contributions from Latin American musicians, poets, and filmmakers in order to discern what their work can tell us about alternative modes of aesthetic thought and practice. The second is to establish relations and create a dialogue along aesthetic and ideological lines among select poets, musicians, and filmmakers with the aim of providing a larger and more nuanced picture of this vital decade's cultural history. Third, in order to articulate the aesthetic and theoretical foundations of decolonial aesthetics, I turn my attention to intellectuals with loci in philosophy, history, and the social sciences, and explore how concepts such as coloniality of power or decolonial thinking might apply to cultural and literary studies. Finally, I examine how sensing these artworks otherwise through decolonial aesthetics elicits a different look at antipoetry, *nueva canción*, and third cinema as a means of rethinking the construction of the cultural canon between 1960 and 1975, but also of seeing what these artworks can offer today, particularly given their renewed profile in Latin America.

To conclude, as I argue in the following chapters, antipoetry, *nueva canción*, and New Latin American Cinema were interested in seeking a new means of expression. These movements were concerned with changing the way language (in poetry, music, and film) was used in their artistic media. By producing artworks that were self-aware and concerned with artistic propositions, defining new directions for music, poetry, and cinema, these artists and their works allow us to understand that current interests in decolonial aesthetics in Latin America also need to be mindful of its precursors and what they have offered to contemporary articulations of aesthetics.

1

Sensing Otherwise

> The colonized intellectual, however, who strives for cultural authenticity, must recognize that national truth is first and foremost the national reality. He must press on until he reaches that place of bubbling trepidation from which knowledge will emerge.
>
> Frantz Fanon, *The Wretched of the Earth* 161

> Marginalia of a given epoque doesn't simply become its memorabilia; it might contain the kernels of the future.
>
> Svetlana Boym, *The Future of Nostalgia* 31

Sensing and thinking about the past can easily fall prey to the power of nostalgia. It is in this light that Boym's words become a critical invitation to rethink how we treat cultural texts from the past and the place we assign them within our cultural canon today. By drawing attention to "our cultural canon," the intention here is not to rekindle or rehearse debates about which texts edify a shared laundry list of cultural artifacts closely linked to ideas of mastery or an immanent quality of perfection, whether in the spheres of the literary, music, painting, or other arts.[1] Instead, in *Sensing Decolonial Aesthetics in Latin American Arts,* the interest lies in the exploration of two interrelated concerns, namely, locating the place of specific texts of antipoetry, *nueva canción,* and New Latin American Cinema, and proposing a framework through which we might sense otherwise (in other ways) artworks constituted as marginalia to Latin America's cultural canon and Western traditions. To define the marginality of an artwork is to be conscious of one's position in relation to it in temporal, ideological, affective, and aesthetic terms. For someone interested in championing the aesthetic values of artworks as canonical objects, the poetry of Roque Dalton or the music of Violeta Parra, to give two examples, were deemed as marginal in their own time, since they appealed to popular sectors of Salvadorian and Chilean populations or those aligned with the political left under the influence of Marxism. Today, they are seen as mere products of their historical and political contexts and thus assigned a place as side-notes to Latin America's larger historical and cultural narrative or regarded as minor artworks. Even if some might argue that these artists have become canonical, one might ask how often Violeta Parra's *Décimas: autobiografía en verso* (1970) or Dalton's *Taberna y otros lugares* (1969) appear as mandatory readings for doctoral exams or in poetry courses. Despite their somewhat disputable canonicity, I would argue that they are examined with a certain nostalgia, to echo Boym, for the unfulfilled promises of the 1960s. To invert Boym's phrase, the artworks that serve as the foundation for *Sensing Decolonial Aesthetics* became memorabilia due to their relative status as marginalia in their epoch and today. I am interested, however, in following the critical invitation inherent in Boym's phrase, which is to revisit artworks labeled as marginalia or memorabilia with a critical look toward the past, as a way to open new critical possibilities in the present and future.[2]

It is precisely this way of thinking about the role of the present in the making of the future that links Boym's words to Frantz Fanon's radical thinking. In the epigraph above, Fanon presents a challenge to the intellectual who intervenes in processes of cultural production in the aftermath of independence and who must ground his art by questioning the modes of artistic expression available to his craft. The artist as intellectual must be aware of the failures that await if he does not realize "he is using techniques and language borrowed from the occupier" (Fanon 160). Fanon's strategy is to establish a marked distinction between two types of colonized intellectuals. On the one hand, there is the artist as intellectual who merely succumbs to unearthing a nation's traditions without realizing that social and political struggles alter the meanings of such traditions, along with the significance of the nation's past. Here, for instance, we can think about *indigenista* or social realist authors in the first half of the twentieth century in Latin America. This same artist forgets that "modes of thought, diet, modern techniques of communication, language, and dress have dialectically reorganized the mind of people" and that such modalities of culture undergo "enormous radical transformations" (Fanon 161).

Foreign and local cultural products shape people's forms of knowledge and their ways of sensing through a dialectical relationship that erases differences and, instead, proffers products that meet the tastes of mainstream audiences and what the market wants to sell. On the other side, which we might today call the decolonial side, the artist as intellectual looks for the place from which radical change can give way to transformed knowledge, which is key to the creation of artworks that are in tune with the challenges and needs of the nation straddling its status as a postcolony and neocolony. The emphasis here is placed on seeking the most pressing issues and challenges in a given society, while intuiting the effects of these knowledges on the future. The intellectual as artist, then, must forge new knowledge from sites of turmoil and instability to continue aiming toward art that is critical, effective, communicative, and "authentic" to a nation's present concerns. For some contemporary readers, Fanon's critical challenges may seem anachronistic, and for others, they may seem resolved issues. However viewed, these challenges will serve here as a companion to the examination of select works of art, broadly conceived, emerging from Latin America in the long decade of the 1960s, precisely because thinking about the role of the artist as intellectual, as producer of culture, as someone putting forth aesthetic propositions by crafting artworks are not superseded or resolved concerns.

Fanon's propositions in the early 1960s were moving in a similar direction to Mario Benedetti's thinking in that tumultuous and key year of 1968 when Benedetti argued that rather than following modeled or preestablished paths toward artistic creativity, underdeveloped parts of the world ought to create art by taking a certain ethics of rebelliousness as its point of departure. A deep sense of social justice must accompany this ethics, but it must also display its own critical means through which places like Latin America can interpret their own history and art through their own means and in their own terms (57). Benedetti is advocating here for an ethics of rebellion that defies the uneven and interrelated structures of power—or what Aníbal Quijano decades later termed the coloniality of power—that dictate the modes of production, distribution, reception, and consumption of arts within Latin America and elsewhere in the world. The rebellious artist is concerned with engagement with a wider audience, rather than how his or her work might be received by critics who build canons ("críticos de sostén") or critics seeking to prove why certain works lack merit or value ("críticos de derrumbe") ("Subdesarrollo" 51). As such, the artist who engages with such an ethics, according to Benedetti, will be in tune with the needs and reality of his social and political milieu.

Thinking about the usefulness of striving toward cultural authenticity (Fanon) or an ethics of rebelliousness (Benedetti) in reexamining artworks from the 1960s in Latin America is partially what provides a foundation for the current project. From today's perspective, the temporal distance that separates our current attitudes toward artworks from those of the 1960s in Latin American renders them as products of what some have called a turbulent decade or as marking the decline of the lettered city.[3] Rather than returning to this decade out of a sense of nostalgia, a renewed ideological utopianism, or in the spirit of revisionist historicism, *Sensing Decolonial Aesthetics* explores how poetry, music, and cinema shed light on new ways of understanding aesthetics as a way of both thinking and doing art whose social and political engagement turns aesthetics upside down by highlighting and uncovering the hidden logic of what Rancière has called the aesthetic regime of art, which serves as a way to discern what is categorizable and "recognizable as art" (*Aesthetics and Its Discontents* 8). It is in this way that I employ decolonial aesthetics to unveil what is occluded by the primacy of aesthetics as linked to distinct legacies and trajectories of philosophical thought. *Sensing Decolonial Aesthetics* considers the ways in which non-philosophical ideas regarding aesthetics emerge from specific works of poetry, music, and cinema in Latin America during the 1960s as indirect responses to dominant and Eurocentric discourses on aesthetics. This project looks at the relationship among these works of art, rather than at works in isolation, while providing a second look at what it might mean to sense these works of art in a diffused light and through different lenses.

To be clear: this study is not about works of art examined purely from the perspective of philosophy or art history. Art here is taken to encompass forms of artistic production beyond what might be on display at a museum or a public installation, although they are not altogether excluded. Instead, *Sensing Decolonial Aesthetics* seeks to broaden what we mean by art and returns our attention to certain genres and concepts within the realm of art by examining their aesthetic contributions. Sensing otherwise can happen if we shift our perception and understanding of what aesthetics has come to mean in academic disciplines—namely, something related to ways of studying the philosophy of art or to literary studies, or simply a discourse that has established categories of taste and traditional models concerned with parameters of beauty or the sublime. To this end, decolonial aesthetics becomes a means to liberate and delink aesthetics from Western or Eurocentric concepts that have become common currency through imperial and global designs.[4]

Aesthetics, *Aisthesis*, and Sensing

Aesthetics is often invoked as both a noun and adjective, but rarely is it qualified or substantially and overtly explained. The underlying assumption is that the meaning of aesthetics is already understood or that there is shared or common history of the usage and underlying references behind the word. This is indeed the point of departure in this section, because if there is an understood lineage and history of aesthetics as a category for discussing art, its precise meanings are rooted in Enlightenment and post-Enlightenment philosophical thought, and its validity or authority is seldom questioned.

Aesthetics, as a philosophy of art, is embedded in a tradition that exhorts and explores the fine arts, while demanding from them scientific rigor. The first remarks found in Hegel's *Introductory Lectures to Aesthetics* already define a clear path to what would become of philosophy of art and how art would be conceived. Hegel announces that the focus of the series of lectures will be on aesthetics, and that their "subject is the wide *realm of the beautiful*, and, more particularly, their province is *Art*—we may restrict it, indeed, to *Fine Art*" (3, original emphasis). Hegel here is defining his usage of aesthetics by linking it to the idealized and restrictive version of what constitutes fine art. More importantly, Hegel draws a clear distinction between art at large and fine art, which is narrowly reduced to specific forms of poetry, painting, sculpture, and, to a lesser degree, to what we now understand as classical music. Part of Hegel's preference for fine arts must be contextualized in terms of how his immediate precursors and contemporaries found ideals (such as beauty or harmony) in Greek art, which later became normative ways of conceiving and delimiting the contours of valued and accepted art. In Hegel's thinking, however, there are other points that are of particular interest for *Sensing Decolonial*

Aesthetics. Toward the end of his opening remarks on his lectures, for instance, Hegel also admits to his preference for the scientific study of art under the possible names of "'Philosophy of Art,' or more definitely, the 'Philosophy of Fine Art'" (*Introductory Lectures* 3). Hegel's reticence regarding the use of aesthetics has to do with the fact that, for him, in the wake of Christian Wolff's *German Metaphysics* (1719), "'Aesthetic' means more precisely the science of sensation or feeling" (*Introductory Lectures* 3). Accepted feelings or aesthetic experiences of the late eighteenth and early nineteenth centuries were restricted to "feelings of pleasure, admiration, fear, pity, etc." (*Introductory Lectures* 3). Despite Hegel's reservations, then, how is it that the philosophy of art came to control aesthetics, understood as a sphere of sensing and knowledge, as well as doing and thinking? Part of the answer has to do precisely with the terms of engagement with aesthetics through the rigor of scientific knowledge, which sought perfection and harmony, but also sought to normalize, categorize, and define modes of sensation, perception, and feeling. Such philosophical discourses fused with *aisthesis*/aesthetics, as related to the senses, which then became the parameters by which art (fine arts) were studied and categorized.

The invocation of aesthetics in *Sensing Decolonial Aesthetics* emphasizes its original linkages with sensorial perceptions, sensorial experiences, and sensuous relationships to art. I am also thinking of sensing the arts as a return to art at large and not exclusively to a narrow relationship between aesthetics and fine arts. Some contemporary philosophers and thinkers have beckoned a shift in aesthetics by drawing attention to the set of possibilities that *aisthesis* can offer. German philosopher Wolfgang Welsch, for instance, understands *aisthesis* as "our modes of sense perception," which go beyond the long-standing privileging of sight as the sense that is most closely linked to aesthetics (182). Bringing *aisthesis* to contemporary debates around aesthetics enables other types of work around aesthetic questions by focusing on the relationships among works of art and hearing, touch, smell, and taste as possible, but not exclusive, ways of sensing. In Rancière's recent work, there is also a return to *aisthesis*, which appears as a way to bring into question the very category of art as it has been understood in the West over almost three centuries. Rancière, for instance, argues that *aisthesis* appears as a concept that elicits discussions of how "we perceive very diverse things, whether in their techniques of production or their destination, as all belonging to art. This is not a matter of the 'reception' of works of art. Rather, it concerns the sensible fabric of experience within which they are produced" (*Aisthesis* x). By turning our attentions to the conditions in which works of art are produced, rather than the way we have received them, the concept of art can be broadened beyond the narrow confines of fine art, which has been the very subject of aesthetic discussions governing sensibilities, tastes, and canons, while also defining what is worth preserving, collecting, exhibiting, admiring, studying, and critiquing. Rancière's project is useful in many ways, since it forces us to look again at the rooted linkages between *aisthesis* and aesthetics. And yet, many of the texts chosen for his study fall under the Western and Eurocentric canon. Commendable, however, is Rancière's effort to move beyond paintings and sculptures by bringing to discussion the emergence of film, decorative art, photography, fiction, poetry, and theater, among other art forms in Europe. *Sensing Decolonial Aesthetics* follows a similar move by engaging with modalities of sensing artworks, while looking at what has been left to gather dust or omitted from the archives of art.

Rancière's recentering of aesthetic questions to encompass the political has caught the attention of renowned scholars of Latin American letters. In a recent issue of the journal *Parallax,* the editor of this special issue, Silvia L. López, focused readers' attention on what Rancière's aesthetic thought might have to contribute to a rethinking of aesthetic modernity in Latin America beyond the tripartite sensorium (the visible, the audible, and the sayable). As inviting as this exercise may be, López devotes much of her attention to reviewing Rancière's work, but not to indicating how his thinking might contribute to a reformulation of Latin American aesthetics per se. This is a task that falls upon the contributors to the issue.

One such example is Bruno Bosteels's article "Global Aesthetics and Its Discontents," in which Bosteels takes issue with Rancière and works through some of the theoretical and practical limitations of concepts such as "the distribution of the sensible" or the "aesthetic regime" when confronted with "the global dynamics of center and periphery, empire and colony, North and South" (Bosteels 386). Bosteels engages with Alejo Carpentier's *The Kingdom of this World* (1949) to test the limitations of Rancierian thought due to its reliance on Western European examples, mainly from France and Germany, and to problematize a facile extension or transposition of such ideas "onto other regions or areas, perhaps even including the Third World" (386). From a brief engagement with Carpentier, Bosteels moves to a discussion of Carl Schmitt's *The Nomos of the Earth* to illustrate the geopolitical limitations and historical blind spots present in Rancière's claim to an aesthetic revolution, and further notes how "today we should rather be surprised that anyone can still present an account of processes such as the aesthetic revolution without taking into account the violent and unequal legacy of colonial expansion" (Bosteels 391). Aside from a brief engagement with Carpentier, most of the examples Bosteels provides to critique Rancière's Eurocentrism in fact come from Western Europe, namely Balzac, Mallarmé, and Huysmans, among others. Bosteels's gesture of pointing to the necessity of seriously accounting for the colonial expansion of Western Europe into other parts of the globe is certainly present in his essay. Yet, that gesture of critique does not fully materialize into more substantial engagements with the examples he provides from an array of Latin American writers spanning from Rubén Darío's first poetic phase and continuing through works by the likes of César Aira or Roberto Bolaño. Without fully endorsing his stance, I do welcome Bosteels's invitation to show the usefulness and limitations of Rancierian thought when confronted with Latin American literature throughout the following chapters.

If in my introduction I argued for the need for decolonial aesthetics to engage with Rancière's concept of "the distribution of the sensible" and Albright's beckoning to move toward "comparative arts" or "panaesthetics," I did so with the aim of opening up theoretical and practical possibilities that a return to *aisthesis* can offer for a decolonial project of rethinking and undoing pervasive aesthetic categories that not only create hierarchical and uneven frameworks, but also continue instantiating a disunity and divisibility of artistic forms. In so doing, sensing otherwise calls for the need to trace relations between artists and their aesthetic propositions insofar as they have a common project of responding to dominant Western aesthetic terms.

For instance, one could think about the relational affinities between Silvio Rodríguez's "Santiago de Chile" from his album *Días y flores* (1975) and Humberto Solás's film *Cantata de Chile* (1976), as both artworks seek to denounce and critique Pinochet's coup d'état in Chile in 1973 and its immediate aftermath. A more detailed discussion of these artworks appears in chapters 3 and 4. Suffice it to say, for now, that a conjoining factor in Rodríguez's and Solás's respective aesthetic engagements is a direct confrontation through the aesthetics of music (lyrics and sound) and film (the visual and sound) with dictatorial politics, primarily through their beckoning of resistance to Pinochet's regime. In the case of Solás, he activates an archive of moments of resistance in Chile that span from the colonial presence of the Spanish and the resistance of indigenous populations, to the mestizo and creole revolution in the nineteenth century, to a worker-led revolt against capitalist forces in the early twentieth century, and how these ultimately connect to the spirit of revolution under Allende's government. The ultimate suggestion, as I read the film, is that Chileans will once again overcome forces seeking to control and suppress their collective subjectivity, or what Rancière calls "the distribution of the sensible" in terms of organized state, police, and military mechanisms used to disperse citizens, and thus more readily control them. In a similar vein, Rodríguez's song traces moments of affective change in Santiago de Chile, which span happiness, falling in love, fear, rage, and ultimately wishing to transform song into an instrument with which to respond to Pinochet's dictatorship. I call on these two examples to illustrate how a critique of coloniality operates on the most subtle levels in art, as in the case of the figures of the early twentieth-century British investors in Solás's film, or as a direct critique of the how the U.S. facilitated Pinochet's coup. One can begin detecting a trajectory or legacy of the "distribution of the sensible" and the coloniality of power in various modalities (race, gender, capital, knowledge, aesthetics, etc.) and how the two can be productively activated as critical tools. In placing these two examples in a brief dialogue, I seek to bring into conversation Albright's model of a comparative aesthetics or panaesthetics in seeking to trace commonalities, rather than distinct differences, among artworks.

While concepts such as the decolonial are of relatively recent usage, the gestures of undoing colonial and Eurocentric legacies of control, including forms of knowledge, cultural production, and affective parameters, are by no means recent. As suggested in the introduction to this work, the genealogy of decolonial interventions, albeit avant la lettre, can be traced to figures such as El Inca Garcilaso and Guamán Poma through contemporary indigenous and Afro-descendant artists such as Freddy Mamani,

Antonio Preciado, or Chocquibtown. The emphasis on the generation of the 1960s has to do with what I perceive to be an unprecedentedly widespread interest in revisiting and challenging Eurocentric categories across various art forms in the name of finding distinct Latin American aesthetic alternatives and responses. For instance, Chilean scholar Patricio Rodríguez-Plaza accounts for some of the ways in which aesthetic questions need to respond in different ways to Latin America's social and political spheres following decades of military dictatorships. Rodríguez-Plaza also points to the need to think about these questions not only in terms of the contemporary, but also by retracing some of these concerns in the *longue-durée,* and he engages in a useful though brief dialogue with Mignolo's ideas on postoccidentalism as a key to rethinking Latin America's relationship to Western European aesthetic genealogies.[5]

Moving in a similar and yet divergent direction from Rancière's and my own, Walter D. Mignolo's recent work has turned to questions linking coloniality of knowledge to questions of aesthetics. For Mignolo, the epistemic sphere is of prime importance in what Aníbal Quijano termed the coloniality of power, in which the political, economic, and epistemic spheres converge to form axes through which various modalities of domination operate (Mignolo, "Lo nuevo y lo decolonial" 37; Quijano, "Coloniality of Power" 549). For Mignolo, the epistemic sphere serves to control modes of feeling—what constitutes knowledge—while also distinguishing between reason and modes of sensing ("Lo nuevo y lo decolonial" 37). Mignolo proposes a liberation of *aisthesis* (which he spells as *aiesthesis*) from what we understand as aesthetics by delinking modes of sensing from rules and norms (as proposed by Kant in his *Observations on the Beautiful and the Sublime* [1767]) that govern and regulate modes of feeling, thinking, and doing art ("Lo nuevo y lo decolonial" 40).

In *Sensing Decolonial Aesthetics in Latin American Arts,* delinking *aisthesis* from aesthetics also means paying attention to what has been left out of discussions pertaining to the Rancierian concept of "the distribution of the sensible," as discussed in the introduction, or to "the aesthetic regime of art" (Rancière, *Aisthesis* xii). The emphasis in the present study is on the exploration of aesthetic interventions emerging from Latin American poetry, music, and film in the 1960s. The examples chosen establish close relationships between aesthetics and politics, but also revolve around questions that seek to delimit which types of poetry, music, and film are valued and the ways in which we sense and experience such artworks. In Rancière's critical language, this divisibility and categorization of the arts is what he calls "the representative regime of art, i.e. a regime in which art in general does not exist but where there do exist criteria of identification for what the arts do, and of the appreciation for what is or is not art, for good or bad art" ("Aesthetics, Inaesthetics, Anti-aesthetics" 219). While the specific examples of poetry, music, and film are situated in countries such as Argentina, Chile, and Cuba, or Uruguay, El Salvador, and Nicaragua, these artworks are also invested in exploring linkages that go beyond the geographical and political borders of said countries. Quite often, in fact, artists such as Mario Benedetti, Mercedes Sosa, or Humberto Solás created art that was deeply in tune with their national realities, to echo Fanon's and Benedetti's ideas highlighted in the opening of this chapter. Yet, their artworks had a way of making people feel the urgency of art beyond national borders. In many instances, the artworks studied here had profound aesthetic repercussions at a transnational level in Latin America.

Sensing and Decolonial Aesthetics

Decolonial aesthetics does not want to become an alternative philosophical model, nor is it intended to supersede the philosophical project around aesthetics that emerged in the West, primarily in Europe. Thinking about aesthetics from a decolonial perspective is more of an option, rather than an outright rejection of modern/colonial European thought (Mignolo, *The Darker Side of Western Modernity* xv–xvi). The decolonial perspective tries to move away from theory per se and seeks to model itself on quotidian experiences of resistance to ongoing modes of subjugation. Decolonial aesthetics emerges from practice, from an investment in linking *poiesis* (as doing) to *aisthesis* (as sensing). In this vein, decolonial aesthetics is simultaneously a way of understanding decolonial thinking through artistic practice and artistic practice through decolonial thinking. Part of the claim of *Sensing Decolonial Aesthetics* is that the non-philosophical views emerging from music, poetry, and film are reflections on aesthetics, by which I mean a return to the roots of the term and what it can offer to critical thinking today. What this return to *aisthesis*, as a form of sensing or perception, forces us to do is to move away from thinking about aesthetics in relation to a pure philosophical discourse on the philosophy of art or with reflections that have to do with scientific or schematic/organized lines of thinking about the function of art and its relation to audiences. A return to *aisthesis,* as linked to the sensory or the sensuous, shows us the occluded side of aesthetics. It points us in the direction of thinking about what is left out, what has been obviated from specific articulations of aesthetics within Western modernity.

Hereafter, then, my invocation of the word aesthetics has to do with this incursion into what *aisthesis* can offer. This is why I emphasize aesthetics through practice rather than as a type of philosophical thinking. Rather than achieving ideals, rather than focusing on a dominant perception of aesthetics or thinking of a system through which aesthetics can be organized, here we are looking at ways in which decolonial aesthetics are linked to local histories, to particular ways of reflecting on the role of aesthetics/*aisthesis* in relation to social and historical conditions as interventions into cultural discourses and dynamics that have often privileged certain types of art over others. Decolonial aesthetics, then, becomes a way to return to the question of which types of art get privileged and the type of attention they receive (critical and commercial, on a local, national, regional, hemispheric, continental or global scale). These questions are taken up in a variety of ways. Of course, looking at non-philosophical propositions on aesthetics does not mean that these particular ways of thinking about aesthetics/*aisthesis* or sensing the arts, which will be hereafter termed decolonial aesthetics, exclude engagement with philosophy or theoretical thinking. I want to emphasize, instead, a type of theory that for Françoise Lionnet and Shu-mei Shih is "becoming a minor of Theory and the becoming theory of the minor" or Judith Halberstam's call for a "low theory" (Lionnet and Shih 14; Halberstam 16). To think about decolonial aesthetics as a low theory or a minor theory, which is to say as a type of theoretical thinking that distances itself from Theory, becomes a useful way to be critical of master narratives and grand theories from which aesthetics has obtained a grounded and yet disputed genealogy. Decolonial aesthetics as theory (with a lowercase initial letter) is at once an intervention in modes of practice and modes of sensing, while also having theoretical implications grounded in local histories. By making a claim for its position as a low theory or a minor theory, my intention here is not to undermine this perspective but rather purposely to avoid

Theory's legacy and its self-positioning in a central stage of discursivity and theorization. Differently put, decolonial aesthetics does not seek to be totalizing. It is actually anchored in its opposite, which is to say that decolonial aesthetics is in tune with its multiplicity, its multivalence, and allows us to view aesthetics through several lenses. *Sensing Decolonial Aesthetics* and decolonial aesthetics itself take their points of departure from the need for undisciplined thinking. If we think of decolonial aesthetics as a type of low theory, then, it "might constitute the name for a counterhegemonic form of theorizing, the theorization of alternatives within an undisciplined zone of knowledge production" (Halberstam 18). As I stated earlier, decolonial aesthetics is invested in exploring the underside, or what has been left out of the legacy of aesthetics as a discipline, and thus locates itself in an undisciplined zone that does not follow the logic and rules of dominant and long-standing articulations of aesthetics.

Ways of Sensing the Nation in Times of Postnationalism and Cosmopolitics

In recent theories germane to literary and cultural studies, the idea of the nation has been greatly resisted and heavily contested. Instead, discourses around postnationalism and cosmopolitics have become common currency in both national literature and comparative literature departments, though these concepts have also been extensively questioned. These debates, of course, are not new, but they have indeed taken on a renewed intensity in the last decade. Despite numerous attempts to announce the death of the nation-state in the face of globalization, Pheng Cheah, for instance, has argued that "Neither the nation-state nor the division of center and periphery have been superseded" (382). Instead, the figure of the ghostly or spectral nation has become a conceptual metaphor to discuss its persistent cycle of life, convalescence, death, resurgence, and haunting. Such a conceptual metaphor "is epitomized by the post-colonial nation, whose haunted life or susceptibility to a kind a death that cannot be unequivocally delimited and transcended suggests the need to reconceptualize freedom's relation to finitude" (Cheah 383). Rather, thinking about the nation as a specter or as having a ghostly dimension, sensing the nation in times when it is resisted, must take into account its contested and difficult past and its present as ways to envision the future.

In entering discussions about cosmopolitanism, we might wonder what is at stake, particularly when we think about who is allowed to enter into such global or cosmopolitan transactions of culture, modes of feeling, and politics through arts. Here we can link this question to Etienne Balibar's proposition in "Toward a Diasporic Citizen?" (2011). Part of the problem with Balibar's position on the freedom of circulation of people across national boundaries, which is inscribed in the International Declaration of Human Rights, is precisely his insistence on exploring the dimension of citizenship while losing sight of what such citizens want, and their self-determination to identify with a given demarcation of space under the rubric of the nation. It is not up to us as academics or intellectuals to make these calls. Balibar affirms that

> Each individual is supposed to have his or her own country, which refers to *membership* as well as *belonging*. I belong to the country whose membership I share with others, this is *my country* as well as *other people's country*, our shared membership makes us part of it as it also makes us its co-owners, as it were. That each of us is said to be able to change place, change nationality, change membership and belonging, "pass" from one country to another following certain procedures, does not alter this structure of belonging; on the contrary, it highlights that it is considered as the rule or norm. (210–211)

Such a position is effective in delineating the dangers of mass migration and what legal discourses have to say about it. Yet, there is no mention of the affective ties linking the migrant or the exile to the idea of nation, or what Guattari calls an "existential Territory" (102).[6] It is objects belonging to art and culture that often help create that linkage to the idea of home, a nation to which one needs to belong, even if academic and global politics and economics would like to think otherwise. This is where sensing works of art otherwise is important from the perspective of decolonial aesthetics. Art from this pivotal and turbulent decade conjures up memories, affective connections, and unprecedented consequences that are still felt today, as I suggest in the conclusion to this book. Discourses on cosmopolitics, globalization, and postnationalism more often than not lose sight of the individual and give primacy to the multitude in looking broadly at the theoretical implications of their own discourses from the perspectives of the state, corporations, and transnational actors (Balibar

223).[7] What these discourses have in common is precisely their unwillingness and inability to account for intangible categories such as sensing and feeling from the perspective of audiences, the people. Decolonial aesthetics allows for an intervention that looks at the imbricated connection between political and affective membership of people in the idea of the nation, as much as that is resisted and thought to have been superseded.

At the heart of cosmopolitics is a certain concern with transcending binaries, whether in discussions around culture or around politics, since "Most of the nations that gained freedom from colonization have tended to form around an idea of power—the totalitarian drive of a single, unique root—rather than around a fundamental relationship with the Other. Culture's self-conception was dualistic, pitting citizen against barbarian" (Glissant 14). Binaries are precisely what lay the very foundation for discussions about culture from a Latin American perspective, though these were heavily influenced by Eurocentric understandings of culture and aesthetics. When thinking about cultural production in Latin America, the binaries of the nineteenth-century distinction between civilization and barbarism as presented in Domingo Faustino Sarmiento's *Facundo* (1845) continued to have an impact well into the twentieth century. Whereas civilization was equated with following European influences, barbarism was represented as a retrograde and backward way of life, referring to peasants and people living in remote spaces with little access to education and knowledge. If ports, capitals, and major cities were the points of contact with civilization (i.e., Western European civilization), working fields, jungles, and plains were associated with the perpetual barbarism and backwardness inherent in the Americas. To move toward progress, thinkers such as Sarmiento proposed to embrace civilization fully at the expense of barbarism, which meant that to become civilized, all traces of barbarism needed to be removed. In terms of cultural production, this amounted to privileging foreign cultural imports over popular culture coming from non-educated, barbaric peoples, while also upholding aesthetics of "buen gusto" (good taste) stemming from neoclassicist and romantic aesthetic ideals.[8]

Such cultural values and mandates had a profound effect among the emerging Latin American republics during the nineteenth century, and would be taken up once again at the turn of the century in José Enrique Rodó's *Ariel* (1900). While Rodó also equated civilization with the admiration and emulation of aesthetic values coming from Western Europe, particularly France, England, and Spain, he also sought to distinguish a Latin American culture from influences coming from the United States. In this sense, Rodó simultaneously presents a Eurocentric and anti-imperialist critique that would pervade much of the next three-quarters of the twentieth century. At the same time, Rodó followed Sarmiento's earlier line of thinking by rejecting barbarism, which was now equated with ideas, values, and tastes coming from popular sectors. Whether popular thought came from the cities or the countryside did not matter. Such distinctions of aesthetic values and sensitivity were projected onto the metonymic contrast between Ariel and Caliban. Whereas Ariel represented the highest form of human sensitivity, knowledge, truth, and the enlightened human being, Caliban stood for materialist and positivist values coming from the United States, but also linked to irrationalism, base emotions, and the raw sensuality of the popular sectors of Latin America. In Rodó's attempt to instill among Latin American youth (to whom the book was dedicated) the desire to emulate European culture and values, there is also the inherent acceptance that Latin America will always remain an incomplete approximation and semblance of Europe without finding its own (autochthonous) means of expression.

Seven decades later, in that long decade of the 1960s, Roberto Fernández Retamar voiced a critical challenge to both Rodó and Sarmiento. For Fernández Retamar, Latin America's cultural ancestor is encapsulated in the symbol of Caliban, which stands for the indigenous, the mestizo, the enslaved, and the one forced to employ the master's language. While the invocation of Caliban is fitting to subvert Rodó's Eurocentric embrace of the symbol of Ariel, Fernández Retamar seems to make no distinctions among those thinkers, authors, and artists operating under the symbol of Caliban. Instead, he creates a litany of names associated with revolutionary or leftist figures (including Simón Bolívar, Toussaint-Louverture, Benito Juárez, Rubén Darío, José Carlos Mariátegui, Alejo Carpentier, Pablo Neruda, Aimé Césaire, Violeta Parra, and Frantz Fanon, among others). Likewise, Fernández Retamar follows José Martí's own rejection of Sarmiento's false dichotomy of civilization and barbarism. As Martí had noted, what exists is a tension between "false erudition and nature" (Fernández Retamar 22).

In the works of poets, filmmakers, and musicians that comprise *Sensing*

Decolonial Aesthetics, in one way or another, there is an awareness of and a reflection on such tensions and binaries. For instance, Ernesto Cardenal's poetry is indebted to his own work with liberation theology, while also being indebted to the poetic example of César Vallejo and the critical thought of José Carlos Mariátegui and Augusto César Sandino. Put differently, Cardenal finds his poetic inspiration in the indigenous peoples of Nicaragua, particularly in the remote area of Solentiname. Whereas previous poets might have gravitated toward the city or looked toward Europe for inspiration, Cardenal looks toward what was once perceived as the root of barbarism, Latin America's indigenous populations. Cardenal is only one example of the artist seeking to challenge the false dichotomies that Martí and Retamar had pointed out almost eight decades apart. After all, to reject one's own roots and dismiss them as barbaric in favor of foreign cultural models can be linked to a pervasive characteristic that has plagued Latin America, namely xenophilia. In this sense, for those seeking high or fine art exhibiting good taste, foreign cultural artifacts, especially if they come from a perceived "first" or "developed" world, are received more favorably than autochthonous cultural products. This is precisely the legacy of the coloniality of knowledge and aesthetics that has become so ingrained, naturalized, and normative that questioning a profound love and admiration for great works of art and cultural models coming from Europe is simply deemed unthinkable, unnecessary, or even heretical.

For Europe, in contrast, the question of determining its culture was never an issue. It was already assumed and accepted as the epicenter and the framework against which other cultures would be evaluated. For Latin America, of course, this meant not defining itself in terms of what it could contribute to aesthetics as a field, but rather merely defending itself as having the right to produce valuable culture and to access what Rancière calls the "aesthetic regime of art" (*Aisthesis* xii). It was not until the generation of the 1960s, perhaps because of that decade's widespread and collective work throughout the arts, that Latin America finally sought to assume its position as producer of culture without imitation or without having to look toward Europe as a model of aesthetic values. It is not that 1960s decolonial artists altogether rejected European aesthetic values, but rather that they were more interested in producing art for consumption by popular audiences of Latin America, and to communicate more effectively with popular sectors than with elite groups.[9]

Keeping in mind these tensions and perspectives surrounding questions of the nation in Latin America, as well as the role of culture, we are reminded that today

> Nationalism is one form of identification confronting the homogenizing forces of globalization. Globalization has two sides: that of the narrative of modernity and that of the logic of coloniality. Those narratives engender different responses. . . . Postnationalism in the West means the end of nationalism, while in the non-European world it means the beginning of a new era in which the concept of nationalism serves to reclaim identities as the basis of state sovereignty. (Mignolo, *The Darker Side of Western Modernity* 5)

Part of the impetus behind this study is precisely this push to think about nationalism as a tangible, affective, and political category that is closely related to modes of sensing and aesthetic sensibilities that serve to reclaim identities precisely at a moment when such identities are often subsumed under broader categories (Latin American, transnational, trans-Atlantic, global/world, etc.) that seek to erase differences and local histories, and give more weight to specific areas within area studies.

Sensing Relations

As discussed in the foregoing sections of this chapter, my interest in aesthetics lies in the possibilities of returning to sensing, the sensuous, and modes of sensibility beyond the visual and beyond works of art that appear in exhibits or installations. In fact, my take on aesthetics focuses precisely on opening up the trove of aesthetics to see what lies at its bottom. A discussion of decolonial aesthetics does not seek to set itself in opposition to European thought. After all, talking about Eurocentric categories such as aesthetics, the novel, literature, or film is inescapable, since these have been historically understood and framed from a European position. This is not say, however, that one cannot resist, reinvent, and redefine what these categories mean. In fact, I argue that this is precisely what my chosen artists have done: redefine, stretch, and contest the limits of aesthetic categories and modes of artistic practice. For the sake of clarity, allow me to state that this project is aware that aesthetics is in origin a Western invention—as a discipline, in its discourse, in its terminology, through to its very foundation in Greek and Latin. German, French, English, and other European languages become part of this lineage of Western languages preoccupied with aesthetic categories. On a basic level, it becomes almost impossible to avoid using such discourse and categories. What we can do, however, is to think about such categories in a different way and not become trapped by using the same rhetoric and terms that have been used to introduce a specific line of thinking that perpetuates a certain Eurocentric epistemological position relative to aesthetics.

Sensing Decolonial Aesthetics is not interested in replicating center-periphery binaries. In fact, what I am proposing throughout the book is that decolonial aesthetics can help us move within and outside such dialectical relations by introducing other sets of possibilities into this discussion. Indeed, through a relational model, it is possible to move away from traditional and well-defined genre studies (i.e., literature as a genre of art or the novel as a sub-genre of literature). What we can do instead is establish particular relations among texts and specific relations within and across particular genres of arts, which is in fact what each of the following chapters sets out to do—finding those relations, tracing linkages and points of connection as we transition from chapter to chapter. In other words, relation here is another way of framing comparisons, since "Comparison as relation means setting into motion historical relationalities between entities brought together for comparison, and bringing into relation terms that have traditionally been pushed apart from each other due to certain interests, such as the European exceptionalism that undergirds Eurocentrism" (Shih 79). My intention is not necessarily to shy away from European discourses or avoid them altogether. In fact, in each chapter there is a consistent engagement with European texts and philosophy. By moving the spotlight away from European texts, however, this project places other modes of thinking and sensing at the same level as their European counterparts, with the ultimate goal of engaging them in a conversation. This is, in part, why there is an investment in exploring non-philosophical ideas and practices emerging from art, precisely because I firmly believe that artworks can offer us alternative models for thinking about aesthetics. An exploration of what artworks can tell us about aesthetics is part of the decolonial move of *Sensing Decolonial Aesthetics,* which seeks a shift in the traditional relationship between aesthetics and arts. Aesthetics, as a discipline, traditionally looks at art objects and thus offers ideas, readings, interpretations, and normative evaluative categories. In addition to this interpretive dimension of aesthetics, in this book I am interested in teasing out from the artworks themselves ideas and positions about aesthetics in relation to sensing. The decolonial move of this book is to place an emphasis on artist and artworks, since they are no longer mere objects of study. Rather, the arts can themselves offer complementary and relevant options to philosophical discourses, which is another dimension of decolonial aesthetics. In short, sensing otherwise allows us to enter into these conversations whereby discourses of center-periphery and binary axes of relation are avoided. Glissant reminds us that "The more it [relation] works in favor of an oppressive order, the more it calls forth disorder as well. . . . Relation is learning more and more to go beyond judgments into the unexpected dark of art's upsurgings. Its beauty springs from the stable and the unstable, from the deviance of many particular poetics and the clairvoyance of relational poetics" (138–139). Unexpected relations come to light, forcing us to sense differently, and enabling us to look at the interrelations of artistic genres. Relational readings or comparisons of the arts enable us to look at what poetry might tell us about music and vice versa, but also at what a particular poet might reveal about another poet's proposition. These points of connection are key to giving a broader and more nuanced picture of the long decade of the 1960s in Latin America.

2

The Poetics of Sensing

Decolonial Verses in Antipoetry and Conversational Poetry

> La literatura vive en relación con su época, pero también en relación con la literatura.
> [Literature lives in relation to its time, but also in relation to literature.]
>
> Roberto Fernández Retamar, "Antipoesía y poesía conversacional en Hispanoamérica"

Following Fernández Retamar's critical suggestion that literature is at once rooted within its time and also exists in relation to literature writ large, one of the goals of this chapter is to establish points of connection and correlation among four distinct and even fragmentary approaches to using vernacular language to write poetry, specifically in examples drawn from Nicanor Parra, Mario Benedetti, Ernesto Cardenal, and Roque Dalton. A second issue that I seek to address is poetry's contribution to a genealogy of decolonial thinking and sensing. To begin engaging with these two questions, there will be two connecting threads: Mario Benedetti and Nicanor Parra.

Benedetti is particularly useful in the present chapter with his articulation of the "poeta comunicante" [poet-as-communicator], since the term encompasses the poetic approaches of Parra, Benedetti, Cardenal, and Dalton. Benedetti defines the poet-as-communicator in two ways. On the one hand, the poet-as-communicator becomes preoccupied with establishing a clear and direct line of communication with his or her reader, and thus invites the reader into a dialogue. At the same time, in Benedetti's conception, the poet-as-communicator bridges historical and cultural gaps, while transmitting changes in generational attitudes

(Benedetti, "Prólogo" 14–15). Moreover, Benedetti ascribes a sense of urgency in political and social terms to the poet-as-communicator's craft, which explains why the language of communication must be straightforward and clearly say what it needs to say. Writing poetry becomes a way to create art that is primarily addressed to an everyday audience, with the objective of delivering a message, inviting the reader into a dialogue, and shifting perceptions of poetry as a form that uses a hermetic and apolitical language that fails to connect with pressing and material concerns of vast sectors of the population. In this conception of poetry's directness, shifting the focus of poetry's primary intended audience is already an invitation to decolonize the legacy of poetry's hermeticism, running from Latin America's romanticism through *modernismo* and many of the historical vanguards.

For instance, critic Alberto Julián Pérez situates the poetic contributions of César Vallejo in his *Poemas humanos* (1923–1938), Pablo Neruda in *Canto General* (1950), and a later generation that includes Benedetti, Dalton, Claribel Alegría, Antonio Cisneros, and Cardenal as contributing and belonging to a progression and growth in social realist art. Regarding this grouping of authors seeking to distance themselves from hermetic poetry and instead move poetry toward social and political engagement, Pérez writes: "La poesía hispanoamericana alcanza especialmente su gran madurez artística con este arte realista socialista, gracias a su feliz incorporación del referente social y politico, la historia y la cultura de Hispanoamérica" [Spanish American poetry specifically reaches its great artistic maturity with this social realist art, which productively incorporates political and social references, and Spanish America's history and culture] (274). Such a grouping under the category of social realist art, particularly in terms of poetry, is appropriate due to the variety of ways in which these poets engage social, political, historical, and cultural Latin American referents. While I tend to agree with this overall grouping as one that aims to put poetry in more direct relation to a heterogeneous questioning of social, political, and historical issues afflicting most sectors of Latin American society, it is also widely known that Benedetti, Parra, and Dalton sought to align themselves more with Vallejo's poetic legacy than with Neruda's, despite the fact that Neruda has been widely read as one of Latin America's most Marxist and more ideologically focused poets of the first half of the twentieth century. While there is value in continuing to read these poets as part of a social realist genealogy of committed poetry, Benedetti's category of poet-as-communicator serves to establish more nuanced distinctions in poetic production and intention among the poets in this group. Part of the act of communicating through poetry implies a heterogeneity in poetic expression that mixes politics and a clear sense of poetry's transformational purpose. Clarity, directness, and openness in communication between the poet and an intended (vast) audience is one of the characteristics I identify as decolonial gestures, particularly in terms of shifting the uses of poetry beyond pure aesthetic pleasure and literary value or worth.

As another way to establish points of connection among Parra, Benedetti, Cardenal, and Dalton, I will employ antipoetry as a second point of departure. In the following section, I will delve more fully into the instability and playfulness of the term "antipoetry." Essentially, however, the connection I emphasize between the poet-as-communicator and antipoetry is best summed up in Parra's words: "poetry is merely life in words. The vernacular, then, has a large place in antipoetry" (Lerzundi 153). In this sense, the poet-as-communicator is preoccupied with finding ways to express what he or she sees and experiences in everyday life by employing vernacular language to communicate with readers. Since antipoetry presupposes that poetry has privileged difficult metaphors, ornate language, and musicality without a discernible connection to real-life concerns, antipoetry turns to the vernacular as a way to counteract "high" poetry. As such, the use of the vernacular becomes a counter-poetics that stands in opposition to and differentiates itself from high poetry, or what I refer to above as hermeticism in poetry. Antipoetry is anti-apolaustic in its conscious creation of poetry that moves away from enjoyment and pure pleasure devoid of social references or political inflections, thus seeking to undo a certain coloniality of poetic language, or what César Vallejo once termed "el proceso hispano-americanizante de nuestro pensamiento" [the Hispanic-Americanizing process of our thinking] (Vallejo, "Una gran reunión latino-americana" 31).

In the following sections, I will explore the ways in which the aforementioned poets employed vernacular language to communicate directly with readers, but also to present a distinct way of writing and doing antipoetry. Given antipoetry's preference for quotidian language, and how the antipoet's socio-poetic awareness must be in the service of social justice, I do not see antipoetry as an exclusively "Parranian" invention or way of writing poetry, though Parra is certainly the foremost and perhaps best-known proponent of antipoetry. It would be a mistake to link antipoetry with Parra in such an overt and exclusive way, since antipoetry is against the practice of turning a poet into an idolatrized public figure. As I will argue and illustrate in the following sections, the choice of quotidian language showcases four distinct-but-related modalities of embracing and expanding upon the poetic possibilities that antipoetry proffers. For the antipoet or poet-as-communicator, poetry does not simply remain at the level of the written word, but must be pushed to its boundaries to come back to life. In doing so, the very literary and aesthetic category of poetry is brought closer to serving a social and political function, and not only a literary one. In essence, the poet-as-communicator draws his inspiration from everyday life and seeks to return to it an aesthetic product stripped of ostentatiousness, unnecessary ornateness, irrelevant imagery, and hermetic language.

But what might one gain from reading antipoetry or quotidian poetry writ large from the 1960s through a decolonial lens? How might this type of poetry already articulate some of the concerns appearing in contemporary theory (in this case coloniality/modernity/decoloniality)? And, in existing discourses around decolonial aesthetics, why does this decolonial stance often concern itself primordially with recent art practices?[1] These are questions that will be more fully addressed in the course of this chapter, but I will provide some preliminary answers here. One of the precepts of a decolonial critique of aesthetics is that aesthetics has concerned itself with establishing parameters within which one may both produce and evaluate artworks and thus distinguish between those works deemed worthy of exhibition, reading, viewing, and enjoyment and those that simply did not conform to the artistic parameters. In the case of poetry, one could extend this type of argument to thinking about the historical prevalence of specific poetic forms (the sonnet or the *décima*), strict preference for meter and rhyme (both as internal rhyme and rhyme schemes), or the preference for high versification, as with octosyllabic or hendecasyllabic verses, traditionally part of the *versos de arte mayor* (usually of nine, ten, or eleven syllables in Spanish). A turn toward quotidian language in Latin American poetry becomes more prominent with the likes of César Vallejo, Luis Palés Matos, or Nicolás Guillén. This emphasis on transforming traditional poetic forms, embracing quotidian and popular linguistic expressions (what I refer to here as conversational poetry), and a sometimes-veiled, sometimes-overt engagement with radical politics (usually anti-imperial and anticolonial) becomes more widescale during the 1960s with the prominence of Juan Gelman, Gonzalo Rojas, Enrique Linh, Roque Dalton, Ernesto Cardenal, José Emilio Pacheco, Idea Vilariño, and Jorge Enrique Adoum, among many others.

As simple as it might seem to us today, these heterogeneous attempts at transforming poetry into a popular art form or, to echo Nicanor Parra, at bringing poetry down from Mount Olympus, are indeed not only foundational to a type of poetry seeking transparency and directness in communication, but also remind us that poetry can and should be directly engaged with the world from which it draws its inspiration. Thus, rather than merely being a distant observer of reality, social conditions, political and social unrest, forms of racial injustice, sexism, and other forms of oppression (a shorthand for the pillars constituting coloniality), the committed poet records in verse, reflects, and responds to such forms of coloniality with poetry, while seeking to expose and critique them in plain language. As I will argue through close readings of select poems by Nicanor Parra, Mario Benedetti, Roque Dalton, and Ernesto Cardenal, reading poetry through a critique of coloniality (a decolonial lens) does not mean that every aspect of these writers' poems, or even their poetic propositions, align neatly with decolonial perspectives. In fact, what we see quite often are uneven approximations of and contributions to the spirit and energy behind the contemporary critical concepts of coloniality/decoloniality. I underscore the pluralization and diversity of positionalities related to coloniality/decoloniality to emphasize the need to think of these theoretical concepts not exclusively in relation to Quijano or Mignolo, but also in terms of the many scholars and non-scholars who have embraced and contributed to an expansion and re-elaboration of these ideas. This, I argue, is part of what needs to happen in a rethinking of the genealogy of decolonial critiques through archival and archaeological work that looks at artists and social actors who have produced various and even incongruous critiques of coloniality through a host of artistic modalities. Simply put, arriving at decoloniality through an exposure of coloniality does not need to take the form of a straight line, nor does it exclusively need to occur through existing discourses from recovered thinkers (Fanon,

O'Gorman, Fals-Borda, Kusch, etc.). Exposures of coloniality can and should appear from heterogeneous optics and positionalities. As I have consistently underscored, my perspective seeks to present art, at the level of philosophy, sociology, or political thought, as a viable and equally important contributor to a decolonization of knowledges, leveling the hierarchy of knowledges. An aversion to engaging with the arts (in this case literary forms), particularly from a decolonial perspective, or even simply giving primacy to certain modes of knowledge (favoring only some disciplines), seems only to instantiate further the very coloniality that a decolonial perspective seeks to expose and denounce. In a recent study, Horacio Legrás takes on this particular issue by focusing on decolonial theory's lack of engagement with literature, and states that "This absence of a literary register is all the more remarkable since literature has been central to the establishment of a postcolonial canon that decolonial authors see as a twin, although differently grounded branch, of the general crisis of colonial reason in the periphery" (19). Echoing Legrás's position, what follows is just such an examination of the poetry of Parra, Benedetti, Dalton, and Cardenal as contributing to "a genealogy of a decolonial ethos" (Legrás 20). Constructing such a genealogy is an ongoing process, and any effort can only be a partial attempt at piecing together the various (and necessarily incomplete) fragments that are constitutive of a decolonial ethos that is not recent, but rather has an extended trajectory.

Antipoetry's Different Modalities

Engaging with a term such as antipoetry presents us with a number of questions. At first glance, with the prefix "anti," the term antipoetry might seem to imply an opposition to or rejection of poetry. Moreover, there would appear to be a conscious attempt on the antipoet's part to distance him- or herself from poetry or to position him- or herself against it. To have a better understanding of how antipoetry differentiates itself from poetry, we need briefly to identify the type of poetry that the antipoet rejects.

In relation to Latin American poetics, the concept of antipoetry has been exclusively associated with Nicanor Parra. In essence, we are dealing with a poetic proposition that has its origins in Chile. Much of the scholarship around antipoetry has almost univocally identified antipoetry with Nicanor Parra, and therefore as a Chilean poetic model.[2] If we take this position as a point of departure, Parra's antipoetry seeks to distance itself from his immediate poetic precursors, namely Pablo Neruda, Pablo de Rokha, Gabriela Mistral, and Vicente Huidobro. Antipoetry, then, stands in opposition to a specific lineage of celebrity-poets in Chile's literary scene and highly lauded poets on an international level. As Alexander Coleman reminds us: "Parra's campaign against the idea of 'poetry' makes him into a literary poujadist; a needler too, a trasher of idols who gleefully spoofs Mallarmé's hermeticism, who deflates Eliot's Christian postures, who jokes with Neruda's bardic rumblings. This onslaught includes attacks against the idea of 'masterpieces' and the attendant sacralization of poetry" (xiv). Coleman's succinct assessment of Parra's antipoetic proposition is accurate, particularly when one thinks of the ways in which antipoetry seeks to distance itself from Neruda's lyric poetry or even the reference to Mallarmé's symbolist poetry, which had been so influential among some *modernista* poets in Latin America. Of equal importance is one of the precepts of antipoetry, by which the idea of poetic or literary masterpieces—the sacralization or aggrandizement of poetry, and by extension of poets—is unjustified and unnecessary practice.

It can be argued that the publication of Parra's *Poemas y antipoemas* (*Poems and Antipoems*) in 1954 marks a before-and-after not only in Chilean poetry, but also in relation to Latin American poetics in general (Fernández Retamar, "Antipoesía y poesía conversacional en Hispanoamérica" 162). In a sense, with this publication, Parra shaped the generation of younger and contemporary poets who became prominent in the 1960s, including Mario Benedetti, Ernesto Cardenal, Roque Dalton, Enrique Linh, Juan Gelman, and César Young Núñez, among others. Additionally, with the conceptualization of antipoetry, Parra reclaimed the collective right of poets to turn to popular poetry, quotidian inspiration, and employ colloquial expressions. After all, as one critic noted: "antipoetry is unadorned, is unlyrical, is nonsymbolist; in antipoetry what you see is what you see" (M. Williams vii).

For Parra, it is important to go back in time to draw inspiration from poets of the quotidian and the vernacular as a way to move forward with his antipoetic proposition, while also demystifying poetry's highly aestheticized, academicized, ornate, lyrical, hermetic, and overly metaphorical tendencies. By looking back to his poetic precursors, Parra also distinguishes between poetic models he wishes to embrace and those from which he seeks to distance himself. For instance, when Benedetti asks Parra in an interview to mention some of the influences that have shaped his elusive and undefined usage of antipoetry, Parra lists the likes of Aristophanes, Lucius Afranius, and Chaucer, all three of whom embraced comedic devices to speak about the follies of their respective societies (Benedetti, "Nicanor Parra o el artefacto con laureles" 44). Among the poetic sources that shaped Parra's proposition, the poet adds Juan Ruiz, el Romancero, *El Poema del Cid,* Quevedo, Gustavo Adolfo Becquer, *Martín Fierro,* and nineteenth-century Chilean popular poetry, among others (Benedetti, "Nicanor Parra o el artefacto con laureles" 44–45; Lerzundi 151–155). Even if antipoetry draws from these traditions, however, there is at the same time a conscious attempt to move away from them. In the same vein, Parra admits to some vague influences from Huidobro, Mistral, and Neruda in his poetry. Parra provides a clue about his vision of antipoetry in the following statement:

> De modo que si ésta es una poesía anti-Neruda, también es una poesía anti-Vallejo, es una poesía anti-Mistral, es una poesía anti-todo, pero también es una poesía en la que resuenan todos estos ecos. (Benedetti, "Nicanor Parra o el artefacto con laureles" 52)
>
> [And so, if this poetry is anti-Neruda, it is also an anti-Vallejo poetry, an anti-Mistral poetry; it is an anti-everything poetry, but it is also a poetry in which there are resonances of all of those echoes.]

Here we find another dimension of antipoetry. On the one hand, Parra acknowledges the influence or echoes of canonical poets such as Vallejo, Neruda, or Mistral, while also reaffirming how antipoetry goes against these poets' legacies. Parra's antipoetic praxis is at once attuned to these poets' work, but only as a way to reject it with the intention of proposing a desacralization of canonized poets.

Since there are echoes of Vallejo's poetics in Parra's antipoetry, it becomes important to trace this point of relation. In fact, Vallejo is a pivotal poetic reference for all four poets in this chapter, precisely because of his legacy in seeking to activate poetry for a political purpose, while peeling back the embedded and overbearing legacy of Spanish language and poetic forms. In an essay that surveys the most salient Latin American poetic figures, Stephen M. Hart suggests that César Vallejo is one of the quintessential poets seeking to join art and politics, particularly in the collection *Poemas humanos* (1939), which "include some of the finest political poems written in the Spanish language" (433). According to Hart, what makes Vallejo's political poetry "retain aesthetic value" is that Vallejo's poetry does not "descend into the ranting of a pamphleteer . . ." (433). While I agree with Hart's assessment, despite the fact that he still operates under a certain Eurocentric aesthetic judgment that is simply at odds with the perspective of this study, it is important to note a simple observation: Vallejo's success and agility in joining poetry and politics rests precisely on his subtlety and his ability to reflect upon everyday events and turn them into political observations worthy of being poeticized. Thus, as much as Parra wants to distance himself from Vallejo by claiming an "anti-Vallejo" stance in his antipoetic praxis, I would argue that Parra ends up emulating Vallejo's subtle engagement with politics through poetry. Another commonality between these two poets, particularly when one thinks about Vallejo's *Poemas humanos* in relation to Parra's *Poemas y antipoemas,* is a turn toward the versification of prose or the mirroring of quotidian speech through complete sentences, dialogues, and monologues, as in the case of Vallejo's poems "El momento más grave de la vida," "Voy a hablar de esperanza," or "Epístola a los transeúntes." In both Vallejo's and Parra's poetry, there is a clear emphasis on an intended audience, a reader, and an interlocutor with whom the poet seeks to communicate. As Hart notes, however, "Vallejo is able to make his political point much more effectively by coining striking poetic images rather than writing straightforward poetry which attacks capitalism directly" (433). This is perhaps one of the most striking differences among the poets in this chapter. Despite a certain family resemblance, to adapt Wittgenstein's concept, there are distinct differences among the four poets' engagement with the directness of language, with how straightforward poetry should be, and with how veiled or direct the "attacks" ought to appear in verse. These distinctions will become clearer in the subsequent sections dedicated to each poet.

Since antipoetry is also anti-everything, and one could extend this claim to examples of conversational poetry, there is a common concern among these poets with a return to simplicity in poetic language, which does not mean simplistic poetry or verses devoid of deep and pressing existential, political, or social questions. For instance, in his attempt to distinguish antipoetry from some of his poetic (hermetic) precursors, Parra attributes the crisis of hermetic or high poetry to the Renaissance: "it occurred to me that that was the source of all the vices of this elegant poetry, of this stuffed shirt poetry that was being written in Chile. . . . I saw that the thing had got off to a bad start in the Renaissance, when poetry was written for the salon, an aristocratic poetry for the upper classes, a poetry eminently conventional; but luckily I went back even further and came upon the Middle Ages" (Lerzundi 152). In his attempt to rehabilitate poetry, not only does Parra go farther back in time for poetic inspiration, he finds kindred voices in classical poets such as Callimachus, Nikarchus, and Archilochus (Lerzundi 152). Furthermore, as one critic has noted, in Parra's antipoetry there is also use of rational discursivity that takes on a tone of explanation in its dialogic or conversational emphasis, and one might even say that antipoetry contains a pedagogic emphasis that brings antipoetry closer to socialist realist poetry, though also questioning the ends and means of an emphasis on historical perspective (Pérez 290).

In this recovery of past poetic forms and a return to a simplicity of language, we find again a connection to Vallejo's own thinking about his poetic milieu when he writes:

> La poesía nueva a base de palabras o de metáforas nuevas, se distingue por su pedantería de novedad y, en consecuencia, por su complicación y su barroquismo. La poesía nueva a base de sensibilidad nueva es, al contrario, simple y humana y a primera vista se la tomaría por antigua o no atrae la atención sobre si es o no moderna. (Vallejo, "Poesía nueva" 12–13)
>
> [The new poetry based upon new words and metaphors distinguishes itself by the pedantry of its novelty, and, in turn, by its complicatedness and baroque nature. The new poetry based upon a new sensibility is, on the contrary, plain and human and, at first glance, one might take it for old or for not drawing attention to itself about whether or not it is modern.]

While Vallejo was describing a type of poetry written in the context of the 1920s, in the aftermath of World War I, in an era of great turmoil and change both in Latin America and in Europe, there are a few keywords stemming from the second description of the new poetry that definitely resonate with the type of antipoetry or conversational poetics of Parra, Benedetti, Cardenal, and Dalton. Vallejo's emphasis on a new sensibility and a return to a simplicity of language to showcase the depths of the human experience, including its horrors, suffering, and multiple modes of oppression, are the seeds from Vallejo's poetics that blossom into a conversational poetics invested in confronting life with quotidian language. In the case of Parra, he displays a distaste for highly ornate, lyrical and metaphorical poetry or poetry that abuses metaphors as a poetic device. Parra wants to strip antipoetry of muddled and highly ornate metaphors and what he perceives as poets' misuse and overuse of them. For Parra, the association of the lyrical with high poetry generated a hermetic product that became highly valorized among certain elite circles but failed to connect with popular audiences. Instead, Parra opts for simple, concrete, and direct language intended to be read and understood by the common reader and audiences. In this sense, antipoetry becomes an effort to create direct communication with audiences without the need for mediators and interpreters (critics) or the deciphering of complex imagery and language.

Furthermore, Parra shows a rejection of the type of poetry that had dominated Latin American poetics well into the first half of the twentieth century. Parra's objection to a certain kind of lyrical poetry is the degree to which it has become delinked and detached from its origins and its relation to the lyre and troubadours, while it has also alienated audiences and negated lyrical poetry's original purpose, which was to communicate directly with and entertain audiences. For Parra, lyrical poetry is linked to perception and the senses and thus is associated with aesthetics, but not the kind of aestheticization that privileges beauty and the ornate. Quite the contrary—in Parra's proposition, he wishes to retain from the legacy of classical and medieval lyrical poetry what he perceives to be a connection with quotidian elements and expressions that denote a conversational approach to bring about communication with readers: "ésta es una poesía que siempre está dirigida a un interlocutor, no a un interlocutor equis sino a un sector . . . de modo que si no se produce la comunicación, yo me siento profundamente deprimido, me parece que he fallado" [This is a poetry that is always aimed at an interlocutor, not at any interlocutor, but at a sector . . . and so, if communication fails, I feel deeply depressed; it seems that I've failed] (Benedetti, "Nicanor Parra o el artefacto con laureles" 50). Clarity and directness in expression, coupled with desacralizing and scrutinizing every possible subject, are perhaps the central tenets of antipoetry as poetic praxis, and what I perceive to be a decolonial gesture of reclaiming and reactivating poetry as a means of directly engaging with audiences.

In short, antipoetry does not stand against the idea of poetry, but only against of a certain conceptualization, execution, and tradition of poetry that has come to dominate poetic output and consumption. As Fernández Retamar notes, "Pero por el mero hecho de ser, ninguna poesía es antipoesía: la única verdadera antipoesía no se escribe" [By the mere fact of being, no poetry is antipoetry: the only true antipoetry is that which is not written at all] ("Antipoesía y poesía conversacional en Hispanoamérica" 163). Far from essentializing popular or folk poetry, antipoetry's claim to revalorize popular poetic forms and expressions appears as a conscious move to take a stand against elitist poetic and aesthetic sensibilities regarding what counted as valid, worthwhile, or beautiful poetry. While antipoetry resists a clear-cut definition, even in interviews Parra has consciously avoided providing a definitive stance or writing a proper manifesto. Nonetheless, Edith Grossman has offered some general goals: 1) to free poetry from the yoke of the metaphor; 2) to use common language as a way to reflect daily life; 3) to localize or use colloquialisms to accomplish the first two goals (Grossman 8–9).

Another important characteristic in Parra's antipoetry is his incorporation of playfulness and comedic devices, which are meant to produce a different sort of aesthetic experience or way to sense poetry: to laugh at the ornate and highly aestheticized, the poetic demi-gods, and the canonized collections of poetry. For the antipoet, nothing is sacred, including antipoetry. Even an antipoem can be self-reflexive and self-critical and poke fun at itself. A good example of this can be found in his collection *Versos de salón* (1962), in the poem "La montaña rusa" ["Roller Coaster"]:

Durante medio siglo
Lo poesía fue
El paraíso del tonto solemne.
Hasta que vine yo
Y me instalé con mi montaña rusa.

Suban, si les parece.
Claro que yo no respondo si bajan
Echando sangre por boca y narices.
(Parra, *Obra gruesa* 84)

For half a Century
Poetry was the paradise
Of the solemn fool.
Until I came
And built my roller coaster.

Go up, if you feel like it.
I'm not responsible if you come down
With your mouth and nose bleeding.
(Parra, *Poems and Antipoems* 67)[3]

As Parra explains in his interview with Benedetti, when he employs "I," it should not be confused with a poetic voice or with Parra as poet. Instead, it is meant to denote a sense of collectivity and belonging (Benedetti, "Nicanor Parra o el artefacto con laureles" 49). As becomes apparent in "La montaña rusa," Parra is interested in taking readers on a roller coaster ride of extreme emotions and modes of sensing poetry, though he rids himself of any responsibility for what the reader may get out of his poetry. At the same time, with the invocation of a bleeding mouth and nose, we see an example of how Parra draws our attention to the quotidian, to the earthly, and avoids any sense of "beauty" in the conventional aesthetic and poetic sense. Instead, Parra presents us with a very graphic and visceral image we cannot escape or confuse with anything else. It does not necessitate extrapolations and does not hide deeper meanings. Antipoetry thus grounds itself in relation to a different aesthetic sensibility, which draws its inspiration from the popular, the quotidian, or simply what the antipoet thinks (deified) poets would deride as unworthy of poetic inspiration. As Parra notes, "What the antipoet looks for is not, fundamentally, beauty, but life, life in flesh and bone; he will settle for nothing less" (Lerzundi 153).

Antipoetry resists the temptation of taking itself too seriously, though at times the thematic preoccupation of antipoets can be somber and serious, particularly with topics such as death and other dark emotions. If any topic can become a source of inspiration for the antipoet, it can also be subverted and turned into a source of lightness. Parra's treatment of certain topics can be associated with a particular view on how poetry needs to have a certain degree of levity if it is going to communicate effectively with its readers. This stance, of course, is very different from the sense of urgency we find in Dalton, Benedetti, and Cardenal. Yet, a common characteristic among the four poets is their embrace of the comedic in relation to poetry. Laughing or poking fun at pain, suffering, authority, oppression, and other forms of power is a key facet of antipoetry's decolonial gesture. In other words, antipoetry demands that we rethink dominant conceptions of what constitutes valid culture from the vantage point of what is perceived as valid, worthwhile, beautiful, or aesthetic poetry.

To establish a connection between decolonial aesthetics and antipoetry, we must remember that Parra's poetic (or antipoetic) perspective lies precisely in the attempt to bring down poetry and poets from Mount Olympus, as he astutely announces in his poem "Manifiesto": "Los poetas bajaron del Olimpo" [The poets have descended from Olympus] (Parra, *Obra gruesa* 211). Parra's references to the poets who have descended and become part of the world are to none other than antipoets, poets-as-communicators, or poets of the vernacular. Moreover, in its decolonial aesthetic proposition, antipoetry embraces everyday language, situations, colloquialisms, irony, parody, satire, and other forms of humor as sources of poetic inspiration for the antipoet or poet-as-communicator. Following Enrique Dussel's call for us to think of aesthetics not exclusively in terms of beauty, the sublime, or other positive aesthetic categories, but in relation to the ugly or the popular, antipoetry becomes an aesthetic and poetic proposition that constantly renews and redefines itself as a way to keep up-to-date with the exigencies of social demands and changes in language (Dussel, *Philosophy of Liberation*). This position is in line with certain aspects of Benedetto Croce's argument about the aesthetic as a science of expression, but also with determining its terms of relation with history and linguistics. In arguing about the relation between aesthetic judgment and questions of uniformity in language, Croce writes that "Language is perpetual creation; what is expressed at one time in words is not repeated save in the reproduction of what has already been produced;

ever new impressions give rise to a continually changing set of sounds and meanings, that is, to ever new expressions" (Croce, *The Aesthetic* 163). Antipoetry or poetry of communication constantly seeks to renovate itself without becoming static or stagnant given its emphasis on the perpetual revitalization of poetic language and its ongoing connection with lived experiences. Rather than standing in opposition to poetic language or creation through verse, as it has been commonly understood, antipoetry seeks to bring poetics back into tune with the rhythms, sounds, words, and sensibilities of the quotidian.

The connection between decolonial aesthetics and antipoetry is an inherent challenge to what has traditionally been favored as valid poetry in Latin America and to conceptualizations of poetic language, as well as to valid perspectives or approaches to appreciating poetry. Since aesthetics are related to perception and the senses, antipoetry opens up the possibility of engaging the senses in relation to poetry. While antipoetry can be aural and visual, it leaves the musicalization of poetry to troubadours, singer-songwriters, or interpreters seeking to adapt a poem into song format. An instance of the correlation between antipoetry and music can be seen with Daniel Viglietti's and Joan Manuel Serrat's respective attempts at setting Benedetti's poetry to music. In the following chapter, for instance, I will explore one example of the connection between poetry and music with a poem Nicanor Parra wrote for his sister, Violeta Parra, to set to music. In terms of antipoetry's visual dimension, we see clear instances of this with Nicanor Parra's turn toward visual artifacts, drawings, and artistic installations, which still retain the written word, but are more concerned with the interplay between the word and image.[4]

In the following sections, I will pay closer attention to the ways in which each of the four poets engages with poetry-as-communication, vernacular poetics, or antipoetry in different modalities. Whereas Parra takes on an anti-everything stance, Benedetti engages with the working class and the struggles of everyday life in urban settings. Cardenal, on the other hand, infuses poetry with liberation theology to grapple with social injustices, particularly with the underprivileged and indigenous peoples. Finally, Dalton takes a militant stance when it comes to writing poetry as a way to underscore the connection between poetic craft and political commitment as a means to work toward social justice.

Nicanor Parra and Antipoetry

Whereas some of the parameters of decolonial aesthetics I demarcated in the introduction and first chapter demand an artist's conscious effort to politicize art, in the case of antipoetry, particularly with Parra, one is able to see the gradations and different approaches by which art can be politicized without the artist overtly doing so. Parra's playful and conscious effort in avoiding disclosure of his political ideologies and stripping his poetry of self-evident political language is another way in which he sought to distance and differentiate himself from Neruda.

If Neruda became associated with Marxist ideology and the Chilean Communist Party, while also actively participating in various capacities in Chile's political life, Parra opted for the exact opposite: no clear commitment to either right-wing or leftist politics. In fact, as one critic noted, "En la poesía de Parra, vemos, no hay una posición política o cultural única, cada posición es capaz de incluir su contrapartida. El autor no se identifica con un solo sujeto, puede alternativamente adoptar todas las máscaras, las 'personas'" [In Parra's antipoetry we see that there is not a single political or cultural position, because each position is capable of containing its counterpart. The author does not identify with a single subject, but can adopt and alternate all masks, all people] (Pérez 291). We can gather, however, from Parra's poetry and interviews where he stands on the political spectrum. This is to say that Parra the man aligns himself with the left, but Parra the poet sees no room for overt politics and ideological tints in his poetry. Of course, there are times at which Parra betrays this apolitical and anti-ideological stance.

For instance, Parra argues that he considers himself a political poet, but not a poet who actively seeks to engage in politics or political life (Benedetti, "Nicanor Parra o el artefacto con laureles" 61). Nonetheless, Parra also suggests how he can be considered a revolutionary poet in the sense that antipoetry seeks to challenge cultural and aesthetic values, which have been passed down. "Un antipoema en este sentido no es más que la punta de un alfiler que toca un globo que está a punto de reventar" [In this sense, an antipoem is nothing else than the tip of a pin touching a balloon that is about to explode] (Benedetti, "Nicanor Parra o el artefacto con laureles" 61). With this statement, for instance, one notices a clear attempt to push the boundaries and challenge cultural notions and values.

The antipoet becomes a political poet by becoming aware of what needs to be exploded in order to open up the way for new values, and antipoetry becomes a response in verse to tumultuous times in which there is no room for being apolitical, or for being abstract when the world around the antipoet is open to questioning, a series of problems requiring questions even if the answers are unsatisfactory or contradictory (Ibáñez Langlois 263–265). To this vision of antipoetry, Parra also adds that artifacts comprise the antipoem. Put differently, an antipoem can be broken down into smaller units that are none other than artifacts (Benedetti, "Nicanor Parra o el artefacto con laureles" 50). Once the antipoem explodes, what we are left with are the remnants, fragments, or verses of the poem.

An instance of such radical changes can be seen in "Cambio de nombre" ["Changes of Name"], particularly as the poetic voice addresses both a reading audience and also fellow poets. For instance, in the first stanza, Parra addresses aesthetes or those interested in what constitutes high art: "A los amantes de las bellas letras / Hago llegar mis mejores deseos / Voy a cambiar de nombre algunas cosas" (Parra, *Obra gruesa* 83). ["To the lovers of belles-lettres / I offer my best wishes / I am going to change the names of things"] (Parra, *Poems and Antipoems* 65).[5] As with this first verse, the second verse evinces Parra's use of irony, and his "best wishes" are not to be taken at face value. Although Parra forewarns the "lovers of belles-lettres" about the changes that will take place, it can be argued that his true and best wishes are summed up in the necessity of changing language. Since language has been exhausted, and is redundant, devoid of any surprises, the antipoet seeks induce a radical transformation in the way we read, write, and interpret poetry, which is to say how we sense verses.

Parra continues in the second stanza by presenting a more straightforward stance on his vision of what constitutes the antipoet's poetic duty: "Mi posición es ésta: / El poeta no cumple su palabra / Si no cambia los nombres de las cosas" (Parra, *Obra gruesa* 83). ["My position is this: / The poet is not true to his word / If he doesn't change the names of things"] (Parra, *Poems and Antipoems* 65). For Parra, the poet's ethical and poetic duty is to transform language, to activate and resuscitate it, to let it speak for itself, but also to ensure that every word carries with it a different connotation. More importantly, it is up to every poet and, in turn, every reader to have a personal dictionary in which words found in poems can be looked up. This implies, of course, that no two readers will come to the same definition or the same understanding of what a poem suggests or implies.

In the remaining parts of the poem, Parra questions why it is necessary to call the sun "sun" or cats "cats." Parra implicitly asks the question: Why should we not change what things are called? To the litany of seemingly random and quotidian objects in dire need of a name change, Parra adds that shoes ought to be called "coffins" ["ataúdes"], since the word *shoe* seems rather arbitrary and does not seem to describe accurately what he sees on his feet. If anything, shoes resemble the shape of coffins, and thus ought to be called what the poet and reader see.

Through antipoetic praxis, Parra presents us with a thought-provoking challenge. It is not enough to radicalize the words we use in poetry so that signifier and signified correlate with one another. Instead, and perhaps more importantly, it is up to each poet and each reader to establish that connection subjectively. Parra seeks to underscore the coloniality pervasive in the acts of writing and reading poetry. When this is done, there is no longer a vertical relationship between poet and reader in which the poet infuses meaning into his verses and the reader desperately seeks to get to what the poet intended. Put differently, the poet and reader become equal partners (a horizontal relationship); the poet acknowledges the reader and demands that the reader take responsibility for drawing meaning from words. Otherwise, the act of establishing a dialogue between poet and reader is incomplete.

Parra concludes his page-long poem by inscribing and openly declaring that individuals (both poets and readers) must design their own dictionary, which implies an ongoing process of renaming objects and thus expanding the vocabulary and possibilities of what can be included in a poem. Parra writes: "Todo sujeto que se estime a sí mismo / Debe tener su propio diccionario" (Parra, *Obra gruesa* 83). ["Every fool who respects himself / Has to have his own dictionary"] (Parra, *Poems and Antipoems* 65). In this instance, having one's own dictionary becomes an act of self-respect and inscribes an urgency to reclaim the reader's subjectivity. Parra reminds us how the acts of reading and interpreting poems are deeply subjective experiences and that, if each individual has her/his own dictionary, an antipoem's artifacts (devices, components, fragments) can be sites of multiple and enriching experiences. In Miller Williams's translation, however, it is problematic to accept "fool" for the original "sujeto." In Parra's original verse, the word "sujeto" denotes subjectivity, and this becomes a key word in his antipoetic proposition of radicalizing and changing the names of things. The word "fool" would seem to weaken the effect of the original verse. Finally, as is characteristic of much of Parra's poetry, he takes a jab at the idea of God and also urges readers to change His name, though "Ese es un problema personal" (*Obra gruesa* 83). ["That is a personal problem"] (*Poems and Antipoems* 65). The conclusion of the poem reiterates the proposition of reinscribing subjectivity into the act of reading. If we contrast the last image of the "personal problem" with the first addressees in the poem, "the lovers of belles-lettres," one can recognize how Parra tossed aside conventions, traditional aesthetic and poetic values, in the first stanza and never looked back. Instead, Parra turned his attention to readers and antipoets, who are arguably Parra's intended audience.

Parra wants his poetry to engage the reader and for his direct language to deliver a message that the reader can gather on his or her own. In this sense, Parra avoids the pitfalls of turning poetry into a tool of political or ideological indoctrination, which thus renders Parra's politics separate from his antipoetic output. This is one of the characteristics of Parra's work: his conscious effort to dissociate or delink antipoetry from politics. As we will see later, however, this is one dimension of antipoetry, but not a definitive one. In the work of Benedetti, Cardenal, or Dalton we find that poetry is more overtly political and ideological as it engages with social issues.

For contemporary critic and poet Martín Espada, Neruda is one of the quintessential poets of the political imagination. For Espada, "Any progressive social change must be imagined first, and that vision must find its most eloquent possible expression to move from vision to reality" (100). One can argue that Parra would reject such association, even if some of his poetry is indeed political or engages with topics related to politics. Parra, like Vallejo, rejects any association with "eloquence" as a means to bring about a vision of social change. Quite the contrary: vernacular language replaces "eloquence" in Parra's conceptualization of antipoetry.

Parra draws from Whitman to rid himself of Neruda, Huidobro, and Lorca as poetic influences. In so doing, Parra finds in Whitman's poetry a model by which to free himself from what he perceives as dominant and suffocating poetry. Parra explains how Whitman allowed him to mark a point of transition between his earlier poetry (before *Poemas y antipoemas*) and what would come after. Parra finds in Whitman a way toward a more horizontal language and poetry oriented toward the everyday reader (Benedetti, "Nicanor Parra o el artefacto con laureles" 43). In Parra's conceptualization, antipoetry can be equated with a type of poetry that takes its cue from life in words. As such, since poetry departs from everyday life, the language it employs needs to connect with it, mirror it, and return to it. If one accepts this a point of departure, Parra explains that poetry can embrace and incorporate a multiplicity of sometimes seemingly irreconcilable positions: "no tan sólo las voces impostadas, sino también las voces naturales; no tan sólo los sentimientos nobles, sino también los otros; no tan sólo el llanto, sino también la risa; no tan sólo la belleza, sino también la fealdad" [Not only feigned voices, but also natural voices; not only noble feelings, but also the others; not only tears, but also laughter; not only beauty, but also ugliness] (Benedetti, "Nicanor Parra o el artefacto con laureles" 51). Antipoetry allows for the inclusion of divergent positions, particularly in relation to aesthetic categories such as beauty or ugliness, but also seeks to bridge the gap between popular voices and sophisticated ones.

In "El pequeño burgués" ["Litany of the Little Bourgeois"], Parra engages precisely with the question of art for art's sake when he writes: "El que quiera llegar al paraíso / Del pequeño burgués tiene que andar / El camino del arte por el arte / Y tragar cantidades de saliva: / El noviciado es casi interminable" (*Obra gruesa* 114). ["If you want to get to the heaven / Of the petit bourgeois, you must go / By the road of Art for Art's sake / And swallow a lot of saliva: / The apprenticeship is almost interminable" (Parra, *Poems and Antipoems* 93).[6] Parra uses irony to poke fun at what has been socially construed as acceptable behavior denoting refinement and good taste. In the remainder of the poem, Parra adds images related to learning to tie a necktie, shave properly, have polished shoes, distinguish between a viola and a violin, and admire works of art in museums, among other conventions. To escape from the vicious cycles of social conventions, Parra concludes his poem by suggesting precisely the opposite of what is deemed proper behavior, thus defying logic. As a possible way of out of the humdrum of modern life, Parra suggests that one ought to "Aparecer y desaparecer / Caminar en estado cataléptico / Bailar un vals en un montón de escombros . . . / Presentarse en frac en los incendios" (Parra, *Obra gruesa* 115). ["Appear and disappear / Walk in a cataleptic trance / Waltz on a pile of debris . . . / Go to fires in a morning coat"] (Parra, *Poems and Antipoems* 95). At the end of the poem, Parra produces a brief list of behaviors, actions, or measures one can take to ensure one will be deemed *persona non grata* in petit bourgeois circles. After all, who in their right mind would dance a waltz among debris or wear a tuxedo to a fire? This is precisely one of the missions of the poem, namely, to challenge social conventions, perceptions, and behaviors, and underscore how certain idiosyncrasies can be subject to mockery.

Parra is also interested in engaging those readers and critics who need absolute and concrete definitions of the type of poetry he writes or what he considers himself. In a poem entitled "Test," Parra presents his readers with two large questions. In the first stanza, Parra lures the reader into trying to define precisely what an antipoet is. To do so, Parra writes out sixteen questions and asks the reader to underline the most fitting descriptions for an antipoet. Some of the questions in this first part of the test that seek to "define" the antipoet are: "Un comerciante de urnas y ataúdes? . . . / Un bromista sangriento / Deliberadamente miserable? / Un poeta que duerme en una silla? / Un alquimista de los tiempos modernos? / Un revolucionario de bolsillo? / Un pequeño burgués?" (*Obra gruesa* 184). ["A dealer in urns and coffins? . . . / A bloody joker / willfully wretched? / A poet who sleeps in a chair? / An up-to-date alchemist? / A revolutionary of the living room? / A *petit-bourgeois*?"] (Parra, *Poems and Antipoems* 145).[7] All of the descriptions offered are suitable and yet incomplete answers to the question. In a way, Parra's exercise forces the reader to accept that the antipoet cannot be neatly defined or reduced to a simple phrase. In short, all of the questions Parra presents in the first half of the test are simultaneously fitting and not fitting, complete and incomplete, when it comes to defining what constitutes an antipoet.

In the second part of the poem, Parra embarks on an even bigger feat, which is to test the reader on what she or he understands as antipoetry. In this part, there are only ten questions, and Parra asks the reader to put an "x" next to the correct answer. In this section, we face a similar problem to the earlier one. All of the proposed descriptions are potentially valid answers, but always remain partial ones. Some of the questions in this section are: "Un temporal de una taza de té? . . . / Un espejo que dice la verdad? . . . / Una advertencia a los poetas jóvenes?" (*Obra gruesa* 184–185). ["A tempest in a teacup? . . . / A mirror that tells the truth? / A warning to the young poets?"] (*Poems and Antipoems* 145). When Benedetti asks Parra to explain what the he intended by the poem, Parra astutely retorts: "Mira, hay tantas cruces como versos. Y quedan algunas cruces pendientes" [Look, there are as many Xs as there are verses. And there are some pending Xs.] (Benedetti, "Nicanor Parra o el artefacto con laureles" 50). In short, Parra playfully reminds us that poetry is not an exact science that can be reduced to a test, a right or wrong answer, or clearly crafted definitions. Antipoetry is a constantly evolving way of writing poetry that steers away from being neatly put into a box. Instead, as Parra suggests in this poem requiring the active participation of its readers, antipoems and antipoetry allow the reader and young poets to form their own opinions, to come up with their own answers, to make the poem and antipoetry their own.

Despite Parra's intention to avoid succumbing to definitions, Parra has also argued that the "antipoet gets involved with everything, even things that have nothing to do with him. . . . Antipoetry is a poetry of commitment" (Lerzundi 154). Such a commitment is clearly expressed in one Parra's best-known poems, "Manifiesto." The poem can be read as an attempt at writing an antipoetic manifesto seeking to distinguish the difference between previous generations of poets and Parra's generation. Parra suggests that his inspiration for this poem came after a trip to China and that it was his attempt at blurring the line between poetry and essay (Benedetti, "Nicanor Parra o el artefacto con laureles" 62). For instance, Parra describes differences in perception of what poetry can do when he writes: "Para nuestros mayores / La poesía fue un objeto de lujo / Pero para nosotros / Es un artículo de primera necesidad: / No podemos vivir sin poesía" [For our elders / Poetry was a luxury item / But for us / It is a basic necessity: / We cannot live without poetry] (*Obra gruesa* 211). Throughout the poem, Parra creates an opposition between high and ornate poetry, as well as urgent or committed poetry. In Parra's view, older poets, even if they claimed to be of the left or socially committed, almost always failed to connect and communicate with audiences. As such, Parra stands for poetry in touch with nature, with the streets, in tune with reality, and not an ethereal or sublime experience or poetry of social protest that merely stays at the rhetorical level. While Parra has been careful not to align himself with a clearly defined political ideology, in this poem one can see how his vision of antipoetry can be employed to effect social change by seeking to reach wider audiences, to make poetry more accessible, and to situate the antipoet as part of society at large and not merely an observer.

Most of the scholarship seeking to trace decolonial gestures emphasizes overt acts of denunciation and undoing of coloniality either through theoretical critique or action. By overt I mean that the decolonial subject's ideological or political stance is easily discernible and leaves little room for doubt or interpretation. A prime example of this would be the writings of Fanon in either *Black Skin, White Masks* (1952) or *The Wretched of the Earth* (1961). When placed alongside Fanon's work, for instance, Parra's poetry lacks Fanon's overt anticolonial, anti-imperial, and politicized engagement with a variety of forms of racialization and infrahumanization. And yet, such an overt absence of politicization and decolonial critique stems precisely from a distinction in locus and means of enunciation. It is not the same for Fanon (as a black Martinican engaged with liberation struggles in the Caribbean and North Africa) to write prose that is fueled by his experiences and observations as someone immersed in such a turbulent period as it is for Parra (as a seemingly white Chilean professor of physics) to write poetry. And yet, not reducing Fanon or Parra to racialized subjects (black Martinican vs. white Chilean) is precisely what I detect as coloniality/decoloniality's true potential in helping us move beyond the embedded legacies of framing how we see and treat artists according to their racialized or gendered subjectivities. More importantly, we should keep in mind that both Fanon and Parra were men of science, though they used it toward different productive and artistic ends. Fanon's career as a psychiatrist became an intrinsic part of his philosophical writings and his revolutionary politics. Parra's training as a physicist and his career as a university professor of physics propelled him to seek poetry as complement and inverse of scientific rationality and to transform poetry in a radical way. Antipoetry and the other forms of conversational poetry discussed in this chapter are indeed political, despite their different gradations of conjugating ideology and poetics. What makes antipoetry political and possessed of decolonial gestures, albeit in an understated way, is precisely its desacralization of everything and everyone central to a normative understanding of society and its institutions of order and reason.

This is why, perhaps, Parra "mocked his readers, he used vulgarity, sarcasm, irony, black humor, comedy, carnivalesque elements, and he made fun of God, religion, and societal institutions" (González and Dotremon 63). Reading such mockery, uses of sarcasm, irony, parody, and displaying critiques through antipoetic verses as political gestures are precisely what make Parra's poetics a challenge to and an undoing of a Western rationality and aesthetics.[8]

Part of the difficulty that most prominent decolonial thought and scholarship presents us with is precisely its emphasis on tracing genealogies of thought that come either from specific genres (such as the essay or other non-fiction prose forms), as in the case of Mignolo's work, or from popular articulations, as in the case of Albán Achinte's or Pedro Pablo Gómez's recent work on decolonial aesthetics. This is perhaps where coloniality of knowledge comes into play, particularly in terms of thinking about which forms of writing are "authorized" to produce "knowledge." In this privileging or authorization of specific genres over others (such as non-fiction over fiction/poetry), a hierarchy of sites and modes of knowledge further instantiates the very coloniality of knowledge that coloniality seeks to critique. The current crisis of the humanities in higher education is a pressing reminder of this tension that coloniality of knowledge underscores. It is rather difficult to find instances of applying such ways of thinking about coloniality or the decolonial to literature, particularly literature not produced by or about indigenous or Afro-descendant subjects. Precisely because of what I perceive to be a reductive equivalence of decolonial thinking in Latin America with identity politics, some scholars of literature and detractors of coloniality/decoloniality swiftly dismiss or prefer to ignore decolonial thinking or critiques of coloniality without a sustained dialogue with decolonial perspectives that may or may not rest solely upon questions related to indigeneity or Afro-descendant politics in a Latin American context. Without entering into a sustained dialogue to build either upon decolonial thinking or critiques of coloniality in order to advance or disprove their theoretical premises, such dismissals are founded upon a somewhat simplistic and reductive understanding of decolonial scholarship, simply because of its identification almost exclusively with Mignolo. As such, and in an effort to trace a "decolonial ethos," to follow Legrás's term, I seek to think about critiques of coloniality and decoloniality in a broader sense by incorporating voices coming from poetry (and other arts) into an archive that is indeed foundational to a more nuanced understanding of discussions around coloniality/decoloniality and its potential uses for Latin American literary and cultural studies.

Mario Benedetti and Poetry as Communication

In many ways, while literary criticism has focused on many aspects of Benedetti's literary production, which includes novels, essays, and theater, his poetry has received limited attention. When placed alongside "full-time" poets such as Parra, Dalton, and Cardenal, among others, the critical reception of Benedetti's poetry has been overshadowed. However, as I will argue in this section, Benedetti was a pivotal figure in the development of a new poetics during the 1960s at the level of criticism and praxis. Benedetti's roles as a critic in his capacity as editor of Uruguayan magazine *Marcha*, and in the formation of Casa de las Américas during his exile in Cuba in the mid-1960s, make him a central figure in foregrounding poetry-as-communication or conversational poetry as an organizational way of grouping together a number of poets with similar affinities and sensibilities (Parra, Cardenal, Dalton, Adoum, Fernández Retamar, Gelman, etc.)

In his prologue to the collection of interviews conducted for *Marcha*, which were later collected in a volume aimed at giving shape to the *poetas comunicantes* (poets-as-communicators), Benedetti argues that the type of poetry produced in the 1960s built upon a tradition of earlier poetry. Benedetti does not see antipoetry, conversational poetry, or poetry of communication as a rupture with previous poetic traditions, but more as a natural continuity or progression (Benedetti, "Prólogo"). One can agree with Benedetti on one level, particularly since poets cannot exist in isolation or with their backs turned away from their precursors. As was mentioned in the previous section, even Parra acknowledged his love-hate relationship with Neruda; as much as Parra is anti-Neruda, there are glimpses of Neruda in Parra. The same could be said about Neruda's poetry in collections such as *Extravagario* or *Odas elementales,* in which Neruda also shifts his attention to antipoetry and conversational poetry. Nonetheless, in Benedetti's assertion about the continuity of poetic traditions, it is important to note that he seems to overlook one of the prime characteristics of poetry and the arts in the 1960s, which is precisely its desire to distinguish itself from artistic precursors and previous artistic movements, and its conscious effort to make a mark by introducing new artistic and aesthetic propositions.

Fernández Retamar makes a similar observation when he argues that the idea of antipoetry and conversational poetry have been around since the nineteenth century. In the case of nineteenth-century Spanish poetry, for instance, Fernández Retamar argues that Ramón de Campoamor was a sort of antipoet who sought to distinguish himself from José Zorrilla (Fernández Retamar, "Antipoesía y poesía conversacional en Hispanoamérica"). Yet, Fernández Retamar is also careful to clarify that antipoetry, as it has been articulated in twentieth-century Latin American poetics, is different in that Parra builds an entire poetic corpus around a poetic proposition that resists definitions.

In thinking about conversational poetry as a type of antipoetry, and particularly its attempts at underscoring the coloniality of poetic language, it should be noted that Benedetti's poetry is deeply concerned with turning every aspect of daily life into a topic of poetic critique. While the concepts of conversational poetry and antipoetry are thought to be exclusively Latin American, we are reminded that the appeal of antipoetics is far-reaching since it becomes a means of questioning the assertion that there is only one way of sensing and doing poetry. To this end, for instance, Glissant reminds us that "The poetics pierces the depths . . . , demands denial where it affirms itself; from a poetics of the poetics of the world emerges an anti-poetics (a negation of the One in the field of the Diverse)" (*Poetic Relation* 200). Like Parra or Benedetti, Glissant argues for a diversification of our understanding of what poetry stands for and for allowing a heterogeneity of voices to contest the idea of a singular poetic voice. In other words, Glissant challenges and seeks to undo the embedded legacy of thinking that poetry must be written, read, consumed, and sensed in a particular (elitist) way. Instead, Glissant argues for a poetics of the world that must arise from piercing and critiquing the embedded legacies of coloniality, which give way to that affirmation of a particular sense of what constitutes poetry—what at times we can call high poetry or simply canonized poetry. For a francophone poet and intellectual such as Glissant, knowing Baudelaire, Rimbaud, Verlaine, or Hölderlin is necessary in order to undo the uniqueness of a certain Eurocentric poetics that prevents an antipoetics as critique from emerging. Put differently, the only way to critique through poetry, and for antipoetry to emerge, is to know the poetic forms, voices, and techniques in order to then be able to turn them upside down and create a new poetics that embraces a multiplicity of voices and experiences silenced by the coloniality of language and aesthetics. This line of thinking can be extended to the Latin American case precisely because the only way to turn toward poetry-as-communication, whether it be as antipoetry or conversational poetry, is to know and turn upside-down the poetic canon as well as the hispano-Americanizing gesture, to echo Vallejo, so prevalent in the history of Latin American poetics. By this, Vallejo meant that, by and large, Latin American poetry has been imitative of the literary trends, forms, and topics coming to the Americas from Spain. One can add to this hispano-Americanizing gesture franco-Americanizing and anglo-Americanizing gestures, which collectively comprise a coloniality of poetic language. In light of this, and echoing Glissant's line of thinking, Vallejo reminded us that we should not forget the ways in which a certain indigenous spirit, an aesthetic of rebelliousness to use Benedetti's words, runs through a certain sector of Latin America, and this was the key to a future poetics of liberation, which I am calling here a decolonial poetics.[9]

Even though I do not completely agree with Benedetti's assertion that there is an unproblematic continuity among the poets-as-communicators and their precursors, I find the concept of poetry-as-communication an effective way to understand why it is that Parra develops antipoetry in Chile, Cardenal turns to exteriorist poetry in Nicaragua, Dalton turns to revolutionary poetry, and Benedetti turns to conversational poetry, all in apparent isolation from one another. As Alemany Bay has argued, it would appear that all of these poetic propositions, which she places under the umbrella of colloquial poetics, developed in seeming isolation and would later come into contact with one another through encounters in Casa de las Américas or through Benedetti as a common poetic interlocutor (Alemany Bay, *Poética coloquial hispanoamericana*). In essence, the four poets central to the present chapter had similar approaches to writing poetry, though with different names for their respective poetic projects. Nonetheless, I argue that all four approaches make use of the vernacular, turn to everyday forms of communication, take on social concerns, and aim to communicate directly with readers. As such, all four poets are responding to previous poetic traditions and position themselves as antipoets in opposition to elitist, ornate, flowery, hermetic, and high poetry. At the same time, however, they also embrace quotidian language and colloquialisms because the ultimate goal is to establish open and clean lines of communication with audiences. In this sense, the antipoet is a poet-as-communicator, but can also be dubbed a conversationalist poet or a colloquial poet. What is important in their poetic outlook and praxis is what they do with their craft and their thematic preoccupations, which distinguish these four poets from one another.

From Benedetti, as a key critic and organizing figure who brings these four poets together, we can turn briefly to examine and illustrate Benedetti's poetic praxis. In his collection *Poemas del hoyporhoy* (1961), Benedetti turns his attention to truly quotidian concerns. We find poems such as "La crisis," which deal with economic crises and the effects of inflation on the poor and working classes. There are also poems dealing with existential crises of the middle class. However, as with Parra, we find in Benedetti a keen sense of humor, and that he takes his poetic craft with a certain degree of lightness. In the poem "Interview," we find what can be assumed to be a dialogue between the poet and his interviewer, though we never get to read the interviewer's questions. They can be gleaned, however, from the responses of the poet. The first question deals with the poet's thoughts on infinity. The poet responds to the question with what appears to be a poetic response, but concludes by affirming that he does not believe in infinity. There is a clear mockery of metaphysical and existential poets and how this poetic voice seeks to distinguish himself from that tradition. This goes back to my earlier point about poetry's function as critique of the sense of uniqueness that surrounds Eurocentric poetics and its ripple effect into a coloniality of poetic language.

The second question of the interview is encompassed by the poem's second stanza. As this question deals with the poet's thoughts on politics, once again, the poet's move is to begin to express what his thoughts are about politics, only to conclude his answer with a negation of politics. The speaker affirms that he is a poet and that poets live with their backs turned to the world. As such, then, poets are apolitical and remove themselves from social and political lives. In the second stanza, Benedetti addresses a different type of poetic tradition, that of a certain kind of political poetry. Benedetti pokes fun at these political poets, who are only seemingly apolitical and only seem to write poetry with their backs turned to the world, social reality, changes of language, and the exigencies of the poetic craft in order to communicate with the everyday reader. The point of this answer is to emphasize the need for poetry and politics to intersect, and also to assert that a depoliticized poetry does not have a place in the context of the early 1960s in Latin America.

The third part of the interview engages with the question of poetic style. As with the previous two questions, the poetic voice also begins by affirming how the speaker draws inspiration from random moments, writes his poetry in bed or on trains, but is always thinking about the future. The answer to this question about poetic style ends with the poet's rejection of style, or rather a statement that he does not believe in style. The fourth and final question of the interview deals with the matter of love and its role in poetry. Here the poetic voice begins to answer in a more honest way and thoroughly accepts how love plays a central role in his quotidian life. His affirmation at the end is that love is a serious matter. The final stanza of the poem is the speaker's request not to publish the interview.

In sum, one can argue that Benedetti's poem "Interview" mocks the elevated and metaphysical tone of poets, as depicted in the first stanza of the interview. With the second stanza, Benedetti pokes fun at those poets who write depoliticized poetry. For Benedetti, socially committed poetry is central to the act of communication. This question of communication is directly connected to the question of style, since conversational style or poetry-as-communication necessitates concrete, direct, quotidian language. Finally, the question of love is also central to the poet-as-communicator, particularly in the poetry of Benedetti, Cardenal, and Dalton. In Benedetti's poetry we find different dimensions of love, ranging from love between lovers, to love and compassion for one's neighbor, to love as a real-life emotion to which readers can relate. Part of the strategy we find in "Interview" is an affirmation that a poet-as-communicator must have firm beliefs about his or her craft, style, and the centrality of politics in his or her work, but also how more earthly and universal questions play a role. Ultimately, for Benedetti the poet-as-communicator must have a defined sense and purpose about the means and ends of poetry. There is no middle ground for Benedetti and no possibility of lacking an opinion on pressing social and political questions and thus a poet-as-communicator must have firm beliefs and stand by them.

In terms of thinking about Benedetti's poems, it becomes useful to consider the purpose of a poem and its sites of enunciation. In light of these topics related to poetic language, for instance, Martin Heidegger wrote:

> Everyone knows that a poem is an invention. It is imaginative even when it seems to be descriptive. . . . The poem, as composed, images what is thus fashioned for our own act of imagining. In the poem's speaking the poetic imagination gives itself utterance. What is thus spoken out, speaks by enunciating its content. The language of the poem is manifold enunciating. (Heidegger, "Language" 195)

Because Benedetti embraces a conversational style of poetic language, his poems might appear as merely descriptive, as social realist to some degree. Yet, as Heidegger suggests, there is a certain inventiveness in a poem, even if it describes the world around us. Part of the poetic gesture is to invent images, to conjure up affective responses through language, and in this way poetry induces an aesthetic effect in its readers. Of particular interest, however, is the emphasis on the act of enunciating poetic content, or rather, that a multiplicity (manifold) of voices emerges from within a poem. By this, I take it that Heidegger is drawing our attention to the multiple resonances that a particular word may have, or its implied meanings. This emphasis on enunciation is different from the one that Mignolo gives to the geopolitical site of enunciation, by which he means that enunciation differs depending upon the location within the house of modernity/coloniality (*The Darker Side of Western Modernity* 94–95). To challenge the embedded legacies of the coloniality of aesthetics, particularly as it plays out in poetry, is already an attempt to make oneself heard, even if those being challenged do not always want to hear or understand such challenges.

A clear instance of this tension appears in a different poem from Benedetti's same collection. A poem that is a bit more personal in tone and somewhat autobiographical, "Cumpleaños en Manhattan" ["Birthday in Manhattan"] was written during Benedetti's only visit to the United States. Given his political stance and his overt denunciation of U.S.

imperialism, after the 1960s Benedetti was repeatedly denied entry to the country. It is no coincidence that among the four poets discussed here, Benedetti's poetry has been the least translated into English, precisely because of his explicit critique of the United States' imperialist attitude and its structural attempts at instituting coloniality in perpetuity.

In the poem, the speaker takes the reader through a walk in Manhattan. The speaker describes a feeling of utter isolation, alienation, and anonymity on his birthday by underscoring how in his 39 years the speaker has never felt simultaneously so alone and yet surrounded by so many people. The cityscape is described in the poem as we walk past skyscrapers and, on the streets, pass others by. The speaker constantly reminds himself that this day cannot be his true birthday. Instead, he will postpone it until February or March, once he returns home to celebrate it alongside family and friends. A recurring image in the poem is how New Yorkers walk for hours without stopping. All of a sudden, the speaker is happy that other Latin Americans (Colombians, Brazilians, Mexicans, Puerto Ricans, Chileans) in New York recognize in him a certain air of familiarity. However, his happiness is rapidly reduced to despair as that moment of being surrounded by familiar faces dissipates all too quickly. This level of affective connection and recognition transcending national borders is one that harkens back to a utopian dream of unifying Latin America that goes back to Simón Bolívar. Yet, in this instance, this recognition of commonality is also one that accentuates Latin Americans' alienation as migrants in a new, foreign, and somewhat inhospitable land that perpetuates the social, cultural, and political unevenness that these migrants experienced back home and from which they were seeking to escape.

In other words, this particular section of the poem reinscribes what José David Saldívar, following Immanuel Wallerstein and Aníbal Quijano, calls Trans-Americanity. As Saldívar notes, Trans-Americanity articulates "that the geo-social and temporal space of Americanity and the coloniality of power involve us in a number of different conceptual axes" (xvii–xviii). As migrants recognize their coloniality within each other and appeal to their shared lived experiences of subjugation, a type of Trans-Americanity comes to the fore to articulate their experiential otherness. "Cumpleaños en Manhattan" concludes with a bleak message in which the poetic speaker feels forgotten, yet calm and inconspicuous—like, he says, a leading zero (in mathematics). This poem prefigures the themes of exile he would take up throughout his life, during his multiple periods outside of Uruguay. Ultimately, in confronting and inhabiting the heart of U.S. imperialism while taking notice of quotidian experiences provides readers with the critical perspective of a visitor who does not romanticize the American dream or its lived experience.

In his collection *Noción de patria* (1962–1963), Benedetti presents us with an epigraph from Parra's poem "Advertencia," in which Parra announces that he is not afraid to get into trouble by writing poetry. This authorial gesture of invoking Parra further corroborates the poetic affinity between Benedetti's and Parra's respective poetic projects, particularly in terms of redefining the uses of poetic language as a means of overt or veiled social and political critique. In the opening poem, which gives the collection its name, the poetic speaker clearly articulates a redefinition of what country or nation has come to mean by invoking a sense of collective yearning for a lost home and the imperative to feel like one belongs to a community. It is that sense of urgency that gives way to a renewed connotation to what nation means, while simultaneously adding a degree of uncertainty about its attainability. While Benedetti has traveled and wandered the world, we get a glimpse of what it is like to yearn for an imaginary home—a place left behind and lodged in one's memory. For Benedetti, the desire to return to his native Uruguay pervades wherever he may be. As such, the sense of alienation, of foreignness, of being an outsider makes him feel like cities and images are just a mirage, artificial, unreal, and transitory. As denoted in Benedetti's concluding verses to "Noción de Patria," the speaker wants to return home to have that sense of collectivity, of belonging to a place and feeling at one with those around him. However, Benedetti also acknowledges that such a return is an impossibility and the precise path toward that return is mere uncertainty. After all, it does not matter how much Benedetti yearns for his homeland; the conditions of return prevail and establish an uncertainty he cannot overcome. The overwhelming feeling of uncertainty and his inability to return are the last images of this opening poem that sets the tone for the rest of the collection, a tone of ongoing desire for homecoming and a never-ending quest to look for that moment when a return home can be completed.

Aside from his engagement with the theme of exile, Benedetti also engages with a mixture of political and religious themes. A prime example of this can be found in "Un Padrenuestro Latinoamericano" ["A Latin American Our Father"] from his collection *Poemas del hoyporhoy*. In this poem, the language of the prayer is infused with a sense that the Lord has forgotten about and neglected everything south of the Rio Grande. The poetic voice beseeches the Lord to turn his attention once again to those who need Him the most, particularly those suffering, the poor, and those living in absolute misery. The poem is both a prayer and also a denunciation of the lopsided divine distribution of wealth and everyday goods necessary for survival. The sense of urgency and the pangs of hunger in the stomachs of those with little food are clearly expressed in his confrontation with God's will simultaneously to give and take away the poor's daily bread. As the poetic speaker clearly suggests, the questioning of God's will is expressed with irreverence and gratitude. The bread, in this case, stands both as a symbol of God himself and also of the material and essential food the poor need to satisfy their hunger and basic necessities. Part of the dissatisfaction the speaker expresses is that God has also deprived the poor of the ability to provide bread for themselves. This poem is thus irreverent in terms of how the speaker confronts God and His will, but also because this confrontation opens up the possibility that the poor might not need to rely upon God's will anymore if they are given the opportunity to secure their own daily bread. In the poem, the collective pronoun "nuestro" (our) is used to denote a sense of community and discontent, as well as the changing times, in which social unrest and protests are leading to a questioning of deeply embedded religious beliefs—that is, of one of the ways in which the coloniality of power has rooted itself, particularly among the disenfranchised or the wretched of the earth, to echo Fanon's words.

The poetic voice takes on a demanding tone with a mixture of irreverence and gratitude, which soon will become indistinguishable from one another. There can be no gratitude for someone who takes food away from hungry mouths. As Benedetti reminds us, daily bread was taken from Latin Americans in the past, but perhaps today it can be given to them once again. If real bread is not possible, a symbolic or religious one will no longer suffice to suppress hunger. The idea of obtaining food becomes an organizational principle and a fixed idea that marks each passing day and every part of a hungry day. Above all, we are presented with the idea that Latin Americans will no longer wait for food to come to them and instead are willing to work even harder to procure it, if only such a possibility presents itself.

In thinking through the social implications of this poem, and its invocation of religious motifs for a poetic critique, we may find it helpful to connect this to Glissant's words regarding the adequacy and power of poetic language: "The poetics no longer requires the adequacy of language, but the precise fire of language. In other words: I speak to you in your language, and it is in my language that I understand you" (Glissant, *Poetic Intention* 46). As I take it, Glissant foregrounds that in times of social unrest, political upheaval, and pressing hardships, lingering on the ornamental function of poetry will not suffice. Instead, finding the adequate words requires that the poet turn to "the fire of language," which is to say, the language that emerges from extreme feelings and that will spark the most sentiments in readers. It is through this common language, and by resorting to quotidian means of expression, that poet and reader can understand each other. In the case of this particular poem by Benedetti, using the form a widely known Catholic prayer and turning it upside down serves to communicate directly with readers in a language that is already familiar (the prayer), though modified for a particular social and political commentary.

Other aspects of the poem engage with U.S. militarization in Central America, the colonial legacy of landowners, peasants, and land distribution, foreign debt, and inflation in Latin American economies, among other topics. As the poor, the indigenous, and the oppressed have succumbed to a long-standing history of social inequities, images of growing non-conformity and social uprisings are also present when the speaker confronts God with the suggestion that His will is present when a citizen turns her or his hand into a fist. The fist, then, becomes a symbol of unrest and protest, as well as of the need to fight against conformity with the status quo. The image of working hands turning into fists ready to fight marks a clear transition in the poem from a sense of collective Latin American passivity to one of a collective shift toward uprisings and struggles, an evocative image of anti-imperial and anticolonial struggles taking place on a global scale in the 1960s. The ultimate decolonial gesture is to invoke the Lord's Prayer and employ it in a more overt political gesture, though in a way distinct from the theology of liberation poetics associated with Ernesto Cardenal. In this particular poem, an implicit suggestion and critique is the role that religion has played in producing and accentuating multi-modal coloniality on its different axes and in different articulations of power (race, knowledge, religion, gender, aesthetics, ontology, etc.). As we will see in the following section, this way of writing poetry that engages with social concerns and religious undertones is one that is best exemplified in Cardenal's poetry, though in a different way and with a less-confrontational tone.

Ernesto Cardenal and Exteriorist Poetry

In Cardenal's work we find a link between liberation theology and poetry, particularly around a depiction of God and Christian beliefs capable of putting an end to suffering and social injustices (DeHay 48–59). By incorporating precepts from liberation theology into his poetry, Cardenal seeks to portray how the average person struggles against oppression, aggression, and unequal distribution of wealth and other forms of capital. Above all, Cardenal is interested in synthesizing the idea of love, which is at once a devotion to his calling as a priest and also a love of mankind, his neighbors, and those who need him the most. In Cardenal's conceptualization of his duty as priest and poet, he cannot just be a preacher, but must also find a way to reinterpret Christian doctrines to bring about social justice for the poor and thus give them a sense of hope (Benedetti, "Ernesto Cardenal: Evangelio y revolución").

As I argued earlier in this chapter, one of the functions of decolonial aesthetics is to inscribe a broader sense of the relationship among the artist, the artwork, and its level of engagement with broader audiences. To this end, for instance, Cardenal opted to teach basic literacy to the people in his colony in Solentiname. For Cardenal, if people do not have a basic sense of literacy, the message of the Gospels and other Biblical scriptures cannot be conveyed. In this sense, we see a connection with Cardenal's Marxist ideology and how the Cuban Revolution also set out early on to remedy illiteracy. Otherwise, the message of a social and cultural revolution would be meaningless and flawed. In a similar way, before even attempting to teach catechism to children, Cardenal took on the challenge of ensuring that children could overcome illnesses and thus premature death, which is linked to the concept of care that will be discussed more fully at the end of this section. In both cases, Cardenal identified basic problems that needed to be addressed before any Christian message could be delivered. The experiences in Solentiname, along with his previous experiences in monasteries in Kentucky, Cuernavaca, and Colombia, gave Cardenal a profound sense of how he could turn his religious calling and poetic work toward a higher and collective purpose (Fernández Retamar, "Prologue to Ernesto Cardenal"; DeHay 48–59).

In an attempt to argue for an aesthetics of Americanity (*estética de lo americano*), Rodolfo Kusch advances the following position: "En general cuando el arte no confiesa, miente, y, por lo tanto, entra en el plano de la diversión. Y la confesión ha de ser de las cosas que vienen desde muy adentro, más allá de la conciencia, de aquel mundo que se halla cerca del germen vital o de que arranca la vida misma" [In general terms, when art does not confess, it lies, and thus it moves toward the terrain of entertainment. Such a confession must be one of those things that emerges from within the depths, beyond conscience, from that world close to the seeds of life or from which life itself begins] (Kusch, *Planteo* 775–776). For Kusch, life, as both the source and inspiration of art, must play a pivotal role in its creation. Works of art must be attuned to the depths of Latin America's neglected realities and truths. It is in this spirit that Cardenal's poetry is invested in creating art that is honest, even at the cost of relegating aesthetics to a secondary role. For it is with honesty, integrity, and social commitment that a politicized undoing of the coloniality of poetic language (a decolonial aesthetics) affects the reader's senses.

In his collection titled *Salmos* (1969) [*Psalms*], Cardenal's poetic voice is one that beseeches God to attend to the immediate and urgent needs of people who have been historically alienated, oppressed, and forgotten. For instance, in his fourth psalm, Cardenal writes: "Óyeme porque te invoco Dios de mi inocencia / Tú me liberarás del campo de concentración" (*Salmos* 11). ["Hear me O God because I call upon you in my innocence / You will free me from the concentration camp"] (*Psalms* 13). Cardenal's tone is not so much a request as a demand. It is meant to reflect how certain groups in society are tired of praying without any response. The underprivileged and oppressed are also tired of the instrumentalization of politics to continue asserting power over the poor. In the same poem we read: "¿Hasta cuándo los líderes seréis insensatos? / ¿Hasta cuándo dejaréis de hablar con slogans / y decir pura proganda?"

(*Salmos* 11). ["How long will leaders be without reason? / How long will you let them speak in slogans / and utter pure propaganda?"] (*Psalms* 13). In this part of the poem, it is not God who is called upon, but rather questions of discontent and frustration are directed at God for allowing politicians to speak in empty political rhetoric, meaningless slogans, and vacuous promises that never materialize. Toward the end of the poem, as a way to appease God and to reassure Him that He is still respected, we get a radical shift in tone: "Apenas me acuesto estoy dormindo / y no tengo pesadillas ni insomnio . . . / No necesito Nembutales / porque tú Señor me das seguridad" (*Salmos* 11). ["I hardly lie down before I am asleep / and I have no pills nor insomnia . . . I do not need barbiturates / because you Lord give me security"] (*Psalms* 14). The psalm concludes with the image of a soothing and comforting God who is capable of clearing one's head of nightmares and preventing insomnia. The speaker finds solace and comfort in knowing that God will attend to his calling and will act upon his just requests to put an end to political repression and the persecution of the innocent under Anastasio Somoza's dictatorship in Nicaragua (1937–1956), Cardenal's home country.

In thinking about Cardenal's exteriorist poetics, particularly in relation to liberation theology in the service of a critique of capitalism and the techniques of politics that enable poverty and suffering, it becomes necessary to pause over one of the possible meanings of liberation theology. In a recent study, Mexican scholar Luis Martinez Andrade has noted the following: "Liberation theology, as a critical and emancipatory discourse, has been instrumental in the process of hegemonic narrative *de-fetishisation*. Through a prophetic and subversive look at the various aspects of modern society—the sanctification of the market, messianic technology, the myth of progress, the ideology of developmentalism, among others—this liberation theology has revealed the sacrificial character of the hegemonic system" (104). Despite Cardenal's conflation of religious and Marxist themes, his poetry has been associated with the line of conversational poetry. Cardenal draws inspiration from Ezra Pound to use poetry as an all-encompassing medium of expression and communication capable of accomplishing just as much as narrative and essays can do. For Cardenal, a poem can engage with topics related to economics, politics, culture, indigenous themes, pre-Columbian history of the Americas, religious topics, etc. As Cardenal argues: "Para mí es muy importante la comunicación con el lector, y siempre he tratado de hacer una poesía clara, ya que siempre estoy interesado en que el lector entienda mi mensaje, e incluso que lo entienda el lector que no está muy acostumbrado a entender la poesía" [For me it is very important to communicate with the reader; I have always tried creating a clear poetry, since I'm always interested in having the reader understand my message, and even in having that reader unaccustomed to reading poetry also understand my message] (Benedetti, "Ernesto Cardenal: Evangelio y revolución" 113). This is perhaps one of the clearest articulations of how his exteriorist poetry, which borrows from Pound's modernist poetics, is repurposed for a particular project of direct engagement with everyday readers and turns poetry into an instrument of social and political critique.

Moreover, in Cardenal's poetry, there is an embedded commitment to trying to write poetry that is at once conversational and yet rigorous in its poetic vision. In this respect, Cardenal differs from Parra's poetic proposition, since Cardenal labels his type of poetry "exteriorist." By employing the concept of exteriorism, Cardenal stands in opposition to the lyrical-oneiric poetry that had dominated Latin American poetics up to his time.[10] In sum, the poetic proposition is one that takes external images as a means by which to express internal feelings, attitudes, and perspectives on the quotidian. Given this approach, anecdotes, proper names, real names, numbers, and dates, among other facts, can be incorporated into the poetic production as an act of communication. In this sense, a poet like Cardenal takes external, verifiable facts as a way to verbalize and ground his own ideas. In essence, exteriorism, as a way of writing conversational poetry or poetry of communication, seeks to bridge a gap between poetic subjectivity and material/external objectivity. Cardenal suggests that his poetry follows the tradition of the Bible, Homer, and Dante, but also of Inuit and indigenous poetics. More importantly, however, Cardenal affirms the following: "toda buena poesía social y política y económica, y toda poesía revolucionaria tiene necesariamente que ser exteriorista" [All good social, political, and economic poetry, and all revolutionary poetry, has necessarily to be exteriorist] (Benedetti, "Ernesto Cardenal: Evangelio y revolución" 121). In Cardenal's conceptualization of exteriorist poetry, he also introduces the idea of the poet as a revolutionary, which is meant to be a way of articulating what he perceives to be the poet's duties. First, the poet must revolutionize language. This alone can be construed as a political act. One does not have to take up arms to be revolutionary. In this sense, for instance, Parra and Benedetti are revolutionary poets of the word and conversational poetic language. Cardenal is a revolutionary poet of the word, but also takes action leading to social justice, whereas Dalton is a revolutionary poet who also engages in guerrilla warfare and armed struggles.

An instance of Cardenal's engagement with revolutionary poetry can be seen in "Psalm 34," in which, once again, he addresses God in a direct way and reminds Him to be on the side of the poor: "Declara Señor tu guerra a los que nos declaran la guerra / porque tú eres aliado nuestro / Grandes potencias están contra nosotros / pero las armas del Señor son más terribles" (*Salmos* 37). ["Lord declare your war on those who declare war on us / Because you are our ally / Great Powers are against us / but the weapons of the Lord are more terrible"] (*Psalms* 41). Cardenal presents us with an image of a God who is ready to fight and struggle alongside those who are persecuted, imprisoned, abused, tortured, and humiliated by those in power. In other words, Cardenal beseeches God to make an ethical decision and side with those who need him most. There is a clear distinction in the poem between two groups that cannot see eye to eye, and God must take a stand, but cannot side with both. Cardenal includes himself among the "us," those who struggle, suffer, and are most underprivileged. Cardenal concludes the poem by enticing God into helping those in need by praising Him through poetry for the rest of the poet's life. As Cardenal notes in a recent collection of essays on this question of God, which seems pertinent to my reading of this particular psalm, "Y cuando Dios nos ama a cada uno de nosotros está amando a todo el universo del que somos parte, aunque sólo los seres conscientes pueden corresponder a este amor" [And when God loves each of us, He is loving the entire universe of which we are part, even though only conscious beings can return this love] (Cardenal, *Este mundo y otros* 58). Ultimately, liberation theology and poetry in the service of social justice emerge as reminders that we are all part of something greater than we are. To believe in God's love is to also believe that His love is directed at every aspect of our world and the pluriverse. It is only in recognizing that sense of love that we can engage in an ethical duty of undoing injustices and calling into question various modalities of subjection. As with most of the poems in this collection, the poetic plea or supplication to a God who has forgotten about the poor is meant to generate a sense of collectivity through a conflation of spirituality, desperation, alienation, and being fed up with current living conditions.

Understanding Cardenal's poetry in terms of liberation theology, particularly in terms of Cardenal's own emphasis on love, is necessary to understanding that our work as readers is not merely to take in words, metaphors, and beautiful images. Instead, this emphasis on love, on a collective, societal, pluriversal love, is linked to what Leonardo Boff has recently highlighted as care. Care is a broader way of experiencing or naming what Cardenal understood as love for one another, in terms of both human and non-human entities, and also our particular love for God, which is also expressed through loving the poor and dispossessed. As Boff noted,

> The fable-myth of Gaius Junius Hyginus transmits to us an ancient wisdom; that is, it is care that binds everything, it is care that brings the heavens into the Earth and that puts the Earth into the heavens, it is care that provides the links from transcendence to immanence, from immanence to transcendence and from history to Utopia. It is care that grants strength to search for peace among the various levels of conflict. Without care that recovers the dignity of humanity condemned to exclusion, the new paradigm of living together will not be established. (143)

In his foregrounding of care as a principle and action that compels us to recognize the historical injustices and deeply rooted mechanisms of oppression that have turned "the wretched of the earth" (Fanon) into the "dispossessed of the earth" (Boff), care, according to Boff, will allow us to strive for the recovery of the dignity of the dispossessed, and the dignity of all humanity. The ultimate goal of foregrounding care is to acknowledge its centrality in what makes us human, an ethos within ourselves that privileges well-being, the *sumak kawsay* (*el buen vivir*), something some of us seem to have forgotten or, at the very least, neglected. Ultimately, Boff calls for humans to recognize within themselves not only the ethical duty to care for the dispossessed, but also how care can be activated as a principle to counteract "ecological degradation" and "the exaltation of violence" on a localized and global scale (144). While some concepts circulated as decolonial theories disengage from theology, as much as they disengage from a Marxist approach to understanding social inequities and the centrality of capitalism in a critique of coloniality, Cardenal's work intersects with liberation theology and he becomes a poet who is foundational to a decolonial ethos, particularly given his preoccupation with the poor, the dispossessed, the racialized, the historically silenced, and the marginalized beings who have been denied a right to exist.

Roque Dalton and Revolutionary Poetry

The late Salvadoran poet Roque Dalton provides insight into his way of conceptualizing poetry, particularly into how *La taberna y otros lugares* (1967) came to be. Since *La taberna* was composed during a time of exile that took Dalton through Cuba, the German Democratic Republic, and Czechoslovakia, Dalton found that, in composing his poetry, he was in fact taking sociological notes based on conversations he overheard from Czech youth and on other observations, particularly in relation to the third part of the collection. As such, Dalton considered his poetry a sociological exercise in which he documented the effects of socialist ideology on the ground (Benedetti, "Una hora con Roque Dalton" 21–22). More importantly, however, in Dalton's poetry we see a form of poetry of communication or antipoetry as a committed and revolutionary act. In Dalton's poetic praxis, he argues that poetry needs to be committed to social change, as well as active and armed struggle against oppression and imperialism (Benedetti, "Una hora con Roque Dalton"; Dalton, *Poetry and Militancy in Latin America*).

Unlike Parra's clear attempt not to disclose his political alignment, Dalton makes no effort to hide his ideological inclinations. For Dalton, poetry is a medium that lends itself to engage with the urgency of undoing or challenging social inequities. In this sense, the poet-as-communicator is also a militant-poet and thus must create art with the intention of denouncing social injustice, but must also be actively engaged with everyday social struggles and the social reality of the people.

In interpreting Dalton's poetics, Hugo Achugar argues that Dalton's poetry "struggles against a system of values that limits poetry to a linguistic adventure with no historical function beyond the development of imagination" (658). This is not to say, however, that Dalton renounces writing aesthetically pleasing or "good" poetry. What changes, however, are the terms, conditions, and categories with which one evaluates poetic works that are at once revolutionary in their political ideology, engaged with larger social struggles, and effecting of profound changes at the level of language and poetics. As Margaret Randall notes about Dalton's influence on writers of his generation: "He taught us, among many other things, that a simplistic sense of 'social realism,' in terms of creative expression, was nothing more nor less than a lack of respect for the work we were doing" (iv). In Dalton's poetic proposition, art was life itself, which is to say that life was the foundation for any type of art. To this end, a poet's commitment had to be to life and not merely a political commitment.

Numerous examples of Dalton's poetic praxis can be found among his poetry collections, including his 1967 publication of *Taberna y otros lugares,* which was awarded the Premio Casa de las Américas in 1969. The organization of the collection is aimed at displaying multiple facets and observations of the poet-as-revolutionary. The first part of book is dedicated to an articulation of Dalton's imagined nation. In his poem "El gran despecho" ["The Great Resentment"], Dalton writes: "País mío no existes / sólo eres una mala silueta mía / una palabra que le creí al enemigo" [Country of mine, you don't exist / you are only a poor silhouette of me / an enemy's word, which I believed] (Taberna y otros lugares 10). Since the idea of country and home Dalton had in mind is nothing but a figment of his imagination and a construction based on an idea instilled by the enemy, El Salvador is defined in a negative way. While Dalton wants to claim El Salvador as his own, he soon realizes that it is an invention or a byproduct of imperialism. In the short poem, Dalton continues to realize that if once he considered El Salvador a small country, with the passing of time, he has realized how insignificant it has becomes as he writes: "pero ahora sé que no existes / y que además parece que nadie te necesita / no se oye hablar a ninguna madre de ti" [But now I know that you don't exist / and more so since no one seems to need you / one doesn't hear any mother speaking about you] (Taberna y otros lugares 10). Dalton defines El Salvador as unnecessary, since it is not essential to anyone. Moreover, with the invocation of a maternal figure, we are reminded of El Salvador's history of colonialism and imperialism, with no one to claim or care for this imagined and then forgotten nation. The poem concludes with full acceptance that his idea of El Salvador was nothing but an invention of his own mind, and that he should be put away in a mental institution for such delirium. In this sense, Dalton realizes that he is himself an expatriate, but also that his country is an ex-patria, or a former country, that is no longer recognizable or one he can call his own.

The rest of the collection presents us with engaging and thought-provoking articulations of exile. Dalton dedicates almost two-thirds of the collection to the idea of country, but from different perspectives. If the first section seeks to engage with a personal quest to come to terms with his own exile and "expatriation," the second section produces fictional characters of English descent who are meant to stand for the neo-imperialist forces that replaced Spanish colonialism in the nineteenth and early twentieth centuries. Put differently, the construction of the collection can be read as an attempt to zoom-in on El Salvador's and Latin America's history of colonialism and its pervasive coloniality. Dalton's third section, about the idea of country, is described from the perspective of imprisonment, which is another of Dalton's facets as a revolutionary. In this section, the idea of country becomes more elusive, since El Salvador seems to turn its back on those in prison by treating them as enemies of the state, as subhuman. The two final sections of the book engage with sociological poetry or poetry written in prose and dialogue form, but also as a reflection on world historical themes and ideological articulations of Marxism among the youth of socialist Europe. Much of the collection was written during Dalton's period of exile, which took him on a journey through socialist countries, including Cuba, the German Democratic Republic, and Czechoslovakia.[11]

As a way to get a better perspective on Dalton's development as a revolutionary poet, we can turn to a posthumous publication comprised of the last set of poems he wrote, under five pseudonyms. *Poemas clandestinos* appears as an attempt to write, publish, and circulate his poetry by passing it off as having been written by one woman and four men of different professions. In her introduction to this bilingual publication, Margaret Randall has suggested that Dalton chose to write in the voice of a woman as a way to come to terms with his own sexism (Randall i–xii). One could argue, however, that the inclusion of a female voice, or his attempt to write from the perspective of a woman, is Dalton's attempt to call attention to how revolutionary struggles have often silenced women's voices.

It is interesting to note that each of Dalton's pseudonyms is presented with a corresponding brief biography, and each has a poetic collection of its own. Vilma Flores, Dalton's feminine pseudonym, suggests in "Sobre Nuestra Moral Poética" ["On Our Poetic Moral"] that she and her fellow "poets" in the volume should not be confused with detached poets who openly attack the enemy; they must rely on anonymity and clandestinity to avoid repercussions. Instead, Flores writes: "Y al sistema y a los hombres / que atacamos desde nuestra poesía / con nuestra vida les damos la oportunidad de que se cobren, / día tras día" (Dalton, *Poemas Clandestinos / Clandestine Poems* 6). ["And we give the system and the men / we attack—with our poetry / with our lives—the opportunity to get back at us day after day"] (Dalton, *Poemas Clandestinos / Clandestine Poems* 7).[12] In Dalton's feminine pseudonym we can discern a clear attempt to call attention to the disparity in gendered power distribution among revolutionary and guerrilla forces. Flores emphasizes how revolutionary women struggle on two fronts: against a common enemy, and against men. Flores evinces a desire for women to be treated equally and for men to fight alongside them in everyday struggle. Other themes found in the poems presented under this feminine pseudonym are questions of love between revolutionary men and women, but also how to spread the message of love and equality among all Salvadorians. If read beyond the context of revolutionary struggle, this particular poem draws attention to the coloniality of gender, as articulated by María Lugones and Rita Segato.[13] Coloniality of gender names a complex and historically embedded mechanism by which gender has been created and rendered normative as a modality of exclusionary practices within a patriarchal, Europeanized society. Lugones, in particular, draws attention to the potential for examining the grid of coloniality not only in terms of race and capitalism, but also in terms of gender, through intersectionality—that is, how modes of racialization and gendering are inextricably linked practices through which power is displayed and by which coloniality is instantiated. If read as a decolonial gesture from Dalton, the poem displays the very tensions of power that have created a hierarchy of power among men and women, despite the seemingly horizontal and socialist goals of revolutionary struggles. More importantly, as the poem suggests, poetry is a means to attack the system, which could be capitalism, imperialism, or patriarchy, all of which converge in what has been termed the coloniality of power.

The remaining four pseudonyms in the collection are men who, in their pre-revolutionary lives, studied law, sociology, and architecture, and one student who demonstrated an interest in liberation theology. Given its brevity and succinctness, one poem, written under the pseudonym of Timoteo Lue, seems to encapsulate Dalton's conceptualization of how to mend the apparent schism that separates poetics and revolutionary work. In "Arte Poética 1974" ["Poetic Art 1974"], the entire poem reads as follows: "Poesía / Perdóname por haberte ayudado a comprender / que no estás hecha sólo de palabras" (Dalton, *Poemas Clandestinos / Clandestine Poems* 34). ["Poetry / Forgive me for having helped you understand / you're not made of words alone"] (Dalton, *Poemas Clandestinos / Clandestine Poems* 35).[14] In short, poetry needs to be in the service of revolutionary action for the greater well-being of others. Poetry cannot stand with its back turned to reality. As such, Dalton, under the pseudonym of Lue, reminds us that poetry is comprised of a number of elements transcending mere words, images, or rhetorical devices. In this brief poem, Dalton also helps us realize how he has forced poetry into submission in order to communicate and understand once and for all what its true essence is all about. To put things differently, and to return briefly to antipoetry's stance as being anti-Neruda, when Benedetti asks Dalton whether he sees himself as being part of César Vallejo's or Neruda's family, Dalton replies: "Mira, yo quisiera ser uno de los nietos de Vallejo. Con la familia Neruda no tengo nada que ver. Hemos roto nuestras relaciones hace tiempo" [Look, I would like to be one of Vallejo's grandchildren. I want nothing to do with Neruda's family. We severed ties long ago] (Benedetti, "Una hora con Roque Dalton" 33).

Poetics of Sensing, or Sensing Poetic Fragments

In her study of César Vallejo's profound contribution to lyric modernity, Michelle Clayton argues for a reading of Vallejo's poetry that privileges "an ethics of the fragment," by which she seeks to distinguish Vallejo's notion of the fragmentary from avant-garde's versions of the term. Instead, Clayton seeks to underscore the fragment in terms of its "centrality to modes of modern subjectivity and collectivism. Poetry in pieces, in other words, as the most responsible mode of lyric modernity" (3). Borrowing this notion of the fragment in Vallejo's poetry, I would like to extend the fragmentary as a critical concept that enables a discussion of seemingly dissimilar poetic modes during the 1960s, a period in which "poetry is afforded very little place, which suggests that in the 1960s—just as today—the aesthetics of lyric poetry was thought to have little to say about or contribute to political discourse" (Clayton 5). In confronting the seemingly disparate and yet conjoined poetics of Parra, Benedetti, Cardenal, or Dalton, we notice a genealogy of the fragmentary that appears in Vallejo.[15] As a genealogy, then, we can understand their claiming a certain ancestry or familial relation that turns these diverse poets into kindred interlocutors constantly seeking to activate an ethics of the fragment in order to foreground the social and political dimensions of their respective poetic projects. Ultimately, such an ethics of the fragmentary seeks to create a resonance of poetry with pressing political questions in a national context, but always with an eye toward bringing together individual Latin American nations (as fragments) in a dialogue with each other through poetry and the arts at large, perhaps in an attempt to correct and advance Bolívar and Martí's dreams of a united Latin America.

The idea of the fragmentary in relation to the arts is one that particularly resonates with the project at hand, especially if we think about fragments in the broadest possible sense. For instance, how do we understand individual song lyrics or a poetic verse, particularly those deemed memorable? In part, reading a verse detached from its whole requires a double extirpation, first of the verse from its poem and then of the poem from its collection. A similar gesture of fragmenting occurs when we listen to a song that belongs to and was intended to be part of an album. Analyzing a scene from a film also requires this type of formal and intentional fragmentation. But this is only one type of fragmentation, interpretive or analytical, among others, including the act of dividing artworks among genres and subgenres. So, how can we make sense of two explicitly fragmentary acts—namely, reducing the scope of study to a few years (the 1960s) and choosing an array of case studies in poetry traditionally deemed incompatible with each other (Parra, Benedetti, Cardenal, and Dalton)?

To provide a preliminary answer, one can turn to Alain Badiou's concept of inaesthetics, particularly as it relates to poetry, and Rancière's response to such an enticing concept. The precise meaning of "inaesthetics" in Badiou's *The Handbook of Inaesthetics* is elusive. It rests on two lines that appear as an epigraph, as well as on a series of readings seeking to show what inaesthetics looks like when we encounter the works of Fernando Pessoa, Stéphane Mallarmé, Paul Valéry, Labîd ben Rabi'a, dance, theater, film, music, and other art forms. Of interest is Badiou's assertion that "The poem is neither a description nor an expression. Nor is it an affected painting of the world's extension. The poem is an operation. The poem teaches us that the world does not present itself as a collection of objects" (*Handbook of Inaesthetics* 29). In seemingly rejecting the Aristotelian model of mimesis, Badiou argues for the poem as an artifact that stands on its own terms and that neither contains nor seeks to replicate the world in a handful of images in verse. Instead, we enter a poem, Badiou argues, "not in order to know what it means, but rather to think about what happens in it" (29). As I take it, Badiou is encouraging a radical shift in our reading practices and methodologies by moving away from privileging interpretation and treating a poem instead as a laboratory in which to think about the "Ideas" suggested in it. Furthermore, Badiou seems to privilege the pedagogical function of the artwork, in this case a poem, "not so much in order to preserve a realm that is proper to poetry or to art, but to preserve the educational value of the Idea" (Rancière, "Aesthetics, Inaesthetics, Anti-Aesthetics" 224). In so doing, then, philosophy turns to poetry as a site from which to think, and thus suggests that literary interpretation is incompatible with aesthetics as a means of arriving at ideas and knowledge of the world. Rancière, for instance, calls Badiou's project ultra-Platonist, given Badiou's aversion to "the notion that the specificity of the arts resides in their respective *languages*. It resides, he affirms, in their *Ideas*" (Rancière, "Aesthetics, Inaesthetics, Anti-Aesthetics" 222, original emphasis). Differently put, in Rancière's reading, inaesthetics becomes a set of reading and interpretative operations that place the arts at the service of philosophical thought. As such, the arts are mere instruments of philosophical thinking, since they symbolize or point to specific problems germane to philosophical inquiry. The specificity of poetic language or music, then, is almost secondary to what poems or songs can offer as events or sites from which to think or test out ideas.

If Clayton is right in her claim that poetry in the 1960s in Latin America was deemed as having little to offer political thinking, we should keep in mind the activation of poetry in Badiou's work not only for pedagogical or philosophical purposes, but also as a way to engage ethics and politics. In Rancière's reading of Badiou's inaesthetics as ultra-Platonism is the claim that "to be a Platonist is to maintain that the question of the poem is ultimately an ethical and political one, that the poem or art is educational" (Rancière, "Aesthetics, Inaesthetics, Anti-Aesthetics" 224). Thinking about poetry's contribution to aesthetic and political thought during the 1960s in Latin America, then, has more to do with claiming the centrality of poetry as poetry for political thinking and with being an integral part of a genealogy of decolonial thinking (a decolonial ethos) than with undermining its aesthetic and affective qualities. Nicanor Parra argued that poetry was nothing but life in words, which is to say that poetry must draw from life, but must also be in dialogue with it. Poetry as quotidian, conversational, and political poetry, then, becomes a direct engagement with, not retreat from, life itself. As Parra put it, "la clave de todo el problema estaba en la palabra *vida,* y la antipoesía no es otra cosa que vida en palabras" [the key to the entire problem rested upon the word *life,* and antipoetry was nothing else than life in words] (Benedetti, "Nicanor Parra o el artefacto con laureles" 51).

In choosing a corpus of poets embracing conversational poetry or antipoetry writ large, I do so with the aim of precisely emphasizing the poetic intention of establishing a clear line of communication, rather than the hermeticism that Badiou so admires in Mallarmé's poetry. This is, in fact, a decolonial critique that could be deployed when facing Badiou's Eurocentric examples of poetry. I would argue that conversational poetry can be theorized or philosophized, but its main purpose is to sense and interpret what it means and not dwell on unraveling excessively complicated metaphors or convoluted language. This is perhaps poetry's clearest contribution to a decolonial ethos, particularly as the four poets discussed here attempt to render the communication between poet and audience as something that operates on a horizontal, rather than a hierarchical, level. Furthermore, in the works of Parra, Benedetti, Cardenal, and Dalton,

I trace specific attempts to place Latin American poetics in dialogue with the transformational and ebullient epoch that was the 1960s by illustrating diverse and fragmentary anticolonial and political positions, which indeed add to a growing decolonial archive.

In Mignolo's recovery of important figures contributing to what he calls "genealogies of thought," he draws upon the work of Algerian Malik Bennabi, the Argentine Rodolfo Kusch, and the Afro-Caribbean Sylvia Winter as constituting such a genealogy of thought in the context of the 1960s. In Mignolo's retracing of a network of "non-national genealogies" of decolonial thinking, he is interested in connecting diverse experiential thinking "through the common experience of the colonial wound—of sensing that, in one way or another, one belongs to the world of the anthropos" (*The Darker Side of Western Modernity* 93). In Mignolo's critical apparatus, *anthropos* is a term he uses to discuss groups of people who have been historically deemed inferior, and who have been marginalized, racialized, sexualized, and experienced other forms of colonial/imperial domination either in their direct experience or simply by virtue of having descended from traditionally marginalized groups. In contrast to the anthropos, Mignolo deploys the term *humanitas* to frame a complex set of formal and often subtle operations that create a hierarchy of domination, and thus enact the very structures foundational to the coloniality of power. *Humanitas* becomes a term used to understand those who are Eurocentric in their thinking, being, and "dwelling," by which he means one's positionality or location "in the house of modernity/coloniality." In this context, one's positionality is not always reduced to physical location, but rather relates to one's understanding of who is capable of knowledge/reason and what the accepted and normative way of rational thinking is. *Humanitas* and the *anthropos*, then, become another way to understand the long-standing division of "civilización y barbarie" emerging from Sarmiento's thinking (*The Darker Side of Western Modernity* 94–95). In the preceding sections, I was interested in exploring how an emphasis on conversational poetry as a return to everyday language is connected to this long-standing project of undoing the sedimented division between "civilización y barbarie," *humanitas* and *anthropos*, those who deploy coloniality and those who endure it. The four poets and other critical voices in this chapter are part of a fragmented and uneven corpus of critical and everyday language seeking to denounce and undo what we now understand as coloniality and, in so doing, compel us to sense poetry otherwise and detect decolonial gestures in verse. Sensing poetic fragments is, of necessity, a set of operations that can work on multiple levels ranging from a purely affective and aesthetic engagement with poetry as poetry (figuring out what a poem means), to enabling poetry's quotidian language to help us think about both historical and contemporary issues in light of coloniality/modernity/decoloniality.

To return to Fernández Retamar's words at the beginning of this chapter, one could argue that conversational poetry (broadly construed) is attuned with its time and literary context and thus engages with the most effective means to redress them. In outlining his understanding of what constituted the difference between art criticism and the history of art, Benedetto Croce distinguished between the critic's proximity to contemporary literature and art, in which case what prevails is "the judging or polemical tone, for which the name 'criticism' seems more fitting; and in that of more remote literature and art, prevails the narrative tone, which is more readily called 'history'" (Croce, *Breviary* 72). For Croce, then, a temporal distance from the literary text or artwork moves the scholar to the side of historical context, rather than criticism, if the latter term is understood as synonymous with polemics. In the preceding sections, however, such distinctions between criticism and historicism have often been blurred in order to arrive at a critique that is attuned to the historical context of the poetry to be discussed, which seeks to reassert its relevance in the shifting poetic language of the 1960s in Latin America. By engaging in close readings to establish points of connection among four diverse poetic propositions, I have sought to shed light on each poet's distinct approach, while moving toward sensing or connecting their seemingly fragmentary positions. If read separately, these poetic positions appear as poetic or lyric fragments, to echo Clayton's idea, that indeed contribute to both poetic and political discourses by politicizing and decolonizing the aesthetic dimension of poetry and aestheticizing politics. Yet, the gesture in this chapter is to read these poetic propositions in their own right, but also relationally, as contributing to a decolonial ethos emerging from poetic verses.

In reference to the radical rupture in poetic production occurring during the sixties when compared to earlier decades in Latin America, Hugo Achugar reminds us how in that decade "an alternative to the hegemonic system emerged" (657). Achugar adds that the rise of a new poetics came about toward the end of the 1950s, particularly with the rise of the Cuban Revolution. During this time, for instance, some of the prominent names were "the Pan Duro group in Argentina (including Juan Gelman), the *antipoesía* of Nicanor Parra, the *exteriorismo* of Coronel Urtecho and Ernesto Cardenal, and the poetry of Fernández Retamar, Benedetti, and A. Cisneros" (657).

While critics such as Fernández Retamar have been pivotal in establishing a clear division between antipoetry and conversational poetry, and subsequent studies have followed suit, I have sought to go beyond this binarism.[16] Instead, it can be argued that labels or poetic propositions have particular significance insofar as each of the poets discussed here attempted to differentiate his work from others,' while also presenting a poetic proposition of his own against previous poetic traditions. Nonetheless, a quick look at the history of the period allows us to see that there are many efforts during the 1960s to establish poetic connections across Latin America. With publications such as Argentina's *Eco Contemporáneo* and *Airón,* the Venezuelan *El techo de la Ballena,* the Chilean *Orfeo,* and Mexico's *Pájaro de Cascabel* and bilingual *El Corno Emplumado/The Plumed Horn,* poets of the 1960s sought to come into contact with one another's work and ideas in an attempt to move toward a poetry devoted to colloquial language (Rostagno 59–87).

Another pivotal figure in his dual role as poet and critic was Benedetti, particularly in his effort to coalesce different poetic approaches (antipoetry, conversational, exteriorist, or revolutionary) under the umbrella of poetry-as-communication. A common denominator that united these four approaches was, in fact, a distinct interest in communicating directly with readers without alienating them through what the poets deemed to be the artificiality and hermeticism of pre-1960s poetic language. Each poetic proposition builds upon another and thus coexists in relation to the others. Once they identified a common poetic "enemy," the paths to counteract said enemy varied, though the final objective of an antipoetic stance did not change.

Parra seeks to disrupt a logocentric understanding of poetic language. In Parra's antipoetry, a disruption of poetic language is primarily concerned with privileging multiple and simultaneous forms of sensing as a form of communication. This becomes even more prevalent in Parra's work when he moves from poetry to *artefactos*, art installations, all of which are antipoetic and seek to engage multiple forms of sensing. In the recent critical assessment of Parra's work, particularly his antipoetic experimentation, Jill S. Kuhnheim has noted Parra's repeated questioning of the nature and limits of poetry. To this end, Kuhnheim writes that "As in his antipoesía, he [Parra] attempted to demystify poetry as he created it" (110). Both in Benedetti as well as in Parra we see an emphasis on returning poetic language to the level of orality and horizontal communication. The image of the gods descending from Mount Olympus in Parra and the figure who walks through Manhattan in Benedetti present us with a renewed sense of each poet's claim to undo and delink the logic that has bound poetry to specific registers governing the modes of sensing, reading, hearing, understanding, feeling, and communicating with and through poetry. In Alejandro A. Vallega's recent work on decolonial aesthetics, he recognizes the necessity of transcending reason and logic in discussions around aesthetics when he remarks that "my suspicion is that at a certain level we are still holding on to the primacy of reason over aesthetic experience as we develop our liberatory and decolonial narratives" (199–200). In Cardenal's poetry, there is an emphasis on establishing new connections between conversational poetry and an ethical sense of social justice infused in the service of those who have been historically excluded from the coloniality of narrative histories central to Latin America. Dalton's poetry reaches new dimensions of decolonial poetics in which there is an emphasis on questioning the very tension that has historically attempted to keep separate aesthetics, poetic creation, and political engagement.

A poetics of sensing operates in all of the aforementioned cases as a way to disrupt, delink, and question the role that poetry came to embody in a world of neglect and marginalization inherent in the creation of poetry as art for specific intended audiences and with defined poetic registers that rendered it only liminally accessible. A poetics of sensing does not have recourse to narrow definitions of the senses, sensing, or the sensuous. In fact, as I have articulated in the sections above, what binds these four poets' approaches to a decolonial poetics of sensing is a radical redefinition of modes in which poetic language can be understood, read, distributed, appreciated, felt, and sensed beyond the contours of written language, established poetic forms, or poetic projects. Put differently, a poetics of sensing necessitates a transcendence of aesthetics as a Western/Eurocentric philosophical project invested in aesthetic categories. Once this happens, and following Enrique Dussel's words, "El arte deja de expresar una belleza equívoca para ocuparse ahora de una de las tareas más urgentes y eminentes que posee el hombre, una tarea inigualable e insustituible: expresar ante la historia, ante sus propios cogestores de la cultura el sentido radical de todo aquello que habita el mundo de los hombres" [Art ceases to express an erroneous beauty in order to concern itself with one of the most urgent and prominent tasks that mankind has, an unparalleled and irreplaceable task: to express before history, before its own cultural bearers, a radical sense of all that inhabits the world] (Dussel, "Estética y ser" 295). Inherent in the poetics of sensing is the poet's attempt to engage and communicate more directly with a broader audience by employing colloquial language, giving the quotidian an antipoetic treatment, which ultimately means bringing poetry back to its original function of communication and its impact on the senses.

3

Decolonial Sounds

Redolent Echoes of *Nueva Canción*

> Time and again the yearning for time has been figured in the topic of music, the art of time.
>
> Marshall Brown, *The Tooth that Nibbles at the Soul* 128

The poetic figures of Nicanor Parra and Mario Benedetti appear as two connecting threads between the type of poetic production discussed in the previous chapter and a specific type of popular music that appeared during the same period. In the case of Nicanor, his indirect contribution to the development of *nueva canción* has to do with encouraging his sister, Violeta, to conduct research in remote areas of Chile as a way for her to compile folk music and traditions that were rapidly disappearing and had been long neglected. These experiences had a significant impact in shaping Violeta Parra's own musical style, lyric compositions, and her incursions into visual and textile arts. Needless to say, Violeta Parra has long been hailed as the founding figure of what would later be termed *nueva canción* beyond the confines of Chile.

In his role as cultural critic, Mario Benedetti makes a critical distinction between the two types of "popular" music. On the one hand, there are popular songs that are merely a product for consumption and enjoyment and easily fit into the category of commercial music. By extension, this type of music produces high sales and acquires its status as popular through high-grossing concerts, large record sales, radio play, and other forms of media exposure. The second type of popular music, instead, shies away from engaging in such mechanisms of commercialization (Benedetti, "La canción como instrumento" 32–34). This type of popular music aims to appeal to a sector of the population that may very well also consume the commercialized type of popular music, though may not quite identify with the escapist or Manichean lyrical constructions of 1960s and 1970s songs in Latin America that often dealt with the topic of love, but failed to engage with social realities. I am thinking here of immensely popular artists such as Angélica María, Enrique Guzmán, or Armando Manzanero. Benedetti also warns against the well-intentioned and overtly political songs that give primacy to ideological content over the craft of lyrical and musical composition. Instead, Benedetti suggests that music must operate within its own set of laws and norms, which simultaneously constitute it as music and art. In other words, music with political content must first stay true to its art and not to politics. When an artist uses overtly political lyrics set to music, Benedetti argues that there is an impending danger of turning art into a mere ideological pamphlet or propaganda presented under the guise of art (Benedetti, "La canción" 33). Benedetti continues his argument by asserting that with popular-political songs, artistic value and merit need to take precedence over ideological indoctrination.

With *nueva canción*, the division between popular songs as art form and lyrics with political content is collapsed. The separation between popular music and lyrics as poetry is blurred in the service of fusing elements from folklore with popular musical styles (i.e., tastes emerging from peasant and working-class sensibilities), as was the case with many of the song styles and lyrics Violeta Parra produced, as well as many of the songs sung by Mercedes Sosa, Víctor Jara, and Silvio Rodríguez. At the same time, the fusion of folklore and popular musical traditions articulated an attempt to bring these musical traditions up-to-date to meet the demands of social and political realities and changing tastes. Put differently, *nueva canción* artists retrieved folk traditions and popular musical styles from the stagnation of form and repetition in performance over successive generations, while exhibiting and maintaining a respect and understanding of the implications that popular arts have for peasants and other sectors of populations across Latin America.

One could go as far as to argue that, in part, *nueva canción* appears as a response to the musical trends coming from the United States and

England as part of a globalized form of counterculture. These forms of musical importation as a neocolonial strategy were seen as a way to mold musical sensibilities, taste, and markets. In the context of the 1960s, *nueva canción* artists created music as an alternative to British and U.S. rock & roll, as it flooded the airwaves, rapidly impacted the tastes and fashions of youth, and spawned a series of groups that took an imitative approach by adapting and translating rock music into a Latin American context. In the Chilean case, for instance, a young artist whose name was Patricio Henríquez took on the stage name of Pat Henry. A similar case happened with the Carrasco brothers who adopted The Carr Twins as their stage name (Rodríguez Musso 60). In the Mexican case, for instance, there were numerous bands such as Los Crazy Boys, Los Teen Tops, Los Camisas Negras, or Los Hooligans doing covers of U.S. and British songs.

In light of this widespread neocolonization through musical sensibilities, and in an attempt to go against the commercial aspirations of record labels and radio industries, *nueva canción* artists, in my view, individually and collectively contributed to an undoing of coloniality of aesthetics through sound. In recovering traditional and so-called folkloric musical styles and instruments such as the *quena* (an Andean flute), *zampoñas* (Pan flute), or the *charango* (an Andean stringed instrument), musicians such as Alí Primera, Soledad Bravo, Amparo Ochoa, Daniel Viglietti, Los Olimareños, Quilapayún, and Inti Illimani, among many others across Latin America, began to create an archive of sounds and lyrics that sought to undo the embedded history of subjugation and domination of indigenous, Afro-descendant, and disenfranchised peoples such as peasants and the poor. In other words, it was through an uncovering of musical traditions that had been historically marginalized (or confined to spaces such as the countryside or popular bars) that *nueva canción* musicians began to respond to the coloniality of power as it operated on levels of knowledge and aesthetics. Popular forms of knowledge transmitted through music were often categorized and hierarchized as folklore or popular in counterdistinction to music of good taste. A clear indication of how dangerous and powerful *nueva canción* became among vast sectors of the non-elite population in Chile is the fact that as soon as Augusto Pinochet rose to power, his dictatorship banned instruments such as the *quena* or the *charango,* simply because "Traditional musical instruments had become so thoroughly associated with the politics of the deposed government that playing them was considered tantamount to subversion" (Morris 123). Not only might playing these instruments have been deemed a sign of ideological subversion, but the instruments themselves served as reminders of their indigenous provenance and that of their musical styles, as well as an allegiance with those who had been historically disenfranchised and had begun to hope for change before the rise of Pinochet's dictatorship in 1973.

While rock music appealed to a certain sector of the youth across Latin America, there were artists who shied away from musical importations and turned their efforts toward recovering autochthonous, folkloric, or popular songs that shared the ethos of revolution, utopian sensibilities, cultural decolonization, a quest for nationalist forms of artistic expressions, and ideologically charged art forms, all of which I read as decolonial gestures. In turn, *nueva canción* became increasingly popular among students and workers, while also emerging as a means with which to raise class-consciousness, validating popular thought and popular art forms, but without neglecting artistic merit or elevating songwriting to new and rarified poetic heights.

Nueva Canción and (Decolonial) Aesthetics

For Edward Lippman, music in the twentieth century moved away from conceptions of aesthetics and turned toward deriving meaning from music. "The question of meaning, then, has superseded the traditional problem of emotional content (which had derived in turn conceptions of emotional expression and emotional effects)" (Lippman 352). Implicit in Lippman's analysis is the scission between aesthetics and meaning as two separate and irreconcilable approaches to thinking about music. Some of Lippman's reservations come precisely from his assumption that music "rarely possesses meaning in the most obvious sense—that of referring to or representing extramusical objects or occurrences" (Lippman 353). Of course, Lippman is primarily concerned with a specific tradition of music (high music) and a particular historiography of musical thought (i.e., Western and, more specifically, European). Left out of Lippman's extensive analysis are musical traditions that are part of a musical corpus that exists at the margins of Western musical aesthetics and is often left unacknowledged within its musical historiography.

This is a point that Carolina Santamaría Delgado has raised to show musicology's insufficiencies to grasp the embedded dimensions of popular knowledge and collective affective memories arising from a musical style such as bambuco in Colombia. Santamaría Delgado goes as far as to argue that the field of musicology is grounded in a certain coloniality of knowledge that demarcates aesthetic domains and does not sufficiently account for non-canonical (popular or folkloric) musical traditions that emerge from indigenous, Afro-descendant, and colonial encounters (Santamaría Delgado 4–7). In a broader Latin American context, for instance, we see a strong current around the middle of the twentieth century that shies away from such conceptions that delink musical aesthetics from meaning, as Lippman suggests. In fact, as we will see throughout this chapter, there is a conscious effort to rehabilitate aesthetics by giving it a political and social dimension, but also by grounding meaning in specific "extramusical" social concerns, historical situations, and political conditions. Moreover, when placing music and lyrics alongside one another, a symbiotic, codependent relationship is revealed in which lyrical composition acquires a specific register of meaning when set to specific musical styles. The same could be argued about specific musical styles (for example, the *cueca*), given that without lyrics embedded in social, political, and historical realities, all we would have would be further folk songs. There would not be anything novel or different about *nueva canción*. Folkloric or "primitive" music has often been categorized as functional in the sense that it is often associated with rituals, ceremonies, or celebrations. In contrast, "high" or cultured music does not necessarily serve a specific function and, instead, it can be placed within the domain of pure art (Nettl 21). For its part, *nueva canción* retained elements of the functional nature of music stemming from folkloric or so-called primitive traditions, but it also aimed to serve as entertainment, though politicized and socially committed, for a specific sector of the population, primarily workers, peasants, indigenous peoples, and students, among other underprivileged and oft-silenced citizens.

It was just this blend of folk musical traditions, instrumentations, dance styles, clothing, and lyrics set to traditional meters that resonated with artistic efforts across Latin America. Musicians within this movement also made a conscious effort to modernize "folk" traditions without falling into the trap of commercialism. This was the case in the later 1960s in Chile, where a number of musical groups jumped onto the commercial bandwagon and often were at the service of the right-wing government instead of critiquing it.[1] As such, it can be argued that there were two movements that aimed to rekindle an interest in folk traditions. The first has been attributed to the direct influence of Argentine musician Atahualpa Yupanqui as a precursor to the new song movements in Latin America and Chilean musician Violeta Parra. The general impulse that gave rise to this movement took on new dimensions and was rearticulated as it spread from its origins in the Southern Cone to other locations across Latin America. The second movement, however, particularly in the Chilean context, merely created music as part of a capitalist enterprise with no particular social agenda and, by extension, few social repercussions. Whereas the first movement sought to connect with disenfranchised sectors of the population while politicizing audiences, the second of these folk movements merely sought to entertain and achieve commercial success. This chapter will be devoted to the first movement, which hereafter will be referred to as *nueva canción*.

In mapping out the Latin American musical landscape, Guillermo Barzuna argues for the conflation and cross-fertilization of musical traditions from Spain, pre-Columbian traditions, African elements, and creole instruments and rhythms (Barzuna 8). While this assessment is partially correct, one of the problems with this sweeping analysis is that it places popular music under the guise of syncretism or acculturation. If one were to interpret *nueva canción* merely as a product of acculturation, we would be negating the centrality of coloniality. In fact, I read *nueva canción* as a way to contest the discourse of acculturation. It is because *nueva canción* seeks to employ musical forms, poetic traditions, and various modalities of oppression carried over from colonial times into the new Latin American republics that the conjoining spirit among *nueva canción* musicians is one of undoing coloniality or the legacies of colonial experience. It is this "undoing" of coloniality via songs that I am linking to the concept of decolonial aesthetics and, specifically, decolonial sounds. *Nueva canción* is invested in reclaiming the idea of the nation by way of reactivating an interest in local and national artistic expressions. At the same time, an interest in articulating art forms at the national level reveals points of commonality with other parts of Latin America, particularly where similar projects vindicating popular culture are taking place. While the discourses of the nation and nationalism would appear as ones of exception (in the sense of working in isolation and for the sole benefit of the national imaginary), those discourses serve to establish artistic dialogues among similar aesthetic-ideological projects across Latin America that share an affinity in politicized creation. In other words, there is a dual sense of belonging: first to a nation, and, later, to a region as a whole:

> La nueva música folclórica en Latinoamérica se ha convertido en un gran movimiento de unidad continental que simboliza la actititud (relativamente amplia y que intenta ser general) de los jóvenes ante las situaciones de sus países. Aunque las canciones son contextualizadas (dentro de cada país en particular), son adaptables a los elementos comunes y constantes de la situación general. (Barzuna 27)
>
> [The new Latin American folkloric music has become a great movement of continental unity, which represents the attitude of the youth (relatively wide and attempting to be general) in relation to the situations in their countries. While the songs are contextualized (within each particular country), they can be adapted to constant and common elements of the general situation.]

It is in this sense that we can speak of a Latin American *nueva canción* movement as opposed to *nueva canción chilena* or *nuevo cancionero argentino* or *nueva trova cubana,* which identify a particular modality of making music with an aesthetic project of national dimensions. However, a national musical movement does not negate the possibility of communicating with and establishing points of contact among different movements at the regional level. Quite the contrary—by having a dual perspective on the musical movements of the period (i.e., movements at the national and Latin American levels), we can shift from looking at context-specific articulations of the movements and how they engage with and respond to a broader regional articulation of the new song movement in Latin America.

Before engaging with the specific movements taking place at the national or regional levels, however, we must turn our attention to the centrality of the singer-songwriter as a figure who is constantly redefining the relationship among folk instruments, contemporary musical sensibilities, and sociopolitical realities. To become a *nueva canción* artist, the singer-songwriter enters into dialogue with a particular musical history that has often been neglected by "cultured" or elite circles. The *nueva canción* artist carves out a space for that derided musical history with conviction regarding its inherent merit and aesthetic value, and how it needs to be reevaluated in the face of the social and political change taking place in most Latin American nations. On a different level, the *nueva canción* artist becomes an aesthete, but not one who is interested in embracing elitist or Eurocentric ideals. On the contrary, for the *nueva canción* artist beauty can be found in the sounds of the *guitarrón* or the *charango* as much as in a violin. As one critic has noted:

> El cantante nuevo resulta, pues, un elemento que hace posible la difusión en grande de la poesía de una cultura musical, y con ellas, de una conciencia de la circunstancia actual de nuestros países; intenta ser, así, un modo de conocimiento y, a la vez, una invitación a desenajenarse y participar en la rebeldía para construir una nueva realidad. (Barzuna 30)

> [The new musician becomes, then, an element that makes possible the wide dissemination of a given musical culture's poetry and, with it, consciousness of the current circumstances of our countries. It seeks to become a form of knowledge and, at the same time, an invitation to unalienate oneself and take part in rebelliousness to build a new reality.]

The *nueva canción* artist becomes instrumental in communicating to the general public the social and political dimension that music can have, as well as the meaning conveyed by means of resorting to particular musical styles or poetic forms for composition. Moreover, the *nueva canción* artist is an agent of social change at both the local and national levels, though she/he shares the labor of change (questioning and attempting to undo coloniality) with other artists across Latin America. Networks of exchange, communication, and creative affinities are created to accentuate the fact that *nueva canción* artists are not working in isolation, but are part of a larger movement with differences in creative approaches and aesthetic propositions, though sharing a broad common goal, which is to turn music into an instrument of communication and entertainment, social activism and denunciation, to evoke emotions and help audiences identify with pressing sociopolitical struggles.

As Fernando Reyes Matta has suggested, when talking about *nueva canción,* one should keep in mind that "This music and poetry are inserted into the popular culture at precisely those points where we find the forms and language of a folklore excluded from the 'culture industry' controlled by the transnational capitalist system" (Reyes Matta 447). In other words, *nueva canción,* as a dual bearer of musical and poetic traditions, seeks to challenge its exclusion from a "culture industry" by challenging the dominant modes of production, consumption, marketing, and dominant tastes. While European and U.S. musical styles were in vogue among youth in Latin America, *nueva canción* appeared as a response to such transnational cultural forces. In this sense, then, *nueva canción* can also be called a "countersong" in that it makes it a point to resist commercial music and other types of cultural importation.[2]

Reyes Matta has also argued that the dissemination and circulation of tapes, the creation of festivals, and the mass appeal of the leading singers of the new song movement helped make the movement one of transnational impact. In the process, however, singers such as Violeta Parra and Víctor Jara have become "renationalized" in the sense that they are not only part of the Chilean *nueva canción* movement, but have also become symbols of political and social struggle throughout Latin America (Reyes Matta 448–49). In Violeta Parra's case, some of her songs have been reinterpreted by the likes of Mercedes Sosa, Soledad Bravo, Joan Baez, and contemporary singer Francisca Valenzuela. Víctor Jara, for his part, has become a Latin American symbol of resistance throughout the arts. In this light, in the following sections of the chapter, the role and impact of select *nueva canción* singers at the national and regional levels will be examined.

Violeta Parra and the Conception of *Nueva Canción*

When thinking about Violeta Parra's artistic endeavors, one is not limited to her musical compositions or poetic output. One must also keep in mind her incursions into folkloristics, painting, and tapestry work (*arpilleras*), as well as her role in showcasing folk songs through her radio shows in Chile.[3] After Nicanor Parra brought his sisters Violeta and Hilda to Santiago from San Carlos, their hometown in southern Chile, Violeta began her career as a singer by performing in *fondas*. From colonial times, and well into the twentieth century, *fondas* were sites where workers went to drink, a space to escape momentarily from their tedious lives, but also as a place where they sought entertainment. In this context, Violeta and her sister Hilda began performing popular tunes and genres of the time, which included Mexican *corridos, boleros, polkas,* and *pasodobles,* as well as theme songs from popular films and radio programs (Rodríguez Musso 48; *Viola chilensis*). Most of these genres were of foreign origin and appealed to popular audiences based on the commercialization of these genres, which were replacing traditional Chilean musical styles. After a couple of years, however, at Nicanor's suggestion, Violeta turned her attention to other cultural enterprises.

Violeta went around Chile from north to south, particularly in the most remote areas, interviewing peasants and folk singers in order to compile a collection of songs that had been passed down orally since colonial times.[4] Violeta's work was part of ensuring that a facet of Chile's cultural patrimony would not die out. At the same time, though she had no formal training in ethnomusicology or folkloristics, her contact with peasants and folk musicians had a crucial impact on shaping her musical aesthetics. As Rodrigo Torres Alvarado has noted, during this particularly creative period of her life in which she developed a "three-way role of researcher, performer, and creator," Violeta developed her own method for collecting popular lyrics and melodies throughout the Chilean countryside (262).

In between trips to remote areas of Chile, Violeta also began a radio show on which she played folk and popular songs using traditional Chilean rhythms (*Viola chilensis*). Furthermore, during this period in which Violeta began finding her true vocation of unearthing silenced voices and traditions and bringing them to a wider public as a mode of resisting the coloniality of knowledge and aesthetics, "she would develop a vast plan of promoting traditional music through radio programs, recording records conceived as didactic, and monographic works, perform in different settings, and initiate her prolific personal creative work" (Torres Alvarado 262). Given her contact with workers, peasants, indigenous peoples, and students during her travels, her radio show had an immediate appeal, and connected at once with these sectors of Chile's population, which immediately identified with the type of music Violeta was airing. One should keep in mind that, at this time, Chilean airwaves were invested in playing foreign music (a form of neocolonialism or coloniality of sound), and it would have been unthinkable to dedicate a radio show to music that elite circles thought belonged to small town festivals or *fondas*. Violeta's use of the radio as a way to disseminate her project of recovering and valorizing folkloric and popular songs became instrumental to bridging the gap between the use of mass media and often-disenfranchised sectors of the population, which included peasants and indigenous populations living in remote areas of Chile, but her work also interested workers and leftist students (Rodríguez Musso 39; *Viola chilensis*).[5] Violeta intended to use the radio as a means of connecting more readily to, and broadening her reach within, her intended audience. In short, by compiling folksongs and employing radio and print media as means of dissemination, Violeta repurposed these popular and neglected traditions as a way to resist the denigration of the sounds and aesthetic pleasures one can derive from such musical traditions.

Keeping in mind how Violeta's artistic project is shaping up at this early point in her career, one could turn to a succinct assessment of her art, which has been defined as having a combination of neofolklore and urban sensibilities (Lindstrom 324). One could extend this assessment to include Violeta's various endeavors in the arts and her work as an "ethnomusicologist" as a way better to understand musical and popular poetic traditions, as she compiled documents from first-hand accounts as a way to preserve them from the passing of time, oblivion, neglect, or complete disappearance.

To situate the origins of popular music in both the Chilean context and across Latin America, Chilean musicologist Osvaldo Rodríguez Musso has argued for the need to think about the origins of popular poetry in relation to the poetic genres that Spanish soldiers brought with them, which include *villancicos, villanelas, coplas,* and *romances* (9). These poetic forms appear as a product of the Spanish colonial enterprise and as foundational to the development of both music and poetry, whether in its stylized or popular versions. According to another musicologist, those who took part in the global counterculture of the 1960s and the *nueva canción* movement in Chile later spearheaded an interest in turning to ethnomusicology as a way to understand the development of popular music (González 249). In other words, with the passing of time, those who had participated in the Chilean *nueva canción* movement became invested in having a more in-depth understanding of the origins of specific musical traditions, the development of musical trends, and tastes.

To return to the context of Violeta Parra's interest in Chilean musical traditions, there were a few reasons for importing foreign musical styles and models into Chile. Because of Chile's presumed lack of mestizo or Afro-descendant musical traditions—indeed, a legacy of Chile's long-standing whitening discourses and practices linked to a coloniality of race—it was easier to import musical styles from other parts of Latin America than to embrace local Afro-descendant, indigenous, or peasant musical styles. As traditional Chilean music relied heavily on stringed instruments, it became easy to adapt instrumentation to foreign musical styles (such as *guaracha* or *corridos*) (González 257). Whereas record companies found it almost impossible to market and catalogue Chilean music via its local genres such as the *cueca* and the *tonada* before the 1960s, in the following decades these genres would be recognized and later valorized as constitutive of a national imaginary by their identification with the construction of Chilean national identity (González 260).[6]

To begin addressing one of the central questions in this chapter regarding the role of women in the development of this music movement, one should note that in Chilean salon culture, female duets or trios were privileged. Furthermore, women were allowed to learn the piano and perform in salons, which became a symbolic space where both genders could meet and interact (González 261). This may seem a minor practice of entertainment and performativity designed for the male gaze and pleasure, but, in fact, one could argue that the presence of women in such traditionally male-dominated spaces corresponds to the growing global presence of feminist ideals and, in this context, an attempt at undoing a coloniality of gender. Furthermore, the salon was also a site where *cuecas* were removed from their rural context and transposed into a space of urban performance. In the twentieth century, the salon also became a semi-professional space where artists first performed before they became famous.

After the mid-1930s, men also began making careers in urban spaces by singing *cuecas* (González 261). *Cuecas* and *tonadas* helped revive internal migrants' cultural memories as they shifted from the countryside to urban spaces. According to Gérard Béhague, the *cueca* comes from a colonial dance known as the *zamacueca* or *zambacueca,* though today it goes by the name of *marinera.* With the passing of time, two distinct dances were derived from the *zambacueca,* namely the *zamba* and the *cueca.* The lyrical composition of the *cueca* follows the form of the *seguidilla,* which uses verses composed of seven and five syllables (Béhague 212). This ongoing process of the colonial imposition of instruments and musical styles is part of an extended and complex repurposing and transformation aimed at bringing to the fore popular knowledges and aesthetic sensibilities that have traditionally been denied space in certain elite, institutional, and academic discourses. Clear proof of this is that a study of such genres would be categorized as ethnomusicology, whereas more respectable and accepted musical composition forms (operas, cantatas, classical music) fall under the purview of musicology. This distinction is one that serves to underscore the hierarchy of knowledges and aesthetic sensibilities constitutive of the modernity/coloniality dynamic.

An example of Violeta Parra's engagement with the *cueca,* as both a dance style and in terms of lyrical composition, would be her song "Cueca de los poetas," which Nicanor Parra wrote for her, though Violeta set it to music. In the first stanza of the song, Violeta praises the beauty of pheasants and peacocks, though she says their beauty is inferior to that found in Gabriela Mistral's poetry. In this case, we are presented with a contrast between the type of beauty found in nature and the beauty reflected in and represented by poetry. In the second stanza, we move from Mistral as founding figure of Chilean twentieth-century poetry to other major poets, namely Pablo de Rokha and Vicente Huidobro. The song questions which of the two poets is worth more. While Pablo de Rokha is a "good" poet, Vicente Huidobro is worth double or triple de Rokha's value. The third stanza is shorter and is dedicated to Pablo Neruda. The stanza begins by recounting Neruda's popularity among Chileans and how he has long been hailed as a poet of the people. Given Neruda's status as the biggest poet in Chile's poetic tradition, the song compares him to the figure of a rooster. The song then comes to an abrupt conclusion in which the rooster (Neruda) is urged to run, as Nicanor Parra will soon come and snatch him away. In other words, Nicanor Parra is presented as a new poetic force who will soon be part of a noteworthy list of poets, but will also supersede Neruda. Given that it was Nicanor Parra who wrote the lyrics to this *cueca*, and Violeta who set it to music and sang it, the song serves as a prime example of the connection between poetic traditions (antipoetry) and musical styles (cueca within *nueva canción*). This is a particularly interesting song and collaboration, because it speaks to the subversive and contestatory nature of decolonial gestures in both poetry and music. As we will see, the lyrics call into question the canonization of poets who have been hailed as foundational to twentieth-century Chilean poetics. By turning this song into a modern *cueca*, the principal decolonial gesture is to call into question how attuned to popular sensibilities poets such as Gabriela Mistral or Pablo Neruda have been. At the very least, and in the spirit of both antipoetry and the *cueca*, humor becomes a means by which to critique and resist the silencing of popular musical traditions, which in this song are leveled by bringing poetic/musical lyrics and the musical form of the *cueca* on even ground.

We should keep in mind that in the late 1950s and into the early 1960s, Violeta Parra traveled throughout Europe, and her stays in France and Switzerland were of particular importance in shifting the nature of her music from traditional folk songs to music with a more overtly political and social content and tone. It was also during this period that Violeta began recording traditional folk songs, and this type of music was well-received in the aforementioned countries. Given her success in Europe, upon her return to Chile, Violeta began to be recognized as a singer-songwriter in her own right. During her travels in Europe, Violeta also developed other facets of her art, which included a one-person show at the Louvre in which she displayed her tapestries (*arpilleras*) and traditional instruments from Chile, multiple performances in the *Quartier Latin*, and making connections with expatriate musicians in France and Switzerland (*Viola chilensis*).[7]

Given the context of her travels and how these shaped the direction her music would take, we are confronted with an "aesthetization of the political" in the sense that Violeta's poetic voice and her music resonate with a committed collectivity invested in effecting social change (Osorio Fernández 38–39). An example of this aesthetization can be seen in Violeta's song "Cantores que reflexionan" ["Singers Who Reflect"], in which she presents the figure of a singer at two different stages of her/his development. In the first part of the song, the artist is merely interested in commercial success and fame and lacks political and social commitment, and, in turn, does not produce authentic and honest art. After experiencing a crisis, the artist finds his own voice and the true meaning of his art in making socially committed music. In this sense, Violeta Parra is presenting an argument that links aesthetics to the realm of the political and goes as far as suggesting that the two domains are inseparable. This perspective echoes with the connections between aesthetics and politics present in Jacques Rancière's work, as discussed in my first chapter.

Throughout the first two stanzas of the song, the singer is invested in seeking fame and earning money, while not being at all interested in singing in the name of truth. In reference to this singer, Violeta sings:

Va prisionero del placer
y siervo de la vanidad;
busca la luz de la verdad
más la mentira está a sus pies.
Gloria le tiende terca red
y le apresiona el corazón
en los silencios de su voz
que se va ahogando sin querer.
La candileja artificial
te ha encandilado la razón
dale tu mano, amigo sol,
en su tremenda oscuridad.
(Violeta Parra, *Gracias a la vida* 18–19)

[Imprisioned by pleasure
and vanity's serf,
he looks for the light of truth,
yet untruth is at his feet.
Glory casts a rigid web
and imprisons his heart,
in the silences of your voice
that is quelling without want.
The artificial bougie
has alighted his reason,
extend your hand, my friend the sun,
to his immense darkness.][8]

Violeta presents us with an indictment of commercial artists who become prisoners to pleasure and the vanity of fame. Instead, the weight of fame and glory becomes a heavy burden for these artists to withstand and it takes a toll on their craft. The artificial spark and joy of performing slowly dissipate and leave these singers in absolute darkness and without a clear sense of where they ought to take their art.

After this moment of crisis, later in the song, the artist has an epiphany in which he finds his own class consciousness and this, in turn, shapes his creative process and redefines the purpose of his craft. Violeta Parra sings the following final stanza:

> Y su conciencia dijo al fin:
> cántele al hombre en su dolor,
> en su miseria y su sudor
> y en su motivo de existir.
> Cuando del fondo de su ser
> entendimiento así le habló
> un vino nuevo le endulzó
> las amargura de su hiel.
> Hoy es su canto un azadón
> que le abre surcos al vivir,
> a la justicia en su raíz
> y a los raudales de su voz.
> En su divina comprensión
> luces brotaban del cantor.
> (Violeta Parra, *Gracias a la vida* 19–20)

> [And his conscience said at the end:
> sing to man about his pain,
> about his misery and his sweat
> and about his reason for being.
> When from the depth of his being,
> understanding told him so,
> a new wine sweetened
> the bitterness of his spleen.
> Today his song is the hoe
> that troughs life,

to the justice of its roots
and to the torrents of his voice.
In his divine comprehension
beams emanated from the singer.]

At the end of the song, the singer's own consciousness is personified and becomes a voice of reason that beckons the singer to address his newfound audience, which is none other than the everyday man. Whereas before the singer had an elite audience in mind, his songs will now reflect the everyday person's pain, suffering, struggles, and toils, and underscore his purpose in society. It is with this newfound understanding that the singer finds solace from his previous internal conflicts vis-à-vis his own craft. In this new facet of his art, the singer's voice becomes an instrument (a hoe) that actively becomes involved with concerns in life, while questioning the very roots of justice and injustice in society. The metaphor of the hoe places an emphasis on the singer's craft as one that is of equal importance or runs parallel to any type of manual labor. By having redefined the purpose of his art, the singer now has a deeper understanding that music must connect with real-life concerns. The lyrics of this song stand as a reminder of Violeta's own preference for "an emic style of performance. 'Emic' in the sense of a deep and emphatic record of the vernacular world and its representation in the heart of the city and its artistic circuit" (Torres Alvarado 265).

Socially and politically committed popular songs defy the political and cultural centralism and bourgeois sensibilities arising from Santiago, Chile's capital (Rodríguez Musso 11). Popular songs, in fact, often describe the experiences of workers, miners, peasants, and those working in saltpeter deposits, as these laborers often live an entirely different reality from that of city-dwellers. While those who had been left out of the city's purview inspired Violeta's musical aesthetics, the experience of oppression and exploitation that Chilean workers in saltpeter deposits experienced also inspired artists during this period, namely Luis Advis's musical composition *Cantata de Santa María de Iquique* (1969) and Humberto Solás's film *Cantata de Chile* (1975).

During 1965, while Chile was undergoing a social and economic crisis during Eduardo Frei's government, there was a musical dispute between Ricardo Alarcón—a musician linked to the *nueva canción* movement—

and a Chilean military officer. According to Osvaldo Rodríguez Musso, the dispute began when Alarcón wrote a *refalosa* (a dance and music style related to the *cueca*) in which he made a reference to the military. In turn, the officer wrote a *refalosa* in which the military's patriotism was underscored. The dispute continued with a number of *refalosas* on each side of the argument. While this dispute came to be known as the "guerra de las refalosas" (war of the *refalosas*), Violeta Parra wrote "Mazúrquica modérnica" ["Modern Mazurka"] as a response to the ludicrous amount of media attention the dispute received during a time of economic and social unrest (Rodríguez Musso 58).

While Violeta chose to write a modernized "mazurka," as the title of the song implies, it is important to provide a brief account of this music's history and the mechanisms by which she modernized this musical style. According to one musical historian, the mazurka, along with the polka, crossed the Atlantic and arrived in Buenos Aires around the mid-nineteenth century in connection to musicals in which both dance styles were incorporated (Santana de Kiguel). These dance styles soon became popular among the elites during the nineteenth century in Latin America, but also among other social classes, as had also been the case in the European context. Moreover, the mazurka and the polka soon spread and became fashionable throughout Latin America. A crucial aspect of Violeta's modernization of the mazurka is her use of a poetic device known as the *jerigonza* in which additional syllables are inserted into words to treat a serious topic in a lighter tone. In this case, however, Violeta uses it as a way to poke fun at the ridiculousness of what has captured the public's attention during the musical dispute of the *refalosas*, when there are serious social concerns more deserving of public attention.

The text of the song begins with Violeta's indictment of those people who are concerned with whether or not "canciónicas agitadóricas" (songs with social and political content) can agitate and create unrest among certain sections of Chile's population. Violeta scoffs at the ludicrousness of the inquiry by stating that only a child would ask such questions. In the second stanza, Violeta continues:

Y he contestádico yo al preguntónico:
cuando la guática pide comídica,
pone al cristiano firme y guerrérico

por sus poróticos y sus cebóllicas;
no hay regimiéntico que los deténguica
si tienen hambre los populáricos.
(Violeta Parra, *Las últimas composiciones de . . .*)

[And I answered the questioner:
When the belly demands food,
it makes a Christian stand his ground and fight
for his beans and onions;
there's no regiment capable of
containing the people if they are hungry.]

Violeta provides a direct answer to the question presented in the first stanza. Her response is grounded in the daily struggles of the people, namely how to survive and obtain their next meal. As Violeta suggests, if people are hungry, they will soon go on strike and there will not be any military or police force that can contain the will of the people to show their discontent and have their voices heard. The singer underscores the agency of the poor as actors in social change. The first two stanzas go hand-in-hand, as the first stanza presents the question, and the second stanza provides an answer that appears self-evident. The seemingly childish question presented in the first stanza as to whether or not political songs can incite people to rebel against the government is grounded in the disjuncture between those asking the question and the objects of the question. Put differently, only those who are out of tune with the needs and realities of workers, peasants, and the poor could conceive of such a question when there are more pressing issues at hand.

In the third stanza, Parra shifts her attention to the role of politicians in keeping people hungry and unhappy. Whereas in the first stanza she was asked about the role of politically charged songs, in the third stanza she asks politicians to ask themselves whether their actions and decisions are more dangerous than verses. After all, they make decisions for an entire population, but if something goes wrong, they place the blame on others and wash their hands like Pontius Pilate. In the fourth stanza, Parra continues putting the spotlight on people of power, namely "caballerísticos almidonádicos" [heavily starched gentlemen], as they are the ones who control the mines and have absolute control over the labor conditions and the types of jobs available to the everyday citizen. This is a direct reference that can be linked to coloniality of power, as discussed by Quijano, in relation to the mechanisms of racialization and capitalism that subjugate certain sectors of the population, even beyond formal political independence. From the comfort of their chairs, Violeta suggests, they keep a tally of those who die in coal mines, with absolute disdain for human life.

By the fifth stanza, Violeta turns her attention to the many massacres recorded in Chilean history. She sings the following:

Varias matáncicas tiene la histórica
en sus pagínicas bien imprentádicas:
para montárlicas no hicieron fáltica
las refalósicas revoluciónicas.
El juraméntico jamás cumplídico
es el causántico del desconténtico:
ni los obréricos ni los paquíticos
tiene la cúlpica señor fiscálico.
(Violeta Parra, *Las últimas composiciones de . . .*)

[History has many massacres
well-printed in its pages:
to carry them out
no revolutionary *refalosas* were necessary.
The always-unfulfilled promises
were the cause for discontent:
neither the workers nor the police
were at fault, Mr. district attorney.]

In this stanza, Violeta returns to the questions asked in the first stanza. If, in the first stanza, it was suggested that political songs might incite people to revolt, in the fifth stanza Violeta suggests that revolutionary *refalosas* (related to the *cueca*) were not necessary in the past as excuse for governments to kill their citizens. Differently put, Violeta suggests that some cultural critics and politicians have used popular interest in *nueva canción* as an excuse to take action against any possibility of revolt. As history shows, however, people have revolted in the past without the aid of revolutionary or political songs. What drove people to revolt has been a litany of unfulfilled promises and a history of discontent, which continue growing with the passing of time and new governments. By the end of the stanza, as though she were respectfully addressing a district attorney, Violeta absolves workers and the police from the weight of history and its numerous massacres.

The final stanza of "Mazúrquica modérnica" places an emphasis on Violeta's own position related to the aforementioned issues raised in the song. Violeta concludes her song in the following way:

> Lo que yo cántico es una respuéstica
> a una pregúntica de unos graciócicos,
> y más no cántico porque no quiérico:
> tengo flojérica en los zapáticos,
> en los cabéllicos, en el vestídico,
> en los riñónicos y en el corpíñico.
> (Violeta Parra, *Las últimas composiciones de . . .*)
>
> [That which I sing about is an answer
> to a question asked by a few jokesters,
> and I won't sing anymore because I don't feel like it:
> laziness runs deep in my shoes,
> in my hair, on my dress,
> in my kidneys and my ponytail.]

Violeta suggests that she has answered the question about whether political songs can affect and mobilize unsatisfied workers in this way primarily because the inquiry was ludicrous to begin with. While the question is apparently not taken seriously, Violeta, in addressing it, in fact provides a very direct and strong statement against social injustice in Chilean society, while highlighting a number of other issues that people should keep in mind instead of being preoccupied with the effects that songs can have on people.

While Violeta's response has seemingly been a humorous one given her use of *jerigonza,* she defiantly and abruptly ends her song by stating that she refuses to continue answering such a ridiculous question and she does not feel like devoting more time to something that does not merit it. Of course, this response is yet another device employed to underscore the seriousness of the issues she has presented throughout the song. The final verses of the song position Violeta on the side of the workers as she reclaims her will to answer a question (i.e., what is the purpose of socially committed songs?) and when to end her response. When Violeta states that she does not feel like continuing to answer the initial question that sparked this song, she attributes her lack of willingness to her own laziness, which runs in her being. In fact, Violeta's laziness is ingrained in her shoes, her hair, her dress, and all the way from her kidneys to her ponytail.

One might wonder why Violeta would end such a powerful song on such a note. I would argue that she is redefining and embracing laziness as a characteristic that politicians and men in power have often attributed to workers and the underprivileged. If workers go on strike, the men in power reason that it must be because they are lazy. A version of this relationship between men in power and workers and how the aforementioned see laborers as lazy can be seen in my discussion of Humberto Solás's *Cantata de Chile* (1975) in the next chapter. In fact, Violeta self-identifies with workers and their rights. She is one of them: "lazy" from head to toe. Once again, she uses irony to mean the exact opposite. While workers have often been labeled as lazy, Violeta rehabilitates such a categorization. After all, and particularly given her humble origins, Violeta often sided with and sang for the underprivileged and the oppressed. In fact, her music has been described as "canto a lo humano y a lo divino" [singing to the humane and the divine], particularly because these are characteristics that describe two constant preoccupations in her music (Rodríguez Musso 39; *Viola chilensis*). While religious imagery appears in many of her songs (as in the reference to Pontius Pilate in "Mazúrquica modérnica"), Violeta is also concerned with very earthly and human issues, particularly those linked to social injustices.

Violeta Parra's art is extensive and cannot be reduced to a discussion of three of her songs, as her legacy and impact are far-reaching. Following her brother Nicanor Parra's advice to turn to the *décima* (a poem with ten verses) as a poetic form to help her express and record her experiences and frustrations, she wrote her autobiography in that form, using it to reflect on her childhood and many of her concerns throughout the years. A few years after Violeta's tragic death in 1967, Luis Advis adapted Violeta's autobiography in *Canto para una semilla* (1972), as the autobiography was linked to Advis's own interest in rethinking whether or not popular music fit into established models of beauty and aestheticized classical music compositions (Osorio Fernández 36–37). If Violeta found inspiration in popular and folkloric forms of poetry and music in her own work, her autobiography inspired Advis to resolve some of his own reservations about popular music's aesthetic values and whether they could be transferred to the form of the cantata.

In thinking about Violeta Parra's contributions to *nueva canción* beyond writing her own lyrics, composing her own music, and compiling popular songs from the countryside of Chile, it becomes important to think of how she has been credited with the role of introducing the *peñas,* as a space for performance and site of more direct engagement with the community. As Torres Alvarado has noted in reference to the centrality of the *peñas,* "At these performance events, a new ritual in which the singer communed with the audience crystallized, negating the distance that had separated them in the nightclub format" (266). In connecting in more personal and affective ways with a community of the dispossessed, Violeta's gesture was important as she moved away from the nightclubs that consumed folklore as a mere commodity that sedimented class-based and racialized difference. In so doing, Violeta sought to engage in an active and ongoing challenge to the relationship between music and performance as objects of commercialization, enjoyment, identification, and liberation. Differently put, these gestures of rethinking the role of the musician and performer in *nueva canción* in bringing her performance to audiences in spaces those audiences already inhabited (popular and disenfranchised areas of an urban space), along with a politicization of music lyrics in unison with a recovery of traditional and popular musical styles, are what I perceive to be the lasting legacies of this movement toward an undoing of the coloniality of sound, or what I have suggested in this chapter as an archive of decolonial sounds.

Particularly for the discussion of the remaining singers in this chapter, Violeta Parra becomes a frame of reference for how to make socially and politically committed songs. Violeta's impact has been widely acknowledged in the formation of a more cohesive movement of the *nueva canción chilena,* particularly among a younger generation of artists, which included her own children Ángel Parra and Isabel Parra, as well as Víctor Jara, Inti-Illimani, Quilapayún, and Patricio Manns, among others. In the following sections, Violeta Parra will continue to be referenced, particularly as we move toward a discussion of *nueva canción*'s articulation as a movement of Latin American dimensions.

Víctor Jara: Lyrics as a Political Weapon

If Violeta Parra is often hailed as the founding figure of the Chilean *nueva canción* movement, Víctor Jara is remembered as a figure who marks a moment of transformation in that movement. His tragic death at the hands of the Pinochet dictatorship only three days after the coup d'état on September 11th, 1973, and the growing repression and violence of Pinochet's regime, compelled many of the leading figures of the movement to seek political asylum in other Latin American countries and in Europe. For instance, Isabel Parra, Ángel Parra, Quilapayún, and Patricio Manns, among others, settled in Paris and continued making music there, while staying closely in tune with political developments in Chile and other Latin American nations (Party 671–684). Víctor Jara's torture and killing in a concentration camp—a soccer stadium that had been adapted to detain and torture potentially "dangerous citizens" in Pinochet's regime—made him one of the first victims of the dictatorship, but also elevated him to the status of a popular idol and a symbol of political resistance. Given the tragic deaths of Violeta Parra and Víctor Jara, as well as their respective contributions to the development of *nueva canción*, both of these singer-songwriters became the most salient voices of a generation of *nueva canción* artists.

It is no wonder, then, that to commemorate another anniversary of Chile's dictatorship, Chilean hip-hop artist Ana Tijoux recently remade one of Víctor Jara's songs, called "Luchín," and released an accompanying YouTube video. My point is that such songs, precisely because of their social and political messages of inequality and disenfranchisement, continue to be as important today as they were in the late 1960s and early 1970s. More importantly, in a contemporary hip-hop artist re-releasing one of Jara's songs there is an implicit gesture of drawing a parallel between the contemporary social, political, indigenous, and student-led struggles going on today in Chile and across Latin America and those that were taking place four or five decades ago. This is why I keep drawing attention in both implicit and explicit ways to coloniality's usefulness as a framework within which to understand these long-standing issues and read decolonial gestures that challenge them. As Madina Tlostanova and Walter Mignolo have argued, thinking decolonially is just as valid and indeed pressing as already-common expressions such as "thinking philosophically, thinking economically, or thinking politically" (17). Furthermore, to think and feel from a decolonial perspective means "formulating the epistemic, political, and ethical basis for global decolonial options *in* the existing world order, which we all witness or take part of today" (17, original emphasis). This is why songs such as "Luchín," whether they are performed by Víctor Jara or adapted in contemporary fashion by Ana Tijoux, are deeply rooted in an ethical and political project of thinking and feeling from the perspective of those Fanon called the "wretched of the earth." This is to say that decolonial thinking and feeling, as gestures of decolonial aesthetics, are deeply connected to those who have been "humiliated, devalued, disregarded, disavowed" for centuries and continue to experience on a daily basis "the trauma of the 'colonial wound'" through entangled mechanisms that render certain people disenfranchised and disempowered due to a complex interweaving of racism, gender, class, and hierarchies of knowledges (cultured vs. popular/indigenous), etc. (Tlostanova and Mignolo 19).

Given this context, and the pivotal roles artists such as Violeta Parra and Víctor Jara played in the formation of the Chilean *nueva canción* movement, a brief comparison of the two cannot be avoided. In fact, one critic has provided a nuanced interpretation of both singer-songwriters, including their marked differences in political ideology and how this shaped their respective works. Whereas Violeta Parra often shied away from closely aligning herself with a given political party or a specific ideology (in a similar way to Nicanor Parra), Víctor Jara made very clear in his writings, songs, and interviews his alignment with Marxist thought (Nandorfy 172–209). Moreover, Jara became an ardent supporter of Salvador Allende's campaign, and continued collaborating with Allende's government (Nandorfy 172–209; Joan Jara). Nonetheless, Jara avoided dogmatism, while still creating songs that dealt with the conditions of workers, peasants, indigenous peoples, and the poor.

As both Violeta Parra and Víctor Jara came from humble origins and were born in the same region of Chile (Chillán), both were equally invested in recording and recovering folk music and lyrical traditions throughout their careers. In fact, it is this common interest that led Víctor

Jara to seek a meeting with Violeta Parra so that the two could exchange points of view on the role and function of folk music in the type of music that became known as *nueva canción* (Isabel Parra 47–50).

Víctor Jara started his career as an actor and later became a theater director and taught acting at the university level. It was during this period that Jara also became part of the musical group Cucumén. Around 1966, Jara began devoting more of his time to creating and performing music, particularly as he came into contact with other artists in a small venue known as the *Peña de los Parra,* which was spearheaded by Violeta Parra's children Isabel Parra and Ángel Parra. The *Peña de los Parra* served as a space where *nueva canción* artists convened to perform and develop long-lasting friendships and collaborative relationships (Mara and Zito Lema; Isabel Parra). His participation in the *peña* put him in touch with other artists, including members of the musical group Quilapayún, whose artistic director he soon became (Carrasco 53–55).

Víctor Jara became fully immersed in the world of music to the point where he recorded and released one album per year, starting in 1969 with *Pongo en tus manos abiertas,* on which some of the members of Quilapayún collaborated. On that album, Jara released "Plegaria a un labrador," which was a song he had written and performed during the First Festival of *Nueva Canción,* and for which he received the festival's first prize. Other albums followed, such as *Canto Libre* (1970) and *El derecho de vivir* (1971). In the latter, there were several songs that indicated Jara's turn to political songwriting, including songs dedicated to Cuba, Father Camilo Torres (a prominent figure of liberation theology), and "Che" Guevara. On the album *La población* (1972), Jara collaborated with theater director Alejandro Siéveking in writing the lyrics, which dealt with the struggles of peasants and shantytown dwellers. For *Canto por travesura* (1973), Jara turned his attention to Chilean folklore; he had compiled many of the songs over the previous several years.

At the time of his death, however, Víctor Jara had been working on an album that would later be released under the title of *Manifiesto* (1973/1974). On this posthumous album, there are several noteworthy songs that encapsulate many of Jara's lifelong concerns. For instance, "Aquí me quedo" ["Here I Stay"] is based on Pablo Neruda's poem of the same name, which appeared on *Incitación al Nixoncidio y alabanza de la revolución chilena* (1973). Víctor Jara and Patricio Castillo, one of the members of Quilapayún, adapted the poem and set it to music (Castillo 56–58). The song begins with a plea for unity, given the growing divide between those who ardently opposed Allende's government and the majority of the population, which supported it.

Yo no quiero la patria dividida
ni por siete cuchillos desangrada
quiero la luz de Chile enarbolada
sobre la nueva casa construida.
Yo no quiero la patria dividida
ni por siete cuchillos desangrada.
(Víctor Jara, *Manifiesto*)

[I don't want a country divided
or bled by seven knives.
I want Chile's light hoisted
Above the newly built home.
I don't want a country divided
or bled by seven knives.]

The song's opening verses provide a dual image of a split in Chilean society. The first stanza suggests a country divided along ideological lines: one part that supports Allende, and the right-wing opposition labeled by the left as the *momios*. The second verse, however, shifts our attention to a forceful divide in Chile in which struggles are turning into acts of violence mostly directed toward workers.[9] Instead of a divided Chilean society, the song advocates for a united Chile as represented by the metaphor of the newly built home.

Despite these political differences in the country, Jara stresses how everyone can coexist: "cabemos todos en la tierra mía / y que los que se creen prisioneros / se vayan lejos con su melodía" [All of us fit in this land of mine / and those who think they're imprisoned / can go far away with their melody] (Víctor Jara, *Manifiesto*). By stating that Chile is his land, the singer reaffirms his sense of patriotism and that his position is in line with entertaining the possibility of dialogue and collaboration. Nonetheless, the singer is also aware that there are those who will claim that Allende's government has "imprisoned" them (the *momios*) in its bid for social justice. If that is the case, those people can simply leave with their repetitive complaints, which are equated with the melody of a song. In the same stanza, the song continues: "Siempre los ricos fueron extranjeros; / que se vayan a Miami con sus tías" [The rich were always foreigners; they can go to Miami with their aunts] (Víctor Jara, *Manifiesto*). The implication in these verses is that the elite have always favored foreign products and culture over Chile's, which is why they ought to join their relatives abroad. Continuously complaining about Chile's social transformations is not productive and can only stagnate any possibility of a truly new society.

In the last stanza, several of the verses are repeated, though the singer clearly sides with the working class. Whereas in the second stanza the voice is conciliatory, here we are told: "Yo me quedo a cantar con los obreros / en esta nueva historia y geografía" [I will stay to sing with the workers / in this new history and geography] (Víctor Jara, *Manifiesto*). If those in opposition to Allende cannot stand the changes in Chilean society, they are welcome to leave. The singer of the song, however, would rather stay and sing alongside the workers, while witnessing the changes in the course of history. The changes in geography can be interpreted as a potential transformation in the redistribution of land and power, which may move the workers and the impoverished from a marginal to a central position in relation to urban planning, power dynamics, and shifts in a participatory democracy.

"Vientos del pueblo" ["The People's Winds"] is another song from this posthumous album that describes Chile's long history of oppression of workers. The first verse in the song illustrates a constant dynamic in Chile, but can also be applied to another Latin American context—that of landowners and people in power abusing workers' rights: "De nuevo quieren manchar / mi tierra con sangre obrera / los que hablan de libertad / y tienen las manos negras" [Once again they want to stain / my land with worker's blood / those who speak of liberty / and have filthy hands] (Víctor Jara, *Manifiesto*). The opening stanza is reminiscent of Violeta Parra's "Marzúrquica modérnica," particularly with the recurring image of those people in power who have "dirty hands" and seek to rid themselves of any responsibility for their decisions and actions. In this song, however, the people in power want to suppress workers by overworking them and even killing them if they protest against their working conditions. The image of the workers' blood staining the very land on which they labor is poignant in establishing a cyclical relationship from which workers cannot escape. Moreover, those in power have a double discourse in which they profess to love freedom, but only for a select few, while they continue to oppress workers. At the end of the stanza, we are left with the image that the hands of the landowners are dually stained, by the blood of the workers and also by constant decisions that sustain a relationship between the oppressor and the oppressed.

Much like the overarching message in "Aquí me quedo," in the second stanza of "Vientos del pueblo," the trope of a divided Chile is highlighted in the following lines: "Los que quieren dividir / a la madre de sus hijos / y quieren reconstruir / la cruz que arrastrara Cristo" [Those who want to separate / a mother from her children / and want to rebuild / the cross that Christ carried] (Víctor Jara, *Manifiesto*). Once again, this stanza presents a clear division between those in power and the poor. The powerful want to divide the poor and continue ensuring that they have a cross to bear. It is in this vein that those in power want to continue endorsing a particular version of history. The song continues: "Quieren ocultar la infamia / que legaron desde siglos / pero el color de asesinos / no borrarán de su cara" [They want to cover up their infamy / left as legacy of centuries, / but the color of murderers / will not be wiped off your face] (Víctor Jara, *Manifiesto*). As with the previous two stanzas, the song contrasts the powerful versus those who have been silenced, punished, marginalized, and abused for centuries. While the actors may have changed, the lopsided relationships of power have not. The ones who murdered and oppressed centuries ago are the ancestors of those who continue the same mechanisms of infamy and oppression today. In this sense, we see a clear example of the coloniality of power, particularly in relation to the continuity of the methods of oppression that sustain uneven distribution of and access to power.

The fourth stanza of the song continues with the same invective against those who have kept the people in poverty while slowly killing them. The stanza also suggests a feeling of being fed up with the course of history and wanting to change it: "Ya fueron miles y miles / los que entregaron su sangre / y en caudales generosos / multiplicaron los panes" [Thousands and thousands were those / who gave up their blood / and in generous streams / multiplied bread] (Víctor Jara, *Manifiesto*). While there have been countless victims of oppression and abuses of power, this stanza exhibits a sense of hope and frustration. On the one hand, the countless deaths of people and their blood have served to continue feeding the rich. On other hand, it is precisely the number of deaths and amount of bloodshed that provide hope and enable those who are fed up to multiply their efforts to put an end to oppression. The imagery of the blood and the multiplying of bread have obvious correlations with religious motifs, but they are present here to support the case of the workers.

The tone of the song shifts in the fifth stanza when the singer professes his desire to live and struggle alongside his brethren. Jara sings the following verses: "Ahora quiero vivir / junto a mi hijo y mi hermano / la primavera que todos / vamos construyendo a diario" [Now I want to live / alongside my son and my brother / the springtime that we are / building daily] (Víctor Jara, *Manifiesto*). Whereas the singer is conscious of how things used to be, his lyrics affirm that there is a new era in bloom. The metaphor of springtime suggests the birth of a new social order, though it is workers and the poor who are working on bringing about a new future. By stressing that the singer wants to live and share a collectively built time of prosperity and change with his family, there is a sense of pride in the effort of building a space and time of transformation on a daily basis. It is not as if the work of changing the social order is ever finished. Quite the contrary—the singer is quite aware that changing people's mindset while challenging the mechanisms of oppression will not take place overnight. Moreover, the labor of transformation and building a new society is equated with any type of manual labor, which requires that workers put in the time and effort to complete an ongoing job.

From wanting to be an active participant in the new future of Chile, the singer becomes defiant in the sixth stanza, when he sings: "No me asusta la amenaza, / patrones de la miseria, / la estrella de la esperanza / continuará siendo nuestra" [I'm not afraid of the threat, / chiefs of misery, / the star of hope / will continue being ours] (Víctor Jara, *Manifiesto*). The singer is aware that not everyone will support these changes in society. The people in power, who are labeled chiefs of misery, will pose a constant threat to the "star of hope" or the "springtime" the people are building. Nonetheless, the possibility of a new future and the hope of being able to enjoy it cannot be taken away from workers.

In the seventh stanza, we arrive at the title of the song, which also acts as a type of chorus. Víctor Jara sings: "Vientos del pueblo me llaman, /

vientos del pueblo me llevan, / me esparcen el corazón / y me aventan la garganta" [The winds of the people beckon me, / the winds of the people carry me off, / these scatter my heart / and fill up my throat] (Víctor Jara, *Manifiesto*). The singer uses the metaphor of the winds to indicate a type of energy that is unstable and cannot be contained. In this way, because the winds are associated with workers, peasants, and citizens working toward social change, they also serve to inspire the singer. It should also be noted that the singer positions himself as an agent who obeys the external forces, which are symbolized by the winds. Since the "winds" operate as the wishes and desires of the people, they also call upon him to become a voice that sings on behalf of the people. In a similar way, the song concludes with an affirmation of the role that the singer-songwriter must play. "Así cantará el poeta / mientras el alma me suene / por los caminos del pueblo / desde ahora y para siempre" [This is how the poet will sing / while a soul may echo me / through the paths of the people / from now until forever] (Víctor Jara, *Manifiesto*). The singer acknowledges his role as a poet of the people and that his craft will live on as long as it is true to the needs of the people. By concluding the song in this way, Jara presents other singers with a challenge by setting an example of the creative and ethical duty that the singer-songwriter must fulfill henceforth. It is in this challenge of denouncing disenfranchisement and a wide set of mechanisms articulated under the concept of coloniality that I detect decolonial gestures in Jara's work, as he draws attention to the need to question and undo long-standing forms of social and economic oppression.

The song that gives the name to Víctor Jara's posthumous collection indeed serves as a manifesto on political songwriting, but also encapsulates many of Jara's own political principles, which carried over into his craft. The song in itself is one long stanza. It does not have a chorus and, as such, it does not conform to a traditional song format. Jara sings the following in the opening verses of "Manifiesto": "Yo no canto por cantar / ni por tener buena voz. / Canto porque la guitarra / tiene sentido y razón" [I don't sing just to sing / or because I have a good voice. / I sing because the guitar / makes sense and has reason] (Víctor Jara, *Manifiesto*). For Jara, it is not necessary for the singer to have a good voice or merely to sing for the sake of singing. In other words, the singer must have a more profound ethical reason to turn to singing. In the case of Jara, however, it is not his voice or a desire to sing that drive him to seek this medium of communication. Instead, it is the guitar, which has become personified, that drives Jara to sing. The guitar becomes an instrument that is foundational to the singer-songwriter's craft, as it is what gives meaning and common sense to any lyrical composition or musical creation.

As the song progresses, the image of the guitar continues to be likened to images of the earth and the freedom of a dove, and it even replaces the function of images of religious items such as holy water. It is in this context that Jara situates his own artwork within a musical movement that Violeta Parra began.

> Aquí se encajó mi canto,
> como dijera Violeta.
> Guitarra trabajadora
> con olor a primavera.
> Que no es guitarra de ricos
> ni cosa que se parezca. . . .
> Que el canto tiene sentido
> cuando palpita en las venas
> del que morirá cantando
> las verdades verdaderas
> no las lisonjas fugaces
> ni las famas extranjeras.
> (Víctor Jara, *Manifiesto*)

> [My singing fits here,
> like Violeta once said.
> Laboring guitar
> with a smell of spring.
> It's not a guitar for the rich
> or anything of the sort. . . .
> Singing makes sense
> when it beats in the veins
> of him who will die singing
> the truthful truths
> and not ephemeral praises
> or about foreign fame.]

By invoking the figure of Violeta Parra, Jara asserts how his music fits within a specific tradition, namely *nueva canción,* and within a national genealogy of socially committed musicians aiming to make music about social justice by introducing critiques of what we now call the coloniality of power. Much like in "Vientos del pueblo," in this song, Jara associates singing and the guitar with the labor of workers. It can also be interpreted as an association with the working class in Chile, especially if we take into account Jara's claim that the guitar is not an instrument that the rich use. In fact, these verses serve as a commentary on how radio stations controlled the type of music that received airplay in Chile, but also on how there were a number of singers who wrote "neo-folk" songs whose lyrics were devoid of any political or social commentary, or of a concrete relationship with pressing issues impoverished communities faced. While apolitical neo-folk music served the interests of the elite, in "Manifiesto," Jara makes evident that the singer must be fully committed to his craft and the content of his lyrics, regardless of the consequences. In retrospect, Jara's words were almost prophetic in the sense that he died defending his ideals, and his imprisonment and torture came about because of his repeated investment in critiquing political power, instead of remaining silent and not denouncing coloniality.

Jara's work toward fostering social justice in Chile through his music is illustrated in most of his songs, though it is most succinctly presented in "Manifiesto." The final verses of the song reaffirm Jara's firm belief in the importance of the type of music he was creating:

> Ahí donde llega todo
> y donde todo comienza:
> canto que ha sido valiente
> siempre será canción nueva.
> Siempre será canción nueva.
> Siempre sera canción nueva.
> (Víctor Jara, *Manifiesto*)

> [It all goes there
> and there it all begins:
> singing that has been brave
> will always be a new song.

Will always be a new song.
Will always be a new song.]

The beginning and end of *nueva canción*, as a song-making practice and a style of social commentary through music, are rooted in the singer's ability to be brave, to be honest with himself and his intended audience, and in the content of his lyrics. This is quite important for an undoing of the coloniality of sounds, because lyric content needs to be honest and believable to the ears of the intended audiences, namely those who have been disenfranchised—the wretched, to use Fanon's words. Furthermore, and to borrow Edgar Ricardo Lambuley Alférez's term, what we end up hearing are other sonorities (*sonoridades otras*) as a mode of resistance, of speaking back to power through lyrics and sounds aimed at empowering the historically disempowered (263–278). Through the simplicity of guitar accompaniment, resistance emerges from within lyrics that employ colloquial speech, solely because of an awareness of the intended audience and that the message of what I refer to here as decoloniality must carry through in a clear and direct manner. In relation to the concluding verses of "Manifiesto," as long as the singer firmly believes in and defends his compositions, a new song will come about. By repeating the last verse three times, Jara suggests that *nueva canción* is not merely a movement that will disappear or that will be censored by those in power. Quite the contrary, as long as there are brave and honest singers, there will be new songs, constantly redefining themselves according to their social and political contexts. The singer and the song-making practices will adapt to the situation, as was the case with many of the *nueva canción* artists who had to go into exile and needed to expand upon their repertoire by incorporating different instruments and musical traditions from Latin America. More importantly, Jara's last verses in "Manifiesto" are hopeful about *nueva canción*'s future by ascribing to the artist the possibility of exploring new means of lyrical and musical expression.

Mercedes Sosa: The Voice of the Silent Majority

If Violeta Parra is considered a foundational figure in the Chilean *nueva canción* movement, Mercedes Sosa can be placed in the same category as Parra, particularly given Sosa's continuous dissemination of Argentine folk music. Sosa's role in what also became known as the *nuevo cancionero* was pivotal in bringing together cultural and musical traditions from various places in Latin America, while she also did covers of other artists in the Latin American movement such Violeta Parra, Víctor Jara, and Daniel Viglietti. Particularly on her early albums, Sosa followed in the footsteps of Violeta Parra by seeking to recover Argentine folk traditions and bringing them up-to-date for audiences in the late 1960s and early 1970s. During the early period of her musical career, Sosa was also building upon the groundwork that Atahualpa Yupanqui had laid in bringing folk music to the forefront during the 1950s and early 1960s.

Among the numerous productions in Mercedes Sosa's early career, and keeping in mind the period studied here, the following albums illustrate Sosa's prolific presence within the *nueva canción* movement: *Canciones con fundamento* (1965), *Romance de la muerte de Juan Lavalle* (1965), *Yo no canto por cantar* (1966), *Hermano* (1966), *Para cantarle a mi gente* (1967), *Zamba para no morir* (1968), *Sabor a Mercedes Sosa* (1968), *Mujeres argentinas* (1969), *El grito de la tierra* (1970), and *Navidad con Mercedes Sosa* (1970). In 1971, Sosa recorded eleven of Violeta Parra's songs in *Homenaje a Violeta Parra*. Some of the songs included on this album are "Volver a los 17," "Los pueblos americanos," "La carta" (with Quilipayún), and "Gracias a la vida." In fact, for many listeners, it is Mercedes Sosa's version of "Gracias a la vida" that has made the song into an anthem across Latin America that celebrates peace and life. It should be noted, however, that Sosa had already recorded a version of this song for her album *Zamba para no morir* (1968). In *Hasta la Victoria* (1972), Mercedes Sosa also did a cover of Víctor Jara's "Plegaria de un labrador." Following this production, Sosa recorded *Cantata sudamericana* (1972), *Mercedes Sosa* (1973), *Traigo un pueblo en mi voz* (1973), and *A que florezca mi pueblo* (1975).[10] Mercedes Sosa continued performing and recording on a yearly basis almost right up until her death in 2009.

One of the main differences between Mercedes Sosa and the other artists in this chapter is that Sosa was not a singer-songwriter. Instead, she performed songs coming from a variety of folk traditions, which ranged from the Argentine *zamba* and the *chacarera* to the Peruvian *vals*. Other songs were composed for her or were compositions by other members of the *nueva canción* movement.

When attempting to describe what Mercedes Sosa means to Latin Americans, one commentator has characterized her as a motherly figure who was able to mediate between Anglo-European cultural influences and indigenous traditions in Argentina, while also advocating for social justice (Bernstein 176). Mercedes Sosa has also been called the voice of Latin America, though she often shied away from such epithets. When asked how she felt about such a label, she once responded:

> It's impossible to be the voice of a continent. . . . Just think about it: from Argentina to Venezuela is six hours by plane. It is an easy thing for reporters to say, but I know perfectly well it is not a reality. I have a great deal of feeling for my continent, great respect and sadness that some things still have not improved. I have sung for Nicaragua, for El Salvador; I sing in Costa Rica for the students and for the people, and they know that I am an artist who feels for every place in Latin America. But to be the representative of the continent is too difficult. (Wald 101)

While this response came at a later point in her career, it still enables an understanding of the magnitude of her presence well beyond her native Argentina. In fact, in Sosa's early music, we begin to see clear examples of how she positions herself as a cultural figure who transcends borders and cultural divides.

As a concept album, *Cantata sudamericana* (1972) is comprised of songs that pay homage to several regions of South America. The opening song, "Es sudamérica mi voz" ["South America Is My Voice"], makes use of a variety of instruments, which include the *cuatro, requinto, charango, maracas,* and guitars, among other instruments reminiscent of Bolivia, Venezuela, and Paraguay. In the opening stanza, Sosa affirms her pride in being born a woman in the Americas, though she also underscores her indigenous and Spanish roots when she sings: "Americana soy/ y en esta tierra yo crecí. / Vibran en mí / milenios indios / y centurias de español" [I'm an American woman / and I was born in this land. / Indigenous millennia / and Spanish centuries / vibrate within me] (Sosa, *Cantata sudamericana*). One can read these lyrics as biographical, particularly given Sosa's indigenous roots. In the opening verses, a hierarchy is created in which the presence of indigenous cultures is more profound and deeply rooted than the Spanish. The contrast is made evident when the weight of indigenous culture is quantified in millennia, whereas as the presence of Spain has only been felt in the Americas for a few centuries. In the same opening stanza, Sosa continues: "Mestizo corazón / que late en su extensión / hambriento de justicia, paz y libertad" [A mestizo heart / beats to its fullest, / hungry for justice, peace, and liberty] (Sosa, *Cantata sudamericana*). These verses are a continuation of the imagery that presents the singer as having mixed ancestry. In this case, however, the mestizo heart can also be read as a metonym that stands for South America as a region. The word "extensión" in the Spanish lyrics evokes an image of South America's geography. Whether the mestizo heart is a reference to Sosa or to South America at large, said symbol stands for the justice, peace, and liberty that the singer is seeking.

The title of the song appears in the chorus, where the singer's voice is not personal, nor speaks on behalf of another. Instead, the chorus advances the idea that South America in its entirety is what informs and inspires Sosa's singing. Moreover, Sosa describes South America as a "foundational country" in its full geographical extent, from north to south and from coast to coast. In the concluding verses and the chorus, the song personifies South America as an aching entity whose pain has seeped into the very core of the singer. It is in this context that, by the last stanza, the singer beckons her listeners to struggle for another emancipation, a more complete undoing of the vestiges of coloniality. This time, however, said emancipation must be a lasting one that will truly free and enable all South Americans (and Latin Americans) to rejoice in their newfound and definitive freedom.

As Sosa sings for the need to strive toward a definite and profound emancipation from South America's long history of suffering, injustices, social inequalities, and armed conflicts within and among its nations, this song is inevitably linked to decolonial aesthetics, particularly as the song acknowledges a legacy of colonial practices that have continued beyond formal political independence. In this song, music and singing become tools to envision an undoing of coloniality by way of decolonial sounds. Put differently, the song employs traditional instruments and musical styles that are linked to lyrics calling for a new beginning, one that must be imagined as a possibility for South Americans to see themselves as brothers rather than enemies. It is for this reason that *Cantata sudamericana* has songs that employ elements of bossa nova, as well as Caribbean and Andean rhythms. The album pays homage to South America's and Latin America's rich cultural traditions, while seeking to employ musical rhythms one would associate with specific parts of Latin America as a way to break down cultural barriers.

In this vein, the last song of *Cantata sudamericana* highlights the urgency of the decolonial project on a regional scale. "Alcen la bandera" begins with the following verses: "Que tu tiempo se acerca, / Sudamérica mía, / con fronteras de flores / y fusiles de mentira" [Your time is near, / South America of mine, / with borders made of flowers / and your make-believe rifles] (Sosa, *Cantata sudamericana*). The singer envisions that South America's time for undoing coloniality—in this case, by reworking and undoing the coloniality of music—is fast approaching. For that to happen, however, borders must be replaced with flowers and guns ought to become mere figments of the imagination. In other words, political and geographical borders and armies will become obsolete in what the singer envisions will be a unified South America. This utopian project, of course, is one that can be traced back to Simón Bolívar's early project of unifying Latin America. A renewed interest in seeking to coalesce Latin American nations is one that must be understood in relation to 1972, when the album appeared, and how the impetus of the Cuban Revolution was waning and dictatorships were budding across the region. Thus, in what I am calling decolonial sounds, the idea is that a challenge to politics can emerge from within an undoing of Western musical aesthetics by affirming the need to reclaim musical traditions and underscoring the urgency of retrieving a common identity rather than emphasizing differences. In light of the song, divisions according to identity politics based on nationalism have been traditionally been used to keep Latin Americans at war with each other and under the control of the political regime in power at any given time. The song seeks to make evident this history of manipulation and oppression through politics.

The song continues presenting images that one can associate with a new beginning. For instance, South America is personified as though it is awakening from slumber and nightmares. For the nightmares to disappear, the chant of the people, a collective voice, must become South America's new reality. South America continues to be likened to a damsel who has been terrorized, whose beauty and innate happiness have been stripped away beyond recognition. At this point in the song, Sosa turns her attention to the following: "Si la muerte me lleva, / no ha de ser para siempre. / Yo revivo en mis coplas / para ustedes, para ustedes" [If death takes me, / it won't be forever. / I come alive in my *coplas* / for all of you, for all of you] (Sosa, *Cantata Sudamericana*). Sosa recognizes the danger in singing about freedom and inciting South Americans to dream of emancipation by accepting the possibility that singing may lead to the singer's own demise. In the event of death, however, Sosa will continue living through her lyrics and her singing for the benefit of all South Americans.

The final message of the song is that liberation is within reach and that it is time to wave the flag of freedom. Moreover, the song places an emphasis on the role that the "guitarras militantes" [militant guitars] have played in creating an atmosphere of hope in which justice, freedom, and happiness can be fully realized. By invoking the image of the guitars, Sosa recognizes the importance of *nueva canción* artists in voicing social inequalities and as agents of social change. As most *nueva canción* artists made use of the guitar to sing about the injustices they witnessed, the guitar became a symbol of political resistance and activism. In the case of Sosa, however, when she performed on stage, she used a drum instead, unlike most of her contemporaries. Despite this difference, one can argue that in Sosa's case, it was her voice and her way of singing political lyrics that served as her principal instrument of militancy. It was through her voice, her primary and most essential denunciatory instrument, that she became known as the "voice of the silent majority" (Schnabel 132).

Silvio Rodríguez and Nueva Trova

Whereas Violeta Parra, Víctor Jara, and Mercedes Sosa were indebted to folk music traditions and instruments native to various parts of Latin America, Silvio Rodríguez was indebted to a style of music known as old *trova,* whose origins lay in the turn of the twentieth century and which was foundational for later Cuban styles such as the *bolero* and *guaracha.* Another major difference between Silvio Rodríguez and the other artists studied in this chapter was their appearance, particularly their choices in clothing and what they came to symbolize. For Violeta Parra, Víctor Jara, and Mercedes Sosa, dressing like the audience to which they were singing, and paying homage to the folk elements from which they drew their musical inspirations, became of prime importance. Thus, often, these artists performed wearing ponchos and other signature peasant garments as a way to create a direct association with popular audiences. Conversely, Silvio Rodríguez presented himself in the fashions of the 1960s and 1970s.

Rodríguez was influenced musically by figures as diverse as Bob Dylan and The Beatles, as well as Violeta Parra and Atahualpa Yupanqui. These foreign influences placed Silvio Rodríguez at odds with the ideological line of Castro's government, in which rock music was deemed subversive and too closely aligned with the perceived decadence and opulence of imperialist and capitalist countries such as the United States and England (Moore 150–151; Díaz Pérez 105).

Attempting to situate Silvio Rodríguez within *nueva trova* and *nueva canción* might also prove to be tricky. Robin D. Moore has characterized *nueva trova* as oppositional and contestatory in its aesthetic scope (Moore 135). One critic has suggested, however, that in choosing the name *nueva trova,* young Cuban musicians sought to distinguish themselves from the *nueva canción* movement taking place in the rest of Latin America, precisely because the latter movement was seen as one of opposition and political resistance (Benmayor 11–44). In the case of Cuba, because a cultural and political revolution was well under way, no such oppositional and denunciatory stance from artists was needed (or allowed). This is not to say that *nueva trova* artists did not see points of connection with the song-making practices of their contemporaries in the rest of Latin America; indeed, there was a convention in Havana in 1967, the First Latin American Protest Song convention, devoted to the genre, which was meant as a common point between *nueva canción* and *nueva trova.* It should be noted, however, that many of the artists who participated in that meeting and who were part of both movements openly shied away from embracing the term "protest song" to describe the type of art they were making. Nonetheless, the 1967 convention was essential in establishing a point of dialogue among the various artists and proponents within both movements.

In addition, *nueva trova* is self-reflexive about its desire for continuity in relation to two distinct sources of inspiration, namely *nueva canción* as a Pan-Latin American artistic movement, and old Cuban *trova*. These two influences converge into a musical style that relies primarily on voice, with guitar as accompaniment. It is the simplicity of its performance and the poetic and suggestive complexity of its lyrics that make *nueva trova* distinct from the larger *nueva canción* movement. In its early form, this style of music became known as protest music, and only in the early 1970s did *nueva trova* gain currency as a term that defined Cuba's particular stance on socially and politically oriented music. It should be noted, however, that as with other *nueva canción* artists, Silvio Rodríguez and his contemporaries also wrote about everyday topics and concerns, particularly love songs with a blend of political or social messages (Benmayor 11–44; Delgado Linares).

For the development of the Cuban *nueva trova,* the support of official state institutions was essential. In fact, it was the Casa de las Américas that served as the first meeting space for many of the *nueva trova* artists. Silvio Rodríguez became a central figure within the nascent movement, to the point where he was one of three singers chosen to represent Cuba at the 1967 Havana event dedicated to the protest song genre. The other two chosen singers, Pablo Milanés and Noel Nicola, became, along with Rodríguez, part of the Grupo de Experimentación Sonora, a group of twelve musicians, under the direction of Leo Brouwer, whose purpose was to create scores for the productions of the Instituto Cubano del Arte e Industria Cinematográficos (ICAIC, the Cuban Institute of Cinematographic Art and Industry) (Benmayor 11–44; Delgado Linares; Díaz Pérez).

A point at which artistic movements and governments coincided was when Castro became closer to Allende's government in Chile. As a result of this, *nueva trova* artists gained recognition in Chile, where politically charged and socially committed songs had gained wide acceptance (Moore 154). This might help explain why there was a truly hemispheric spirit of solidarity against Pinochet when he rose to power. Immediate responses to this dictatorship from the arts came from Humberto Solás in his film *Cantata de Chile* and Silvio Rodríguez himself with his song "Santiago de Chile." Turning our attention to Rodríguez's *Días y flores* (1975), which was the first major *nueva trova* album, one can see a range of themes.[11] Aside from the ideological connection between Castro and Allende, one can see Silvio's homage to Chile for its cultural contribution and for the possibility of social change it represented during Allende's government.

The song "Santiago de Chile" is an anthem that is at once melancholic while also describing the singer's unwillingness to succumb to despair despite the pervasive sense of loss and rapid transformation of how life used to be. The first stanza opens with the singer's strong emotional response to a woman: "Allí amé una mujer terrible / llorando por el humo siempre eterno / de aquella ciudad acorralada/ por símbolos de invierno" [There I loved a terrible woman / crying from the eternal fumes / of that city cornered by winter's symbols] (Rodríguez, *Días y Flores*). Here we get a description of the landscape surrounding Chile as it stands at the foothills of the Andes, but also the scene in the context of the winter season. This accentuates the extreme emotions present in the song. The beloved woman is described as "terrible" and as crying for a symbol of loss that will not dissipate (eternal fumes). The second stanza continues with the imagery and sensorial experiences of winter as the singer describes its coldness, the fog, and rain found everywhere in the "calles del enigma" (streets of enigma). A clue to figuring out why the streets of Santiago may be enigmatic appears in the chorus: "Eso no está muerto / no me lo mataron / ni con la distancia / ni con el gris soldado" [That is not dead / they did not kill it from me / neither with distance / nor with the somber soldier] (Rodríguez, *Días y Flores*). The chorus refers to those memories described in the first two stanzas of the song. The memories of heartache, loss, and winter in Santiago have not died in the singer's voice. Quite the opposite; they are still alive within him, which is why there is an emphasis on making the action of killing those memories impossible. Those experiences are so internalized in the singer that neither the distance of exile nor the militarization that ensued with Pinochet's rise to power can diminish their weight.

The song continues in a similar vein by reminiscing about the friends left behind and simple things that once made the singer happy. By the fourth stanza, we find a reference to the power of *nueva canción*: "Allí nuestra canción se hizo pequeña / entre la multitud desesperada, / un poderoso canto de la tierra / era quien más cantaba" [There our song became small / in the middle of the desperate crowd, / the powerful singing of the land / was what sang the most] (Rodríguez, *Días y Flores*).

As the *nueva canción* movement belongs to the people, it is the collective response ("multitud") to a tragedy and social instability (desperation) that dwarfs the significance of the song ("allí nuestra canción se hizo pequeña"). The weight of *nueva canción* does not rest upon the individual, but rather on a collectivity, which is what assigns the song its strength as it refers to the symbol of the land as a source of labor, but also as a reference to Chile and its population.

The song continues to reference themes of death, shadows, and hatred, while underscoring the speaker's inability to foresee the profound changes that were to come. One might ask at this point why Silvio Rodríguez would write a song as though he were a Chilean in exile. Part of what makes the song so powerful is that the voice captures the conflictive experiences and emotions of a person forced into political exile, while having to come to terms with the ideas of a home and a country that are still alive. Here we see a clear example of how a singer-songwriter is able to transcend the social and political realities of his native country and address international concerns affecting a "familial" population. This song shares the spirit and message of unity and of the transcendence of political borders, as described in Mercedes Sosa's songs.

Another key song from *Días y flores* is one that Rodríguez wrote while living on a fishing boat for several months. The song "Playa Girón" pays homage to the ship on which the song was written, while also serving as a reference to the site where the Bay of Pigs conflict took place. The composition of the song is of particular significance to the project at hand, since Rodríguez seeks to engage in dialogue with fellow poets, musicians, and historians in a collective reconfiguration of aesthetic categories and affective responses to politicized artworks. The song is divided into three distinct parts. In the first part, Rodríguez asks fellow poets for advice on adjectives, which is to say, the precise wording with which to write a poem about the boat in which the song is being written. He is concerned that the poem not come off as sentimental, as avant-garde, or as political propaganda. Moreover, the song must be in tune with the latest developments in poetry, which is to say it must turn to colloquial and conversational expressions, as I have argued in chapter 2. Ultimately, Rodríguez is unsure of whether or not he ought to use direct and simple language in his song. Needless to say, the concerns expressed in the first part of the song are in tune with the poetic projects of the poets studied in the second chapter, as these poets also sought to steer away from the entrapment of sentimentalism, overtly political poetry devoid of artistic merit, or hermetic avant-garde poetry. It should be emphasized here that "Playa Girón" is one of Silvio Rodríguez's most accessible and direct songs. There are no ornate words or metaphors open to multiple interpretations.

The second part of "Playa Girón" turns to musicians. Here Rodríguez asks for their advice on the type of harmonies and polytonalities that he should use to make a song about the men on board the ship. It is as though he is seeking the precise musical language to do justice to the sailors on board the ship and tell their life stories. By the third stanza, Rodríguez turns his attention to the role of historians. As an artist, he shares the commitment of historians to be impartial and be at the service of truth. Ultimately, the singer comes to the realization that it is up to the sailors themselves to write their own stories. Some important characteristics in all three parts of the song are that Rodríguez invokes the assistance of his comrade poets, musicians, and historians. In doing so, the singer positions himself in all three fields. As a poet, Rodríguez must do justice to what he tries to describe through his word choices. As a musician, he must find the right music to complement his poetic craft. Moreover, in each song, he writes a piece of history in honor of truth and social justice. It is because of these three functions of his craft that in all three parts of the song, Silvio Rodríguez says "me urge" [it's urgent]. These three aspects of his art as a singer-musician-historian carry a sense of urgency and a profound sense of ethical duty to craft the best song possible.

In "Pequeña serenata diurna" ["Little Diurnal Serenade"], Rodríguez makes a statement against repeated international allegations that the Cuban Revolution has infringed upon the rights of its citizens. The opening verses of the song thus are: "Vivo en un país libre / cual solamente puede ser libre / en esta tierra, en este instante / y soy feliz porque soy gigante" [I live in a free country, / which can only be free / on this land, at this moment, / and I am happy because I am colossal] (Rodríguez, *Días y Flores*). When Silvio asserts that he lives in a free country, he implies that democratic values are still intact in Cuba. At that moment, because freedom and revolution are in place, he is the happiest he has been. It is that immense feeling of happiness that makes him feel "colossal." Silvio adds that he has a woman he loves and who loves him back without asking for much in return. As the song continues, and as if freedom and love were not enough, Rodríguez sings:

Y si esto fuera poco,
tengo mis cantos
que poco a poco
muelo y rehago
habitando el tiempo,
como le cuadra
a un hombre despierto.
soy feliz,
soy un hombre feliz,
y quiero que me perdonen
por este día
los muertos de mi felicidad.
(Silvio Rodríguez, *Días y Flores*)

[And if this weren't enough,
I have my singing,
which I gradually
mill and restore,
inhabiting time,
such as it fits a lively man.
And I would like to be forgiven,
in this day,
by the dead of my happiness.]

Asking for more than happiness and love is inconceivable, though Rodríguez has plenty more for which to be thankful. His voice and his singing are yet other gifts that transcend the passing of time. With Rodríguez's singing, he has control over his voice, which is something he can adapt ("mill and restore") according to the circumstances. His absolute joy, however, is not something he takes for granted, as he can only enjoy it now because of those who died in the early days of the revolution to transform Cuban society. While "Pequeña serenata diurna" is a celebratory song, it is also a song of mourning and remembrance of those Cubans who cannot enjoy the freedom for which they fought. The last verse suggests a sense of eternal indebtedness to the martyrs of the revolution. In reference to this song, Chilean *nueva canción* artist and critic Patricio Manns notes, "When Silvio Rodríguez makes millions of people tremble with one line (note: one single line) in which he makes the beautiful declaration: 'I live in a free country . . . ' in three seconds he washes away thirty years of infamy and calumnies leveled against his country by thousands of mercenaries of the pen, at a cost of millions of dollars" (Manns 194).

In the same way that Violeta Parra, Víctor Jara, and Mercedes Sosa were proud of their roots and were committed to effecting social changes in their respective contexts, Silvio Rodríguez is proud of forming part of revolutionary Cuba, to the point where today he is a member of Cuba's national assembly. Rodríguez's connections to *nueva canción* are also still prevalent. In his recent CD, entitled *Segunda cita* (2010), he has a song entitled "Carta a Violeta Parra" ("Letter to Violeta Parra") in which he updates her on what has taken place in Latin America since her death. As the only one of the four singers discussed here who is still alive today, Silvio Rodríguez remains a salient voice of a movement that continues to have an impact among younger contemporary listeners in Latin America.

In light of this brief discussion of lyrics and music, it is important to talk about their connection to how we sense sound and its decolonial potential. In her book *Sensing Sound,* Nina Sun Eidsheim contends that sound and music are not only about aurality, but also about a "tactile, spatial, physical, material, and vibrational" set of sensations or multisensorial phenomena that are "at the core of all music" (8). Put differently, Eidsheim argues that when thinking about music and how to discuss it, we tend to privilege one of the senses (hearing), while neglecting a discussion of how we might have a multisensorial experience relative to music. I agree with this claim, since immersive experience shapes the field of musicology and sound studies. For me, what is important is to come up with a way of understanding how we sense the past in the present through music that can be categorized as popular as opposed to classical or operatic, or as folkloric as opposed to other popular genres prevalent in the 1960s across Latin America. Sensing *nueva canción,* and the archives of decolonial sounds, including lyrics, a recovery of popular and indigenous instruments, melodies, and musical styles emerging from popular and rural spaces represents a set of challenges, because when listening to an extant

LP or a CD, we often experience aurality of both the musical components, or what Eidsheim calls "figures of sound" (pitch, timbre, tonality, etc.), and lyrical composition. In this chapter, I have privileged a discussion of lyrical composition given its centrality as politicized (decolonial) lyrics during the 1960s within the *longue durée* of musical styles in the Americas. Of particular interest are the ways in which the politicized lyricism of *nueva canción* intersects with a recovery of traditional and folkloric musical forms such as the *cueca* or the *zamba*. In the decades preceding the rise of *nueva canción,* there was not such a widespread and overt politicization of lyrics in genres such as the *bolores, rancheras,* or the *cha cha cha*. The overt politicization of lyrics in *nueva canción* is what helps it coincide with the radical shift in poetry and film during the 1960s. If we are lucky today, we may sense and experience archival footage of performances through online platforms such as YouTube or as part of documentaries or biopics. What remains in the archives of decolonial sounds, either in their original form or in terms of song covers, are primarily lyrics.

Decolonial Sounds

Throughout this chapter, I have stressed the importance of music lyrics to help reframe the importance of *nueva canción* within the specificity of the political and historical contexts in which specific songs and artists emerged. Likewise, at various points, I also argued about the efforts these artists made in recovering specific musical traditions, reworking them for modern sensibilities, and imbuing them with the political and social urgency of reclaiming musical legacies that had been historically excluded from discussions of musical aesthetics. It is in this sense that Violeta Parra's continuous efforts in working with the *cueca,* the *refalosa,* the *mazurka,* and other genres can be read and discussed as a way to engage with a delinking of Western musical aesthetics from the Latin American projects that emerged during the 1960s. In reclaiming musical traditions, and putting them at the service of social commitment, artists such as Víctor Jara, Mercedes Sosa, and Silvio Rodríguez sought to engage more concretely in exploring the political dimensions of music-making at the national and transnational levels. In this way, when I discuss song lyrics, these must be understood as sounds in themselves and not strictly as written language. *Nueva canción,* then, as a register of historically inflected decolonial sounds, necessitates a renewed framework for the listener to move beyond the instantiation of its lyrics or the seeming datedness of its instrumentation. Instead, as decolonial sounds, the music of *nueva canción* is both inscribed within its time and exceeds it through memory, representation, and adaptations.[12] In short, the lyrics set to music must be imagined as active speech emerging from a particular moment of Latin America's cultural history that continues to have a deep resonance in our times.

So, how might we understand the emergence of music from the perspective of musicology, rather than cultural theory? For literary and music critic Lawrence Kramer, musicology serves the following function.

> Musicology . . . simply picks up where music leaves off. It turns on music the same kinds of attention that arise, at times, spontaneously, in making music. It does not add a process of interpretation to the presence of music but joins a process of interpretation that the music has made present. In doing so it acknowledges and augments the power of music to be not only something understood but also a medium of understanding no less effective than the texts that traditionally constitute "literature in the European and modern sense" and the images that form the texts' doubles and opposites. (Kramer 288–89)

In making this claim about the relationship between musicology and music, Kramer would seem to have in mind a specific approach to interpreting music and, by extension, a very concrete definition of what constitutes music, from which there can be very little deviation. By invoking terms such as "tradition," "European," and "modern," Kramer seemingly obviates other types of tradition that are also modern, even if they may not be entirely European, though they are of European influence. One need only mention the plethora of instruments, particularly the guitar as a foundational tool for *nueva canción,* that are European by design. Yet, what distinguishes the pan-Latin American movement described in this chapter from the type of approach Kramer advocates is the conscious efforts of Violeta Parra, Víctor Jara, Mercedes Sosa, and Silvio Rodríguez to serve as cultural and temporal bridges between folk traditions and modern musical sensibilities. If music is what enables the interpretive process, as Kramer suggests, one cannot help but wonder if the same "power" he ascribes to music would be applicable to popular music and songs with political content. As Kramer makes a claim for music as something not merely to be "understood," but also as an object that leads to understanding, it would also appear that he has a very specific register of the type of texts (musical or literary) that might open up to interpretations and create a repertoire of suggestive images.

Part of what is embedded in this approach to understanding and interpreting music is linked to the "loss of radical sensibility" with the introduction of the *ego cogito*, which has traditionally privileged reason "over the irrational body, sensibilities, affects, intuitions, and memories" (Vallega 199). Interpreting and sensing music from a decolonial perspective, including lyrics and instrumentation, requires a radical shift in our understanding of what constitutes aesthetics or what aesthetics is for, and in whose service it works. So doing, and thinking about the genealogy of decolonial sounds discussed in this chapter, requires that we think about the generation of *nueva canción* musicians not merely as responding to the spirits and ideologies of the time, but as having made redolent contributions to a rethinking of how to sense and experience music that is colloquial, rooted in popular traditions, and critical of power, and that reclaims the centrality of popular forms of knowledge, while positioning collective sensibilities emerging from below at the center of aesthetic discussions. To sense sounds from a decolonial perspectives requires a "learning to unlearn and relearn," which is to say that we must be willing to forego long-standing categorizations of *nueva canción* as just *nueva canción*, and begin thinking and sensing these musicians' collective contributions to a genealogy of decolonial sounds in their exposure and contestation of various modalities of coloniality (Tlostanova and Mignolo 15).

As I have argued throughout this chapter, *nueva canción* was part of a broader countercultural movement that took place in individual Latin American countries, but expanded onto the region at large. As a countercultural movement, it stood at odds with foreign influences and national cultural elitism, while actively seeking to validate folk traditions, popular registers of lyricism, quotidian concerns, and engaging directly with workers and peasants as an intended audience. After all, *nueva canción* was fueled by a nationalist sentiment in which a rediscovery and revalorization of indigenous and folk traditions were employed in response to imperialist and commercial influences coming from the United States and

Europe (Vila 1–17). *Nueva canción* has also been characterized as songs having "an impact on the *pueblo,* who identified both with the message, which portrayed them sympathetically, and the music, with its catchy dance rhythms and simple melodies" (Bernstein 170). It is with an intentional shift in the music-making practices that valorize the national over the foreign, the traditional and folk over the modern, political and social content over apolitical and commercial demands, and the crucial role of the singer-songwriter as an agent of social change that decolonial aesthetics becomes a useful interpretive tool. It is the artist who has to be in tune with the tastes and fashions of his or her time. The artist has a choice either to conform or challenge them. As Marshall Brown has put it, "Aesthetic value abolishes time; to be the latest and best is to stake a claim that none hereafter may escape from your sway" (Brown 101). In the case of *nueva canción* musicians, however, they did not seek to become merely popular or just a fad. Instead, they sought to make a profound and lasting impact by marking a before and after in the historiography of music in Latin America and thus abolishing time, as Brown would suggest. More importantly, the artists studied in this chapter actively sought to break the artificial boundaries that separated high and popular music or values that gave preference to the former over the latter.

4

Decolonial Visuality and New Latin American Cinema

> As a continent, we had begun to recognize our own voice, our own image, and though our response to this discovery was somewhat extreme, it was also a necessary stage of our development.
>
> Humberto Solás, in Burton and Alvear, "Interview with Humberto Solás" 32

In the concluding words to his coedited volume *Empires of Vision* (2014), Martin Jay reminds us that integral to the multilayered forms of imperialism are the uses of vision, visuality, and "the visual to achieve its ends. The spectacle of imperialism is always a screen behind which a far less attractive process unfolds. Although resistance to that process also can draw on visual practices, it too is never predominantly an affair of the eye or the gaze" (Jay 618). In making these remarks, Jay is aware that the visual was only one of the ways in which European empires sought to control their colonies and that any partial attempts at resisting "the spectacle of imperialism" certainly subverted, reinvented, and contested the very aesthetics of the visual that empires employed and introduced to control and subject the colonized. Any discussion of decolonial visual aesthetics, particularly in relation to the language of cinema, must begin with an acknowledgement that cinema and its various aesthetics emerged from the United States and Europe and rapidly made their way to other parts of the globe, including Latin America. Much of the early cinema in Latin America engaged and closely mirrored both European and Hollywood sensibilities and film aesthetics.[1] It is in this sense that the epigraph to this chapter emerges as Humberto Solás's reflection on New Latin America Cinema filmmakers' efforts to shift and resist the "spectacle of imperialism," to borrow Martin Jay's words. If the work these filmmakers produced was "somewhat extreme," and yet necessary for the undoing and challenging of Western film aesthetics, as Solás admits in this 1978 interview with Julianne Burton, it was because of the pressing necessity for new, if imperfect, cinematic practices to contest the coloniality of vision and visuality.[2] By this I mean the Western/Eurocentric framing of visual practices and aesthetics, which had widespread repercussions elsewhere in the world. As Nicholas Mirzoeff has succinctly put it, "The authority of coloniality has consistently required visuality to supplement its deployment of force. Visuality sutures authority to power and renders this association 'natural'" (Mirzoeff 6). It is precisely this "natural" association that links authority and power by using visuality (or the right to see) that the New Latin American Cinema filmmakers sought to undo, contest, and reconfigure through a decolonial gesture characteristic of their aesthetic propositions and films.

As a response to the co-opting of visuality to justify the use and abuse of power through imperial designs, one may consider countervisuality as a way to engage in a decolonial delinking and undoing of the historical embedded and naturalized nexus connecting power to visuality. In this sense, Mirzoeff argues that "Countervisuality is the assertion of the right to look, challenging the law that sustains visuality's authority in order to justify its own sense of 'right.' The right to look refuses to allow authority to suture its interpretation of the sensible to power, first as law and then as the aesthetic" (Mirzoeff 25). To reframe countervisuality *as* the right to look necessitates a reexamination of the articulations that subsume sensing, the sensible, and the sensuous into structures of power, which have been normativized and embedded in scientific, legal, and artistic discourses. Inherent in Mirzoeff's argument is the need to redefine and rethink the aesthetic from a decolonial perspective leading to countervisuality. It is in this way that the aesthetic propositions emerging from New Latin American Cinema can be considered an archive of countervisuality, which needs to be reconsidered as such.

To revisit the work of this generation of filmmakers with a particular eye to their respective visual aesthetic propositions, it becomes important to turn to Michael Chanan's seminal assessment of their work. In his introduction to *Twenty-Five Years of the New Latin American Cinema* (1983),

Chanan argues that the various cinematic articulations taking place in Latin America during the period he studies comprised a heterogeneous movement bearing the name of New Latin American Cinema. This movement starts with Fernando Birri's documentary film school in Santa Fe, Argentina, in the late 1950s and continues to redefine its aesthetics with Glauber Rocha and Brazilian *cinema novo*, as well as the emergence of a prominent Cuban film industry. In places such as Chile and Bolivia, among other countries, what we find are isolated cases of filmmakers seeking to take on some of the creative challenges posited by the aforementioned filmmakers and their cinematic manifestos (Chanan 2–8).

While the label for this movement certainly underscores the novelty of aesthetic film propositions and shares with other art forms the emphasis on a radical break with previous models and ways of making films, this label also simultaneously downplays the transformative effects of the various types of filmmaking of this period. The groundbreaking influence of this period's films is not merely their distinction as "new" cinematic alternatives to previous efforts. Whereas the term New Latin American Cinema certainly encompasses a number of the alternative and politicized approaches to and modes of filmmaking that began in the late 1950s and continued into the 1980s, this label is also useful in finding the connections among the explicit cinematic visions, political projects, and aesthetic propositions that Fernando Solanas, Octavio Getino, Tomás Gutiérrez Alea, Humberto Solás, Glauber Rocha, Miguel Littín, Jorge Sanjinés, and Raymundo Gleyzer, among others, articulated in their own films and in their writings in relation to a reading of their projects as producing decolonial visual aesthetics.

The conjoining moment that gave a certain degree of coherence to this film movement was the 1967 film festival in Viña del Mar, Chile, in which many of the aforementioned filmmakers came together to showcase their work, start a collective dialogue, and share perspectives on their respective national film industries. As a result, a document was produced that would lay the foundation for the formation in 1974 of the Committee of Latin American Filmmakers. From this founding document, the use of the term New Latin American Cinema became common among scholars and filmmakers, who adopted the term as an umbrella under which various modalities of filmmaking could come together. From a statement in that document, one can discern the common agenda among filmmakers:

> El auténtico nuevo cine latinoamericano solo ha sido, es y será el que contribuya al desarrollo y fortalecimiento de nuestras culturas nacionales, como instrumento de resistencia y lucha . . . y el que aborda los problemas sociales y humanos del hombre latinoamericano, situándolos en el contexto de la realidad económica y política que lo condiciona, promoviendo la concientización para la transformación de nuestra historia. (Anonymous 545–546)
>
> [The authentic New Latin American Cinema has been, is, and will be that which contributes to the development and strengthening of our national cultures, as instruments of resistance and struggle . . . and one that engages with the social and human problems of Latin Americans, situating them in the context of an economic and political reality that conditions them, and promotes consciousness toward the transformation of our history.][3]

The founding document for the Committee of Latin American Filmmakers makes a profound and explicit case for the use of the term "New Latin American Cinema" in relation to political cinema linked to the grounding of national cultures. Infused in the language of this document is a certain Fanonian spirit in which national culture serves as a mode and tool of resistance against colonial enterprises, but must also be critical of its own colonial legacies, which in today's critical language we now call coloniality. In fact, Fanon's thinking is present as early as the opening intertitles of Solanas and Getino's *The Hour of the Furnaces,* particularly in the film's first part dealing with "Neocolonialismo y violencia" [Neocolonialism and Violence]. Within the first six minutes of images of violence, we read quotations from the likes of Aimé Césaire, Fidel Castro, and Che Guevara, among others. The film quotes Fanon: "El hombre colonizado se libera en y por la violencia" [The colonized being becomes liberated in and through violence] (05:38). The ideas quoted in this film, the Fanonian spirit present in Solás's interview serving as the epigraph to this chapter, and the foundational document "Constitución del Comité de Cineastas de América Latina: 1967–1985" all draw from Fanon's *Wretched of the Earth.*[4]

Given New Latin American Cinema's original intended role as an instrument of resistance and struggle, I am also arguing for its interchangeability with the term third cinema, which comes from Fernando Solanas and Octavio Getino's manifesto, "Toward a Third Cinema." In that manifesto, they argued for a third alternative or a third way of making films, delinked from Hollywood models or European aesthetic influences. As Solanas and Getino succinctly put it, "*[t]hird cinema* is, in our opinion, the cinema that *recognizes in that struggle the most gigantic, cultural, scientific, and artistic manifestation of our time*, the great possibility of constructing a liberated personality with each people as the starting point—in a word, the *decolonization of culture*" ("Toward a Third Cinema" 18, original emphasis). For Solanas and Getino, third cinema became a means to challenge and question the way art, history, politics, and national culture had been articulated. The project of third cinema is one that acknowledges a profound schism between two versions of culture: a "dominant" one and an "inferior" one. As Chanan has argued, "The need for a third cinema was a consequence of the conditions of neo-colonialism which had ruled the evolution of cinema in Latin America" (3).[5] For Solanas and Getino, film served as an effective tool with which to contest and subvert previous hierarchical models of culture. In the following section, I will draw an explicit connection between the New Latin American Cinema as a decolonizing cinematic endeavor and decolonial visual aesthetics as a theoretical tool to examine the ways in which filmmakers sought to challenge dominant film aesthetics.

Decolonial Visual Aesthetics and Third Cinema

In *The Future of the Image* (2009), Jacques Rancière posits a differentiation between the concepts of the image and the visual (2–3). For Rancière, the image stands for or refers to external referents. As such, one could argue that the image always lends itself to interpretation. The image is suggestive and always concerned with the reality it seeks to represent or encapsulate within a frame. In contrast, for Rancière the visual is self-referential. While the visual could also lend itself to interpretation, its self-referentiality renders it apolitical and concerned with the field of aesthetics, particularly an aesthetics invested in the idea of pure pleasure and entertainment derived from art. Moreover, Rancière complicates this initial distinction when he argues that "The image is never a simple reality.

Cinematic images are primarily operations, relations between the sayable and the visible, ways of playing with the before and after, cause and effect" (*The Future of the Image* 6). In other words, while the image may stand for reality, it never represents it in a simplistic or one-dimensional manner. In being represented through an image, particularly a cinematic image, reality fragments itself into what remains outside the film and what is captured inside a frame. In this way, the cinematic image creates an ulterior reality based on a set of codes and registers that communicate to the audience that the images they are seeing are neither purely real nor entirely fictional.

While Rancière's argument is helpful to a degree, his dismissiveness of the term "visual" needs to be complicated. Whereas Rancière focuses on isolated images, which is to say fragments of a whole work of art such as a film (a discussion that appears toward the end of chapter 2 of this book), the visual refers to our ability as audiences to grasp and look at a work of art in its entirety. That is to say, as viewers of a film we can make sense of a series of images and how they connect to one another because we are engaging several of our senses. In a different work, Rancière argued that aesthetics is connected to the domain of the perceptible and to politics ("The Rationality of Disagreement" 43–60). As such, by engaging our senses, especially our sight and hearing, aesthetics is reinserted into the equation. By arguing for the importance of the visual, however, I am following Rancière's articulation of aesthetics as a political activity by design. Put differently, I am arguing for the need to articulate the "visual," which is to say the viewer's ability to make sense of images, as a political praxis.

In a different though related sense, I am making a claim for the need to distinguish among different types of aesthetic practices. For one, in using the term visual aesthetics, I am differentiating artworks seeking primarily to affect and engage our sight from those artworks that engage sight along with other senses and other modes of sensing needed to come close to a decolonial aesthetic experience. The project at hand is not interested in advancing the long-standing articulations of "aesthetic experience" as a passive act or as one that delinks entertainment from political engagement. It is at this juncture that decolonial visual aesthetics comes into play as a category that specifically addresses and engages with artists whose works have purposely challenged Eurocentric/Western articulations of aesthetics. More importantly, decolonial visual aesthetics acknowledges the existence of visual aesthetics embedded in the coloniality of power, while challenging it by shifting cinematic techniques, cinematic codes, intended audiences, and modes of representation.

At this point, it becomes necessary to specify how decolonial visual aesthetics is related to or enables a reading of third cinema and New Latin American Cinema. We should keep in mind that the concept of third cinema came about during a time of anticolonial struggles for independence in Latin America following World War II. It is in within that context and anticolonial/Fanonian "spirit" that Solanas and Getino saw Latin America as existing in a neocolonial stage of its history. Despite seeming to have formal political autonomy, the political control in Latin American nation-states was in the hands of a select few, while national economies were heavily dependent upon foreign capital. This also helps to explain why the dominant discourse in films such as *The Hour of the Furnaces* is closely in line with dependency theory and its articulation of the center-periphery dyad. Although Solanas and Getino did not use these terms, what they called a neocolonial phase in Latin America was none other than coloniality, which is to say a continuum of colonial modalities of oppression and control that validate those who can be in power and define those cannot have access to power. As argued throughout this book and developed more fully in the next chapter, it is under coloniality that knowledge is also codified. Only a specific line of knowledge (Eurocentric/Western) has been assumed as universal and valid, while negating the possibility of other forms of knowledge that deviate from this model.[6] Making an argument for the need to rethink aesthetics, Solanas and Getino write: "Ideas such as 'Beauty in itself is revolutionary' and 'All new cinema is revolutionary' are idealistic aspirations that do not touch the neocolonial condition, since they continue to conceive of cinema, art, and beauty as universal abstractions and not as an integral part of the national process of decolonization" ("Toward a Third Cinema" 19). Whereas in today's critical language the concept of the nation is less-favored, particularly in relation to categories that look at the transnational or the global, Solanas and Getino's remarks are still relevant in an effort to look at aesthetics and the arts anew from a decolonial perspective. This perspective will, in turn, have an impact at the individual, communal, national, and global levels. Rather than falling into "idealistic aspirations" or "universal abstractions," I am arguing here instead for a reexamination of instantiated and specific attempts to shift, delink, challenge, and decolonize modes of sensing, particularly under the rubric of New Latin American Cinema.

It is at this juncture that third cinema and decolonial visual aesthetics intersect. Third cinema appeared as a critical intervention in theory and praxis that acknowledged the need to reframe aesthetics, as well as what constituted valid art and cinema. As one critic has put it, "The praxis of Third Cinema, i.e., the call for action of these films, within the context of production, leads us to view the aesthetic of Third Cinema as a form of ideology; that is, the films point toward a confrontational cinema and an aesthetics of liberation" (Gabriel 6). Just as third cinema did not merely accept the established ways of making film coming from Hollywood or Europe, it also did not complacently accept ideas of "beauty" or what could be considered "beautiful" in film. Decolonial visual aesthetics names artistic interventions that reframe, challenge, question, and rearticulate established conceptions of what constitutes cinema or what can be labeled aesthetically pleasing, beautiful, or entertaining. More importantly, decolonial visual aesthetics does not concern itself with presenting entertaining, visually pleasing, or beautifully constructed images. Quite on the contrary—as a way to undo neocolonial ways of conceiving film aesthetics, films espousing the principles of third cinema aim to engage audiences in dialogue rather than complacency and mere spectatorship, and thus move toward what Rancière has called "the emancipated spectator."[7] The images and themes treated in third cinema seek to draw upon the sensibilities of workers, peasants, and students. Instead of being essentialized or romanticized, workers and peasants are depicted in a "realistic" manner in which the everyday issues affecting them are treated in a more profound way, rather than superficial or Manichean constructs fitting into pre-established cinematic models or formulas. In the following sections, I will explore some of the ways in which the films discussed in this chapter presented different models of making documentaries and fictional films, while moving toward aesthetics that challenged established models.

Fernando Solanas and Octavio Getino: *La hora de los hornos* and Third Cinema

La hora de los hornos (1966–1968) [*The Hour of the Furnaces*] serves as the Grupo Cine Liberación's prime example of how films can serve as a laboratory for defining the language to be used in the making of an alternative to Hollywood or European cinema. As the film was being created, Fernando Solanas and Octavio Getino organized small screenings in clandestine locations to obtain feedback from and engage in dialogue with workers and students. One could argue that these small screenings and dialogues with viewers were foundational to the final construction of the film and are, in themselves, a decolonial gesture challenging the hierarchical relationship and critical distance between filmmaker and audience. In fact, at various points in the three parts of the documentary, which runs over four hours, there are intertitles or black screens at which point the film was meant to be stopped so that the person screening the film could update the audience about specific political situations or open up the floor to discussion. As such, the film was conceived to be an organic and horizontal film-viewing experience seeking to undo modes of instantiating the coloniality of knowledge. In this exchange and dialogue, ideas coming from workers, students, and peasants in the audience were just as valid as (and perhaps more valid than) those presented in the film. In 1968, upon completion of the film, *The Hour of the Furnaces* was screened internationally and received an outstanding critical reception at film festivals, including an award at the Pesaro Film Festival.

The documentary informed the critical language and theoretical proposition of a new kind of filmmaking that would shape the region, as well as subsequent politically committed African and Asian cinema. As such, the documentary and the manifesto "Toward a Third Cinema," which appeared in 1969, were instrumental in the development of critiques of colonialism (coloniality) throughout the world. In fact, the manifesto makes explicit the language and approach to filmmaking that Solanas and Getino set out to embrace, particularly when using terms such as "films of decolonization" or "cinema of subversion" ("Toward a Third Cinema").

It would be impossible to talk about third cinema in Latin America without studying *The Hour of the Furnaces* by itself and then looking more closely at the critical language it creates, as well as its aesthetic-ideological proposition. As mentioned earlier, the film is divided into three parts, which are simultaneously independent of and complementary to each other. If we interpret the documentary as an extended visual essay, the first part serves to introduce the historical, social, political, cultural, and economic background of Argentina and Latin America. The opening of the documentary, "Neocolonialism and Violence" is divided into thirteen subsections, which include a discussion of history, Argentina as a nation-state, forms of quotidian violence, Buenos Aires as a port and symbol of centralization, the oligarchy, systems of power, political violence, neoracism, dependency, cultural violence, Eurocentric and universal cultural models and forms of knowledge, ideological wars, and possible solutions and options to the aforementioned problems. In recent critical discourse, all of these areas have become central to discussions around the coloniality of power, being, knowledge, gender, race, and aesthetics. As such, reading this film from a decolonial perspective means viewing this documentary as part of an archive of images seeking to challenge the coloniality of representation, or what Alejandro Vallega has called "the coloniality of images." In so doing, Vallega articulates a position similar to that of Mirzoeff's concept of visuality in which what is explored is who represents whom and through which visual registers and means. Following Quijano, Vallega argues that the coloniality of images points to an issue in which "the colonized see themselves through a *Eurocentric image*" (201, original emphasis). A way of undoing this Eurocentric construction of images is to find modes of self-representation, or seeing oneself, that come from the visual register of the European cinematic gaze, but use visual modalities that are inherently oppositional, critical, and subversive of Eurocentric optics and visuality. This is why, for instance, there is an emphasis on distinction in the adjectives used in third cinema or imperfect cinema, which seeks to distinguish itself from hegemonic visualities coming from Europe or Hollywood.

In the opening intertitles, it is made evident that the film addresses how neocolonialism and everyday violence take place in Argentina, and by extension, in the rest of Latin America. However, Cuba is purposely left out of the discussion, as the filmmakers acknowledged its status as the first liberated Latin American nation-state. The film also makes use of a black screen and interspersed images of violence and social unrest, accompanied by texts that complement the images. In so doing, Solanas and Getino ensure that the images will not be misinterpreted, and they are also correlated with concrete examples from history.

In the opening subsection of part one, a discussion of Latin American history and the history of colonialism is of prime importance to setting the stage for the rest of the documentary. The discussion of history in this section centers on a discussion of Spain's colonial presence (colonialism) and how England has taken over from Spain and become a neocolonial power in Latin America through investments and banking. While Latin America exported raw materials in the nineteenth century, England sent the finished products back to the Americas. The discussion of history then shifts to the relationship that Latin America has had with the United States, particularly in reference to the Monroe Doctrine and the Big Stick, which led to multiple U.S. military interventions in the region. At the time the film was made, the narrator was able to count forty-one U.S. military interventions across Latin America in the twentieth century. The film also asserts that the Organization of American States conceals and perpetuates this history of neocolonialism and U.S. intervention. For the narrators, while in the nineteenth century Latin American states were divided and pitted against one another, in the twentieth century the idea of Pan-Americanism continued serving the practices and discourse of neocolonialism.

The second subsection of part one focuses on Argentina's history as a nation state. This section gives an account of Argentina's population, its natural resources, its centralization and overpopulation around Buenos Aires, etc. The third subsection focuses on forms of quotidian violence. Images of factory workers, coal miners, and farmers are used to illustrate or put a face to everyday violence. This section also addresses the problem of uneven distribution of land—who owns it versus who works for it and who profits from it. The discussion of the distribution of land has parallels with Raymundo Gleyzer's *México, la revolución congelada* [*Mexico, the Frozen Revolution*] (1971), which will be discussed toward the end of this chapter. Finally, the section presents an argument in favor of the disenfranchised or the wretched of the earth, to echo Fanon's term, particularly when they lack basic utilities: running water, sewers, electricity, etc. For Solanas and Getino, these are problems that are experienced on an everyday basis and are forms of violence and oppression in very tangible and experiential terms.

The fourth section focuses on Buenos Aires as a predominantly white, Eurocentric city. The section makes the argument that Buenos Aires is Argentina's center of neocolonialism or coloniality. The fifth section turns its attention to the role that the Argentine oligarchy plays in perpetuating neocolonialism. For Solanas and Getino, the oligarchy is comprised of cattle ranchers, as well as the rural landowning families who are the "owners" of the country. In the sixth section of the film, the military is presented as the enemy and as a constitutive component of the system of oppression. This section also makes the case for various forms of internal colonialism, particularly in relation to the agricultural, cattle-raising, and industrial oligarchies.

The seventh and eight sections deal with instances of political violence and neoracism as other modalities of neocolonialism. The ninth section is about the history of economic, political, and cultural dependency on Spain, England, and the United States. The tenth section emphasizes how illiteracy and pedagogical/educational colonization are two ways in which cultural violence is perpetuated. The eleventh section makes a case for Latin America's fascination with European and seemingly universal forms of culture and models of knowledge. This section illustrates how Latin America has yet to produce culture and knowledge that steer away from or questions widely accepted Eurocentric models. A discussion of ideological wars is the main topic of the twelfth section. The images presented in this section show how Buenos Aires was fully immersed in the global counterculture of the 1960s. As the film makes evident, these foreign influences had very little to do with Argentina's reality beyond the dominant spheres of culture.

The final subsection of part one argues for the need to engage in a transformative revolution that engages with all the problems presented in the preceding twelve subsections. As the narrator in this section states, "En su rebelión el latinoamericano recupera su existencia" [In its rebellion, the Latin American being recovers its existence] (*La hora de los hornos*). These are the concluding words of the first part of the film. They also encapsulate several of the concerns presented throughout this section, particularly in advocating for the need to seek liberation as a way to validate the everyday person's existence in the eyes of his or her oppressor. In other words, the final statement in the section presents us with the critical challenge of rethinking the everyday person's ontological position within a spectrum of coloniality that seeks to continue colonial forms of oppression into neocolonial times. These words are also invoked and strategically placed in relation to a last image of Ernesto "Che" Guevara's death. The film zooms in on Che's face with its open eyes and advocates for the need to struggle even to the point of death. The need to engage in a profound liberation movement is equated with taking the risk of losing one's own life for the collective well-being, as was the case with "Che" Guevara.

The second part of the film, "Acto para la liberación" ["Liberation Act"], focuses on the ten-year period from 1945 to 1955 in Argentina, during Juan Perón's first government. For Solanas and Getino, this government became a symbol of what sets the stage for actual liberation. If Perón's government changed the political system from a position of power, its inclusion in the film is meant to make recent history a referent of the type of revolution that Solanas and Getino are advocating. The third part of the film, entitled "Violencia y liberación" ["Violence and Liberation"], is concerned with what took place after Perón's government. Some of the topics discussed in this section include how theory can be transformed into praxis and lead to a revolution. The third part of the film also questions whether or not pacifism and non-violence are viable options with which to lead a revolution. This part of the film also links struggles in Argentina with struggles in Africa and Asia. The concluding part remarks how violence is the only way to combat oppression and power, and be liberated.

If we interpret the three parts of the film as three sections of an extended visual essay exposing various modalities of coloniality, we could conclude that Solanas and Getino started with a discussion of Latin America as a whole and its history, and how Argentina can be situated within that history of colonialism and neocolonialism. The first part of the film is essential to discussing what gave rise to Peron's government and how this government sought to remedy some of the existing problems in Argentine society. The third part of the film also focuses on Argentina's situation during the 1960s, and seeks to draw parallels between the types of struggle and forms of neocolonialism present in Argentina and liberation struggles in the rest of Latin America, Africa, and Asia.

Accompanying the release of *The Hour of the Furnaces*, Solanas and Getino wrote a brief statement in May of 1968 that served as the founding document for the Grupo Cine Liberación (Liberation Cinema Group). The concluding words of the document are:

> *La hora de los hornos,* antes que un film, es un *acto*. Un acto para la liberación. Una obra inconclusa, abierta para incorporar el diálogo y para el encuentro de voluntades revolucionarias. Obra marcada por las limitaciones propias de nuestra sociedad y de nosotros, pero llena también de las posibilidades de nuestra realidad y de nosotros mismos. (Solanas and Getino, "Primera declaración," 10)
>
> [*The Hour of the Furnaces* is an *act* rather than a film. It is an act toward liberation. It is an incomplete work, open to incorporating dialogue and to the meeting of revolutionary wills. It is a work marked by our society's limitations and our own, but it is also full of the possibilities of our reality and of ourselves.]

By stating that *The Hour of the Furnaces* is an act rather than merely a film, Solanas and Getino are arguing for the need to change the way we experience and view films. *The Hour of the Furnaces* is not a film for viewing pleasure or complacency. Quite the contrary; the active participation of small audiences, and the opportunity for dialogue, are essential to the screening of the film and inherent in what I have been tracing as decolonial gestures of denouncing modalities of oppression, but also in shifting the dynamic between filmmaker and audiences. Solanas and Getino crafted this film as a text that could be stopped and opened to discussion much in the same way that one might do with a difficult passage in a written text. The directors do not assume that the film is self-evident, with a fixed meaning, or that it provides answers. Instead, as they suggest in the quotation above, the film remains an open text in which the viewer and audiences can inscribe their own readings that lead to further questioning of what they call neocolonialism, or what in today's critical language we understand as a stage of coloniality's *longue durée*.

Turning our attention to "Toward a Third Cinema," which appeared in 1969, this particular manifesto is one that is invested in questioning the history and nature of art, science, culture, and thought in "neocolonized" nation-states. In other words, the manifesto is not merely a film manifesto that argues for the need to conceptualize and put into practice a third way of making films that is different from the Hollywood norm—"first cinema," so to speak—and Western culture's attempts to offer an alternative to Hollywood, or "second cinema." It also argues for the need to transform culture, art, science, the history of knowledge, and cinema. Third cinema, then, is an intervention in all those fields, a way of critiquing normative and Eurocentric ways of perpetuating the coloniality of knowledge and aesthetics. If Hollywood set the standards for filmmaking in terms of techniques, aesthetics, technology, and distribution, and established a star system, then auteur cinema, French New Wave, and even Brazilian *cinema novo* sought different directions in those areas, but were limited by the particular set of cultural models. Second cinema emerges as an attempt at cultural decolonization, while still operating within the conceptions of Western/Eurocentric aesthetics and adhering to cinematic language, modes of production, and distribution employed by first cinema.

For Solanas and Getino, without second cinema as an initial attempt at cinematic decolonization, third cinema would not have been possible. Thus, in their self-definition as a third option to making cinema, Solanas and Getino are likewise acknowledging their indebtedness to second cinema, while being critical of its limitations and shortcomings. When thinking of the direction of third cinema, two basic requirements must be met: "*making films that the System cannot assimilate and which are foreign to its needs, or making films that directly and explicitly set out to fight the System*" (21, emphasis in original). *The Hour of the Furnaces* certainly meets both requirements, as it is a film that was not readily assimilated by the global/Western cinematic system of images, cinematic techniques, and mechanisms of film distribution, while also openly challenging in a decolonial gesture this very system of visuality. In fact, one could argue that all the films studied in the present chapter meet both of these basic requirements of third cinema.

At this point, one needs also to question whether or not there are marked differences in making documentary and fiction films under the concept of third cinema. For Solanas and Getino, films have the "capacity for synthesis and the penetration of the film image, the possibilities offered by the *living document*, and *naked reality*, and the power of enlightenment of audiovisual means [which] make the film far more effective than any other tool of communication" ("Toward a Third Cinema" 21). In making *The Hour of the Furnaces*, the directors certainly make use of the "living document" by going to the streets, fields, and private spaces to capture what was happening at that moment of Argentina's history in the mid-1960s. They also made use of the living document, or "naked reality," by including images from mass media, archival footage, and scenes from other films. For instance, throughout the first part of the film, Solanas and Getino employed images from Fernando Birri's *Tire Dié* (1958), León Hirzman's *Maioria absoluta* (1964), and Joris Ivens's *Le ciel-La terre* (1967). By including images from these films, Solanas and Getino seek to establish a relationship with films that have served as a cinematic foundation for what would become third cinema. Other film referents in Solanas and Getino's filmmaking style as they were making *The Hour of the Furnaces* were Glauber Rocha, Joaquim Pedro de Andrade, Tomás Gutiérrez Alea, Santiago Alvarez, and Jorge Sanjinés (Caetano 60).

It should be underscored that "Toward a Third Cinema" is concerned with the role of cinema as a component of a larger transformative process that needs to take place at the aesthetic-political level. It is not merely a film manifesto, but an essay on how culture needs to be rearticulated from the vantage point of "the people." For Solanas and Getino, the elite circles of society are merely filters for foreign modes of thinking (coloniality of knowledge). The elite think and operate within a dominant culture—as a system of oppression, or coloniality of power—and do not see a need to change it. They are fully satisfied with the status quo and the system that has kept them in power for so long. It is the elite's inability to see beyond its social circles and interests that has caused Latin America's cultural development to stagnate and has positioned it as a receptor and imitator of culture. In the role of receptor, it is impossible to produce works of art that steer away from pre-established models. Reception of culture without producing and exporting a culture of one's own maintains what Mignolo has termed the colonial difference, which is an imbalance in power by means that perpetuate Eurocentrism as the core of a global system, while relegating the rest of the world to a peripheral status (Mignolo, *Global Histories/Local Designs*).

When Solanas and Getino showed parts of *The Hour of the Furnaces* to students, workers, and activists, they realized third cinema's new potential: "the *participation* of people who, until then, were considered *spectators*" ("Toward a Third Cinema" 26, original emphasis). The film-viewing experience depended on those who organized it and those who attended.

This is to say that third cinema, particularly with a film like *The Hour of the Furnaces,* demands the active participation of its audience engaging in dialogues during and after a screening. This film and its accompanying cinematic manifesto changed the way political films were made, particularly during a time when discourses of liberation and decolonization were circulating in Latin America, Africa, and Asia. The film and the manifesto proved that political action could coincide with artistic merit and that aesthetics could be placed in the service of undoing coloniality. More importantly, *The Hour of the Furnaces* sought to transform the relationship between a film and its viewers. If before film had been used as on object of entertainment, now it became a medium through which to question and contest history and the present. A concern with history and the present as ways to imagine the future became a common interest beyond the documentary form and beyond Latin America's southern cone. In the following sections, we will turn our attention to examples that take the challenge of third cinema to new registers, in other Latin American contexts, and in both fiction films and other genres.

Tomás Gutiérrez Alea: *Memories of Underdevelopment* and Revolutionary Cinema

Gutiérrez Alea's *Memorias del subdesarrollo* (1968) [*Memories of Underdevelopment*] is based on Edmundo Desnoes's homonymous novel, published in 1966. Aside from being a criticism of the Cuban bourgeoisie that left the island after the 1959 revolution, the film posits the problems of coexistence between bourgeois life (remnants of capitalism) and a sociocultural revolution that is solidly in place. Ultimately, the film seeks to underscore the insurmountable disconnect between these opposing states of mind (coloniality and an attempt at decolonization) and social realities. In many ways, the main character in the film, Sergio, embodies these tensions. Sergio decides to stay in Cuba despite most of his family and friends migrating to the United States. But Sergio's lifestyle and frame of mind are out tune with socialist Cuba and its newly implemented social policies.

Memories of Underdevelopment's opening sequence is devoted to Afro-Cubans dancing, and as part of the diegetic soundtrack we hear Afro-Cuban drums. This sequence suddenly comes to a halt and things shift to the film's narrative, particularly the exodus of Cubans leaving the island in 1961. In fact, we have a sequence of images of the airport in Havana and affluent families emigrating, mostly to the U.S. One could interpret the inclusion of dancing, celebration, and visual referents to Afro-Cuban culture as signs of the positive and triumphalist atmosphere that had pervaded Cuba since 1959. By contrasting these images of celebration with Cubans seeking to emigrate, the film portrays the ideological tendencies between those who supported Castro's government and those who opposed it. Those who left the island were the ones who would benefit the least from the revolution, because of the loss of their private property or companies in the redistribution under socialism. In contrast, the Afro-descendant and formerly disenfranchised Cubans benefited the most from Castro's new government.

From this opening, the film narrative turns our attention to Sergio, the film's protagonist, whose voiceover guides the film. Images of Sergio on the balcony of his apartment serve as our first introduction to him. From that vantage point, Sergio looks at the city through a telescope and admires the changes in the cityscape. At this point, Sergio states: "Todo parece tan distinto. ¿He cambiado yo o ha cambiado la ciudad?" [Everything seems so different. Have I changed or has the city changed?] (*Memorias del subderrallo*). From this moment onward, Sergio tries to answer these questions as he constantly tries to figure out what is becoming of Havana and who he has become in this revolutionary process, now that all the people he once knew are gone.

Gutiérrez Alea makes conscious use of Hollywood conventions such as over-the-shoulder shots to introduce characters, tracking shots to establish the type of rooms and apartment Sergio lives in, or details such as Sergio's wardrobe. By employing these film conventions, Gutiérrez Alea ensures that audiences will situate Sergio as a petit bourgeois who is out of place in Cuba's new social and political milieu. In fact, by having Sergio look at the city and its inhabitants, and resorting to inner dialogue, the film shows Sergio's alienation from everything and everyone around him. Furthermore, our central character is not interested in what the future may hold for Cuba. Instead, Sergio is invested in the past as he looks over objects that remind him of his wife—lipstick, furs, a monocle—while listening to a recording of a conversation between them. As these objects evoke memories for Sergio, they can also be interpreted as symbols of decadence of Fulgencio Batista's pre-revolutionary regime. These objects are remnants of Sergio's previous life, but they also stand as symbols of the uneven social hierarchy before the revolution.

Early in the film, however, Sergio begins to discover answers to the question of whether it is the city or he who has changed. Through Sergio's perspective as a mere bystander and observer of the social changes taking place, the camera follows the quotidian experiences of women—how they walk, how they dress, and what they eat. It is as though Sergio is trying to make sense of his fellow citizens. Sergio's alienation is such that he yearns for the times when Cuba was called the Paris of the Caribbean. For him, under Castro's regime, Havana now looks like a Tegucigalpa of the Caribbean, a possible reference to the longstanding history of U.S. intervention in Honduras and how the country's economy and governance had been weakened during the first half of the twentieth century. Comparing Tegucigalpa to Havana brings into the fold a subtle critique of U.S interventions across the Americas. By contrasting medium shots depicting scenes of everyday citizens in Havana with Baroque non-diegetic music, the film suggests that it is other people who have changed, not Sergio. In fact, Sergio wonders what the meaning of life must be for them, but his concern is empty, detached, particularly since he sees himself as different from the rest.

The film also presents what those Cubans emigrating or wanting to leave the island are thinking. In a conversation that Sergio and one of his friends, Pablo, have prior to the latter's departure, Pablo lauds people from the United States for knowing how to do things. Pablo is trying to fix his car, so that he can turn it over to the Cuban government. Only upon handing it over will Pablo be allowed to leave Cuba. From this conversation, the film suddenly shifts to Sergio's inner thoughts about the hunger that Cubans withstood under Spanish colonialism and how hunger affects children everywhere in Latin America and is one of the leading causes of death. It is interesting to point out that this scene echoes a similar point made in *The Hour of the Furnaces* regarding Latin America's problems with malnourishment and how extreme poverty has claimed more victims in the region than the entire casualty count of World War II. This scene is a prime example of inherent coloniality in Sergio's thinking in his supposition that hunger and social inequities belonged to the nineteenth century under Spanish rule and that U.S. intervention at the turn of the nineteenth century led to social progress and economic growth. Sergio's failure to see how such uneven distribution of wealth affects and disenfranchises vast sectors of Cuba's population positions him within the modernity/coloniality/decoloniality spectrum. In other words, Sergio assumes a linear historicity of modernity as progress (colonialism, independence, post-independence), without being capable of acknowledging what this linear discourse veils (coloniality or the perpetuation of modes of oppression beyond formal independence). Decoloniality, then, becomes a non-option, for it first needs the acknowledgment that coloniality exists in order to move beyond it, critique it, and seek to undo it.

Memories of Underdevelopment has several scenes interspersed throughout the film's narrative, which at first glance would seem to disrupt the narrative flow, but end up enhancing the narrative by contrasting Sergio's careless and bourgeois attitude with his observations on Cuba's underdevelopment. One could mention here three different scenes related to Sergio's love interests to illustrate this point. In one sequence, Sergio fantasizes about his maid, Noemi. As Sergio and the maid are having a cup of coffee, there is a voiceover describing Noemi's baptism. The scenes of the baptism are idyllic and Sergio imagines himself embracing her; Vivaldi's *Spring* is used as background music. This dream-like sequence shifts to Sergio gazing on Botticelli's *The Birth of Venus*. With these references to Renaissance art and Baroque music, the film suggests Sergio's detachment from what is going on outside his apartment and his refusal to let go of his bourgeois sensibilities and his preference for Western aesthetics or high art, which negate the possibility of sensing popular forms of visual or aural art forms.

In the next sequence, Sergio bumps into a young girl. This teenager, Elena, wants to become an actress, and Sergio introduces her to people he knows at the Instituto Cubano de Arte e Industrias Cinematográficas (ICAIC). While they are having dinner, Sergio asks Elena why she wants to be an actress, to which she responds that she is tired of being herself. Sergio replies that actresses repeat the same gestures, the same words over and over. The film shifts to images of five (Hollywood and European) films in which images of women are repeated. Most of the images are sexual, particularly of women showing their breasts, and of men and women about to have sex. In hearing Sergio's statement that films are made up of repetitive dialogue and scenes and observing repetitive

Hollywood imagery, one can argue that this sequence serves as a direct commentary on Hollywood cinema, its formulaic approach to filmmaking, and even a coloniality of visual registers and visuality as a form of controlling and subjugating women by reinforcing gender roles—what is now called coloniality of gender. In other words, this is Gutiérrez Alea's commentary and stance on what it means to make imperfect films under the Cuban Revolution, which is to depart from cinematic formulas and change the approach to filmmaking by turning a film into a set of visual cues aimed at interrogating modes of domination or coloniality.

In a different set of scenes also centered on Sergio's relationship with Elena, Sergio becomes bored with her and realizes the following: "Siempre trato de vivir como un europeo y Elena me hace sentir el peso del subdesarrollo en cada paso" [I have always tried living like a European and Elena makes me feel the weight of underdevelopment with each step] (*Memorias del subdesarrollo*). Sergio wants to make Elena more like his wife, Laura, and for Elena to suit and share his own tastes. Particularly in view of Sergio's statement about underdevelopment, one can argue that Gutiérrez Alea wants to make the case that underdevelopment has to do with Sergio's state of mind, in which he assumes a position of inferiority in relation to European culture. This position is illustrative of coloniality and thus the need to move toward the decolonial as an option to the coloniality of knowledge, aesthetics, and being. In other words, to be a Cuban or a Latin American is insufficient and incomplete, since one needs always to strive to be like Europeans in their accumulation of knowledge and refined taste, which from Sergio's perspective creates an ontological hierarchy (Europeans as superior to Latin Americans) involving the virtue of intersectionality of race (white) and knowledge (European).

The film shifts its narrative to a flashback of Sergio's affair with a young German woman, Hanna, prior to his marriage. In fact, throughout this sequence, Sergio admits to falling in love with Hanna, who he thought was more mature than the underdeveloped Cuban women around him. Hanna and her family decide to move to New York, but Sergio cannot go as he is in charge of the family business, a furniture store, which is to say he is bound by his capitalist and familial ties to the island. Sergio argues that he does not want to go New York empty-handed, but in the process of his obsession with work, he is forced to let go of Hanna. This flashback is introduced in the film to illustrate how this relationship has transformed his attitude toward work and toward women, two of the main themes in the film. Now that the revolution is in place, Sergio does not work, and survives on what he receives from renting out properties he owns—a reminder of the familiar capitalist ties that bind him to the island and why he chose not to leave with Hanna. Memories of Hanna haunt Sergio and become a reference point to which other Cuban women can never compare, given her beauty, maturity, and overall development. Implicit in this discourse are threads that can be connected to an embedded coloniality, but also a Darwinian and even positivist perspective on the alleged superiority of the blonde German woman over any mixed-race or black, and thus impure, Cuban woman. Sergio's idealization of and fascination with all that Hanna represents as a symbol of European/Western beauty, intelligence, sophistication, self-assurance, and maturity cannot be matched by any woman coming from the Americas. Read from this perspective, what we see in this film is Sergio's own entrapment and stagnation on the island due to his inability to recognize his own coloniality of mind as something that ought to adapt to the changing times under the Cuban Revolution. Gutiérrez Alea's inclusion of this sequence is also reminiscent of Latin America's fascination (starting as early as the foundation of the Latin American Republics in the nineteenth century and continuing today) with that which is foreign, particularly European, at the expense of what is local, indigenous, Afro-descendant, or popular, and thus assumed to be inferior or flawed. This xenophilic gesture is one that is constitutive of coloniality and one that the decolonial seeks to unveil.

The film's exploration of Sergio's character eventually leads to a conclusion in which he finds himself alone. With the revolution, there has been a rupture in society that Sergio cannot bear. For Sergio, everything about the past falls prey to the seemingly successful aura of the Cuban Revolution, allowing Cuba's prerevolutionary past to be forgotten in the current state of underdevelopment. In this existential crisis, Sergio assumes his nothingness, his own symbolic death, and sees himself as too old and as having little to contribute to society. While dwelling in his existential crisis, Sergio looks at pictures of his youth and likens his life to that of a monstrous vegetable. If this monstrous vegetable can be likened to a visual representation of coloniality, is it even possible to uproot it, given its deep sedimentation in the collective mindset? Because the revolutionary discourse in Cuba is all about "the people," Sergio finds himself in complete isolation, as he thinks he is the only one who speaks coherently. Prior to the revolution, Sergio was considered "respectable," and now he is forced into a position where he is one of "the people," though he rejects this new role without being able to identify himself as the problem, let alone connect in any significant way with vast sectors of the population.

The film's finale suggests that Sergio does not know how to act and cannot adapt to the changes around him. Instead, he becomes static and petrified in his sense of his superiority in relation to what he perceives to be the widespread underdevelopment that plagues Cuba and its citizens. While the film is primarily concerned about Cuba's situation in the revolution and its people, it also served as a model in its day for how to make ideologically charged fiction cinema to critique long-standing modes of domination, or what can be called coloniality of power. Gutiérrez Alea presents us with a new set of aesthetic choices to make fiction films in a region that is trying to define its own cinematic language as a tool of social and political critique.[8]

Humberto Solás: *Lucía*, Historical Reevaluations, and Melodrama

Humberto Solás's *Lucía* (1968) takes its viewers through three distinct moments of revolutionary history in Cuba, namely 1895, 1932, and an unspecified year in the 1960s. Humberto Solás, Julio García Espinosa, and Nelson Rodríguez cowrote the script; García Espinosa's participation is of particular interest given his theorization of an imperfect cinema. Distinctive of Solás's film style is the careful mixture of melodrama, social critique, and surrealist imagery. As in many of the early ICAIC films, Leo Brouwer was responsible for the musical compositions here, particularly in creating music that accentuated the film's melodramatic tone.

As one of the three films that redefined third cinema in 1968, *Lucía* confronts us with the role of women in Cuban society at three distinct moments of social unrest, and serves as a way to reflect on the absence of women's voices during this period of transformation. Focusing on three distinct moments of revolution in Cuba (1895 against Spain and the U.S., 1933 against Machado's regime, and a year in the 1960s in the midst of the Cuban Revolution), and using conventions of the melodrama, the film takes a keen interest in using the medium as a tool for understanding the role of history in the composition of contemporary society. Lauded as one of the masterpieces of the period, it also remains one of the most enigmatic in its treatment of female characters and their participation in political struggles and societal transformations.[9] This film provides a stark contrast to *Memories of Underdevelopment*.

The character of Lucía in 1895 is submissive, conforms to the norms expected of unmarried women, follows what her mother expects, and yet, when she is surrounded by her female friends, is playful and girlish. In conforming to these gender roles and attributes that are constitutive of the coloniality of gender, the film inserts a question: Is it possible for this Lucía to challenge the coloniality of gender and engage in political action? The first encounter between Lucía and Rafael accentuates their playful flirtation with each other, which marks their initial relationship. The women support and help the revolutionary cause by sewing clothing and hammocks for the Cubans fighting against the Spaniards. In this first part of the film, there is a heavy emphasis on prioritizing women's work and labor. In the first scene, in which the women are sewing, one of the female characters wishes to take a break from work and chat instead, while Lucía makes a case for talking less and working more. In fact, she argues that if anyone is going to win the battle between the Spaniards and the Cubans, it will be the "mambises," a reference to the Cuban guerrilla fighters fighting for independence. This alludes to anti-Spanish and anti-colonialist sentiment reminiscent of Latin American nineteenth-century texts. In this subtle attempt to take a leadership role within a domestic and feminine space, Lucía begins to show signs of wanting to insert herself in political struggle, albeit from a distance.

The relationship between Lucía and Rafael is marked by the latter's deception as he seeks a relationship with Lucía as a way to find out more information about the rebels' plans and location. Rafael serves the interests of the Spaniards and Lucía symbolizes the spirit of a thwarted pro-independence and nationalist sentiment that fails to materialize. Among the rebels is Lucía's brother, Felipe, who is killed by the Spanish forces. As a response to this betrayal, the passivity, submissiveness, and naïveté that were emblematic of Lucía's character are exchanged for madness and a desire for revenge as she stabs Rafael to death. One can read this violent gesture as a moment in which Lucía radically challenges gender roles aimed at keeping her in a domestic space (coloniality of gender) and takes it upon herself to become involved in political struggle by killing

Rafael, a symbol of colonial allegiance and the persistent coloniality of power—Cubans wanting to perpetuate Spanish modes of domination.

In contrast, the second part of the film focuses on 1933 Lucía and her affair with Aldo, a revolutionary fighting to overthrow Cuban President Gerardo Machado's regime. In this section of the film, the role of women shifts. Here we no longer have a seemingly submissive and naïve female character. Indeed, this Lucía decides to leave the comforts that her well-off family can provide and take up work in a tobacco factory. Aldo, as the male figure, is still the symbol of revolutionary struggle and resistance, but Lucía also becomes politically engaged as she participates in strikes and actively supports Aldo. In relation to Lucía from 1895, this period's Lucía shows the progress made by women in Cuban society, which is to say progress toward challenging and undoing the coloniality of gender. Nonetheless, the elements of melodrama and personal tragedy, both of which are distinctive of Solás's style, are inescapable. Aldo is killed during one of the attempts to overthrow Machado and Lucía is left to suffer in silence and with the added weight and responsibility of carrying Aldo's child. The relationship has not only awakened but deeply affected Lucía's consciousness, thus enabling the possibility of a change in her condition in a patriarchal society constitutive of coloniality of gender.

In the third section of the film, the 1960s Lucía has characteristics of the initial submissiveness of Lucía from 1895 and the progressiveness of Lucía from 1933. It is clear that this period of the story, which is left open-ended, takes place in post-revolutionary Cuba. Lucía has just married Tomás, and they are still in a honeymoon phase. However, we soon find out that Tomás still thinks and behaves like men did before the revolution, as he is resistant to change and wants to keep Lucía in confinement, not allowing her to leave the house or see friends and relatives unless he is present. Tomás's jealousy is such that when the illiterate Lucía has the opportunity to learn how to read and write, her husband nixes the idea. For the lifestyle Tomás wishes for his wife, and in the agricultural rural context they inhabit, Tomás cannot and does not want to understand why women would want to learn how to read, have access to education, or work outside the home. In other words, Tomás is perfectly content to uphold the modes of domination that have been put in place to oppress women, and thus to uphold a coloniality of gender by denying Lucía access to knowledge, which may lead to her emancipation. Tomás thinks that laboring at home ought to be sufficient for Lucía. Yet, in the spirit of revolution, she escapes from Tomás's obsessive and archaic control with the help of a literacy volunteer sent from Havana to teach everyone in town how to read. In her desire to rebel or to escape her husband's control, all Lucía wants to do is to work and be able to move freely without having to ask her husband's permission. At the end, Tomás chases Lucía around the salt dunes where she has gone to work, while she resists his repeated attempts to take her back home to their previous living arrangement and modes of domestic, emotional, and psychological control and domination so key to the pervasiveness of the coloniality of gender. Although the style of this third part of the film is comic, this last section resolves some of the tensions present in the two previous representations of women during revolutionary times in Cuba. Lucía of the 1960s exhibits a rebellious persona that echoes the liberation of women taking place in other parts of the globe through second-wave feminism. Moreover, the third section makes the case that under Castro's government, the role of women is central to the advancement of a profound revolutionary process, as it challenges the embedded structures of patriarchy that have sustained gendered modes of domination leading to the coloniality of gender.

Even if the film is heavily invested in entering into dialogue with the past, such an exercise is meant to be a critical reflection on the present. For Solás, the past helps us arrive at a better understanding of a nation's cultural, social, and psychological articulations, which shape everyday life and social mores (Caballero 165). In a broader sense, for Solás, *Lucía* also serves as a critical reflection on the relationship among Latin American nations, which Solás identifies as one of isolation rather than interaction. As Solás writes, “El problema más importante de los incentivos que me planteó el filme fue buscar un modo de expresión nacional que, de genuino, trascendiera el ámbito isleño y se insertara como aspecto de un modo de expresión latinoamericano” [Among the most important incentives with which the film confronted me was to search for a mode of national expression, which, if genuine, would transcend the scope of the island and become an aspect of a mode of Latin American expression] (Caballero 165). Even though the film was attempting to engage in a historical study of the trajectory in the liberation struggles in Cuba and the place of women in them, in fact, the film could also be read as a reflection on the future direction and struggles that need to take place elsewhere in Latin America to avoid repeating the failed emancipatory experiences of the likes of Lucía from 1895 or the Lucía from 1933. The film's progression from subtle to overt modes of overturning and challenging patriarchy is the most prominent way in which I see Solás's work as one that displays decolonial gestures toward undoing or, at the very least, questioning the sedimentations of patriarchy that give way to the coloniality of gender. In other words, the film can be interpreted as an exercise in underscoring the need to decolonize gender in Latin America's patriarchal societies at the discursive and experiential levels (Lugones, "The Coloniality of Gender"). One could argue that Solás's use of melodrama serves as a way to engage the film with a historical reflection on the progressive liberation of women, but also as a reminder of what remains to be done to avoid the pitfalls of revolutions spearheaded solely by men. Moreover, the film advocates for the centrality of women in revolutionary causes. This is a concern present in subsequent films by Solás, including *Cantata de Chile,* though to a different degree.

Humberto Solás: *Cantata de Chile,* Neo-Baroque Sensibilities, and Melodrama/Tragedy as Critique

In contrast to *Lucía, Cantata de Chile* (1975) is not concerned with Cuba or the role of women per se, but rather with workers in the north of Chile. This is not to say, however, that women are not depicted positively in the film. On the contrary, the role of women is of prime importance in enabling the saltpeter miners' revolt against their oppressors. In this section, I am interested in reconsidering the ways in which Solás crafted his film *Cantata de Chile* (1975) as a means of engaging with politics and history beyond the borders of Cuba. In this film, Solás establishes temporal shifts that move from nineteenth-century Chile to pre-Columbian times and then to 1970s Chilean society. The bulk of the action of the film takes place in 1907, though there are temporal shifts to correlate the struggles taking place in the early part of the twentieth century with the colonial and independence periods. Toward the end of the film, there is also a correlation between the 1907 revolt and the popular revolts of the mid-1970s. Through a nuanced examination of Chile's history of oppression, Solás is able to focus on questions of labor and foreign capital in Chile, particularly in relation to miners and exploited laborers in Iquique, which led to the massacre of Chilean miners in 1907. By engaging with history, particularly the tragic massacre in Iquique, Solás creates a highly ambitious film in which he blends his signature emphasis on visual and aural tropes linked to melodrama with a highly politicized film aesthetic that incorporates sculptures, paintings, techniques from theater, and the constant use of a choral piece composed specifically for this film. This amalgamation of artistic media in its political vein is what I call decolonial film aesthetics. To ground my analysis and theorization, in this section I will draw on Walter D. Mignolo's and Madina Tlostanova's work, as well as other critical texts that enable an examination of Solás's slippery conjunction of the tragic with melodrama.

Recently the work of Walter D. Mignolo and of Madina Tlostanova has focused on articulating how decolonial aesthetics might work. For Mignolo, what lies ahead is precisely the challenge of uncoupling aesthesis (in its original meaning of sensorial experiences) from aesthetics which, after Kant, became synonymous with discourses around beauty, the sublime, aesthetic pleasure, and evaluative categories (Mignolo, "Aisthesis decolonial" 10–25). While more contemporary works on aesthetics do not necessarily rely on these categories, they still rely on the same logic of positing a normative aesthetics that originates from Europe and now the U.S. In a similar vein, Madina Tlostanova is attempting to liberate aesthesis from this normative aesthetics that still persists today (Tlostanova 10–31). While their works focus primarily on pictorial art, as well as modes or places of exhibition, in my own work I have extended decolonial aesthetics to other art forms, in this case film, precisely as a way to return to language that enables us to think about how we can sense the arts anew, while also allowing space for voices and works of art that are not created to satisfy or meet normative aesthetic expectations.

In this sense, then, Solás's interest in the correlation between film and history continues in *Cantata de Chile,* particularly because the film serves as a tool with which to look at the history of British investment in Chile and the legacy of economic imperialism. In fact, the film presents pointed critiques of nineteenth-century British imperialism, as Britain controlled Chile's saltpeter mines, and the country became a neocolony under British economic investment. Aside from looking at the mechanisms by which workers were oppressed by the bourgeoisie (Chilean and foreign investors), the film is meant to elicit a reflection on the rapid transformations in Chilean politics and social repression after Pinochet's coup d'état. This film, then, can be read as an example of Solás's interest in historical analysis and social critique beyond Cuba.

As part of Solás's aesthetic style and choices, for instance, during the battle scenes from the War of the Pacific (1879–1893), he makes heavy use of blue and red when focusing on the common citizen engaged in battle. The film suggests that it was foreign investors and the elite who came out as victors in this struggle. To accentuate this perspective, the foreign investors are depicted as though they are watching the battles from a balcony. The color used to envelop their shadowy presence is gold, which is symbolic of the money they continued making at the expense of a territorial dispute among neighboring countries—Chile, Bolivia, and Peru. When dealing with the 1907 massacre, in order to draw parallels between that revolt and Chile's history of struggles since colonial times, the director invokes the figure of Lautaro, who led the Araucanos' victorious revolt against the Spaniards in the 1550s. As the miners share stories around a bonfire in the 1907 scenes, they invoke Lautaro as a mythical figure of popular resistance, which leads the miners to identify with Lautaro and what he symbolizes: a continuous struggle in their country from colonial times into the early twentieth century. To mark the temporal shift and to differentiate 1907 from the colonial period, Solás makes use of dark colors and dim lighting in the former.

Another way in which the film seeks to establish a parallel between time periods involves the same actors playing roles in 1907 and in colonial times, changing costumes and embodying those fighting for independence in each era. To denote this shift, aside from the changes in costume, Solás uses reds and brighter light in the colonial era. In this part, the film presents a discourse on how independence was available only to a select few, while there was continuity in the unevenness and oppression of the poor and workers. When asked about how much improvisation has gone into his filmmaking style, Solás responds that in the case of *Cantata de Chile,* scenes were rehearsed about an hour before shooting. Solás adds that up to ninety percent of the actors were, in fact, Chileans living in exile and were thus non-professional actors. These actors worked on the film "as a political activity for the liberation of their country" (Burton and Alvear 32).

The film's main narrative takes place in 1907. As the saltpeter miners are convening to march toward Iquique, where they will meet other miners, they begin to dance the *cueca*. Bolivian miners soon join them. As music forms an important part of the aesthetics of this film, the traditional *cueca* instrumentation incorporates Bolivian wind instruments. This can be seen as a sign of transnational workers' solidarity and as an effort to put behind them the events of the War of the Pacific. At this point, the scene transitions to a panoramic image of workers marching with Chilean, Bolivian, Argentine, and Peruvian flags waving. At various points in the film, Solás defies cinematic convention by having workers march toward the camera, while at other times they march from left to right or right to left.

After meeting with the owners of the mines in which they work, demanding better salaries, and having their demands dismissed, the saltpeter miners decide they must fight for a popular democracy and a government ruled by and in favor of the workers. As this is perceived as a revolt against the government, the military gets involved, and soon begins shooting at the miners. While the miners are defending themselves with rudimentary weapons such as picks and knives, the film transitions to the scene of a protest in the 1970s. The film concludes with a repeated chant of "el pueblo unido jamás será vencido" [a united people will never be defeated]. Even as the images fade out, the repeated chant continues to be heard.

Colonial indigenous insurgencies, nineteenth-century armed struggle for independence, miners' revolts at the turn of the twentieth century, and political demonstrations in Chile during the 1970s are seldom the first scenarios we imagine when confronted with the task of thinking about why tragedy matters today and what it means to contemporary audiences. In Humberto Solás's *Cantata de Chile* (1975), these moments of Chile's history are woven together to explore why tragedy, in the second half of the twentieth century, should neither focus exclusively on a traditional tragic protagonist nor on single tragic event. The film focuses instead on articulating different dimensions of collective tragedy, whether in the guise of an entire country or concerning groups that have fought against different agents of subjugation. It is this history of resistance that enables the staging of historical tragedy, or rather a series of historical events that have a tragic aspect. To examine what Solás does with his film that might enable a discussion of tragedy, I will focus on four different aspects: the film's engagement with the tradition of the cantata; a shift from a single to a collective protagonist; moving from a single event as the source of history to drawing connections among several historical events to delineate the contours of historical tragedy; and the formal components taken from theater and painting that are present in the film. By looking at *Cantata de Chile* from these perspectives, I argue that Solás produces a choral film, one that highlights specific events from Chile's history to emphasize the impact of tragedy upon its citizens as a collectivity, and that the filmic representation of these tragic events necessitates the use, variations, and conjugation of techniques/language stemming from music, theater, history, and film.

In an interview conducted over a decade after *Cantata de Chile* was released, when asked if it was one of his most ambitious and provocative films, Solás replied that from an aesthetic perspective, the film could be qualified as such. For Solás, the problem the film presents in terms of communicating with an audience is that it is a "choral film," which means that Solás incorporated elements of choral music, theater, and painting into the medium of film. It also means that the action does not focus on a single protagonist, but rather on a group of miners. In terms of the musical composition for the *Cantata de Chile*, the film relies heavily on music for melodramatic effect, and Patricio Manns wrote lyrics for the opening cantata. Manns was among the many Chileans who went into exile after the rise of Pinochet, and was also a pivotal figure in the Chilean *nueva canción* movement. At various points in the film, characters recite poems by Pablo Neruda and Violeta Parra, which are used to draw a connection between the historical struggles of the turn of the twentieth century and Chile's social and political repression in the mid-1970s.[10] The Cuban National Symphony also provided music, particularly to accompany the cantata. For moments of high tension, as with many ICAIC films, Leo Brouwer provided the musical arrangements. In terms of the incorporation of art, the film employed sculptures made by the students at the Escuela de Bellas Artes San Alejandro, which is Cuba's most prestigious and oldest fine arts school.

As one can see, the film aimed to make use of several art media to convey a political and historical message regarding workers' rights. More importantly, the film served as Cuba's homage to the atrocities that Chile had just endured a couple of years prior to the release of the film. Perhaps because of the incorporation of certain film techniques along with other art forms as a way to discuss Chile's historical struggles and its relationship to its society's situation in the mid-1970s, Julianne Burton and Marta Alvear have dubbed *Cantata de Chile* an "interpretive documentary" (32). By this, Burton and Alvear suggest that the film aims to interpret social reality by employing suggestive art media, which may not be readily associated with Chile's situation under Pinochet, though they certainly denote it. In a different interview, Solás added that when he was making this film, Paolo Ucello's *The Battle of San Romano* (c. 1435–1460) had heavily influenced him, which may explain the marked Renaissance and Baroque visual undertones present in the film (Caballero 184). Altogether, *Cantata de Chile* is a highly ambitious film that embraces these various art forms to accentuate the melodrama of social oppression in Chile's history.

As Darlene J. Sadlier reminds us in her recent assessment of the use of melodrama in Latin American cinema, the prefix of the term comes from the Greek word for music (*melos*), and became associated in the first half of the nineteenth century with theater that employed musical arrangement to "heighten emotional climaxes" (2). In the latter part of the nineteenth century, the usage of the term morphed to include "plots featuring spectacular actions, improbable twists of fate, intense expressions of emotion, last-minute rescues, and vivid conflicts between bad and virtuous characters" (2). Furthermore, Sadlier notes that in Latin America, melodrama as a term linked to film has wider implications in that it may refer to "domestic dramas" but also to "historical epics in which family life is viewed in relation to larger national issues" (3). In *Cantata de Chile,* however, Solás makes use of non-diegetic music, in fact a choral piece composed by Patricio Manns, which gives its name to the film. The title of the film, which is to say the cantata, is linked to a specific tradition of music that has its origins in the late seventeenth century and eighteenth century in countries such as Italy, France, England, and Germany (Joncus 513–540). Thus, as we can begin to see, Solás is referencing a well-established film and theater tradition in melodrama, but also makes an allusion to Baroque music, which was initially used in religious domains and later became part of secular music. Through this referencing, appropriation, and subversion of genres, we see glimpses of what I am referring to here as decolonial aesthetics. In addition, however, the tragic, historical, and collective events treated in *Cantata* lead us to engage in an evaluation of the film's engagement with the tragic.

Distinguishing between tragedy and melodrama in theater, Helen Foley writes that "In contrast to tragedy, stylized acting, gestures, and facial expressions could serve in the plays to counter linguistic ambiguity. Tableaux and freezing of the action distilled and underlined specific emotional moments; music helped to define character and heighten tension and pathos" (5). One could argue that Solás resorts to these conventions in *Cantata*. While critics may view Solás's use of these conventions exclusively in light of melodrama, in fact, I see the use of these conventions as a way to collapse the distance between tragedy and melodrama. It is well-known that Solás resorts to melodramatic components and neo-baroque aesthetics in his films (as critics have charged, and he has admitted several times). Yet, tensions, suffering, and other characteristics of traditional tragedy are not readily resolved in his films. In this sense, then, Solás employs specific conventions of melodrama in relation to tragedy as a way to give it some contemporaneity, to complicate the critical division of the two genres.

In most conventional tragedies, a particular event is taken as the basis for the action. Such an event is developed, as well as the tragic protagonist. In *Cantata,* instead, the only event that is even partially developed is the massacre at Iquique, while the other historical events are succinctly presented as a way to provide background for the massacre, to draw parallels between the past and present, and to encourage reflection on the connections between past and present tragedies. The difference between conventional tragedy and the type of tragedy we have in *Cantata* is that usually the source of tragedy is an isolated event, whereas in the film we have several events that serve as background for a larger tragedy—a tragedy that then reflects a continuity of tragedies, of woven histories told from the perspective of below, often forgotten and treated in isolation. The tragedy, then, is a way to discuss how the tragic works in relation to a country or nation-state. In essence, the nation becomes the tragic protagonist. The workers are also the tragic protagonist. The weight of tragedy in the film is not carried by a single, isolated figure.

For instance, in Euripides's *The Bacchae,* the real tragic protagonist is not really any individual actor or figure, but instead, the city (in this case

Athens). In reference to the timelessness of Greek tragedies and their impact on our contemporary world, Helen Foley argues the following:

> Tragic individuals are fundamentally inseparable from their social world; domestic tensions among its elite characters are observed by choruses that preserve a public dimension to the action. Character is illuminated through public speech, difficult choices, and action; protagonists struggling to live a moral life take responsibility for outcomes that can be imposed on them for a range of reasons from within and without. The plays are not didactic; there is no clear triumph of good over evil; many plays arguably lack a firm sense of closure. The questions they pose are not resolvable, but confronting the past and cultural memory is critical to moving forward. (Foley 2)

If we take into consideration this critical invitation, then, in a sense, what Solás is doing is transforming Chile into the tragic protagonist in a longstanding tradition of tragedies. In other words, while the actors in the tragedies may change, the site of the tragedies remains the same. These tragedies are often not connected in our contemporary and ahistorical minds. Or rather, they are often understood and treated as isolated and unconnected events or moments in history. The traditional focus on the tragic has involved paying attention to particular figures, names, and actors. Instead, what Solás is doing is to shift the attention and really place the emphasis on what these events have done to Chile. In so doing, Solás moves from that general and abstract level of focusing on the idea of Chile to treating the nation-state as the tragic protagonist and focusing attention on the parallels that we can draw, the connections that can be made among colonial times, the late eighteenth century, the early nineteenth century, the early twentieth century saltpeter mining tragedy, and the early 1970s, with the aftermath of Pinochet's dictatorship as Chile's most recent tragedy. In a sense, then, the film explores the archives of tragedies in order to explore how each tragedy in isolation, but also all collectively, comprise a multilayered aspect of a country's history. The film is also exploring how a country's collective memory can be a source of these traditions and registers of historical information, while drawing attention to what might be left out, what is communicated or forgotten in the process of remembrance. The film thus forces its viewers to look at tragedy from a variety of perspectives, not just from a single/isolated perspective grounded in history.

Whereas in classical tragedies the source of the action and the drama is usually a story that is built around mythology or mythological figures, in *Cantata* what we have is a conglomeration of traditional history, events left out of history, oral traditions, and the mythical foundations of the nation-state itself. These are perspectives that are usually left out of official historical discourses and official history. What Solás does is use all these different levels of historical discourse to build a fragmented narrative about the tragic protagonist, which is the country itself. The fragmentation that appears in the film is intended to allow viewers to draw parallels between the tragedy of Iquique in 1907 and the colonial resistance of Lautaro and the Araucanos, and see the connections between the struggles for independence and what took place in colonial times. These events should be seen as a continuum among independence, labor rights, and labor struggles in Chile, or rather as a continuum of modalities and histories of resistance to coloniality. This, in a sense, also allows one to draw parallels between what happened in those three particular historical times and the history of resistance in Chile, which reached its most profound form in the aftermath of Pinochet's rise to power from 1973 to 1975. While the story is fragmented, Solás is trying to break away from the traditional model that looks at history as a linear narrative. The film portrays history as a source of non-linear tragedy, a tragedy with multiple layers, parallels, and points of correlation, which the viewer must then connect to make sense of them.

When asked about whether or not he has a specific audience in mind when making films, Solás has alluded to the difficulty of gauging one's audience and how they might respond to political films. To illustrate his case, Solás discusses the reception of *Cantata de Chile*, which the crew and collaborators hoped would have been more successful and received a stronger critical reception in Cuba. Instead, due to the Cuban audiences' politicized film-viewing experience, the political issues raised in *Cantata de Chile* were not particular enlightening, as they did not advance or clarify the debates around Chile's political situation under Pinochet. Solás adds that the film "turned out to be more appropriate for other sectors of Latin America where the issues raised by the Chilean experience are still confused and distorted" (Burton and Alvear 32).

In discussing what he tried to achieve in making *Cantata de Chile*, Solás categorizes his own film as an experimental work in the sense that he aimed to "achieve a convergence between form and ideological components" (Burton and Alvear 32). He notes that the film included elements from popular theater and iconography, and played with the temporal display of images, which was meant to encourage an allegorical interpretation of Chile's political climate, though this was also applicable to other countries that had "passed through the stages of colonialist and neocolonialist domination" (Burton and Alvear 32). Of the films studied in the present chapter, *Cantata de Chile* is the least-available and least-known in the United States, which is one of the reasons why I have discussed it here at some length. In fact, only a couple of universities have it as part of their collections. While the film's reception may not have been favorable, its ambitious interplay of theater, sculpture, painting, music, and cinematic techniques produced a film that deserves reevaluation on its aesthetic merits and for what it aimed to achieve at the time of its release, given Pinochet's regime in Chile and the rise of dictatorships across Latin America. While *Cantata de Chile* has often been overshadowed by more "authentic" or critically acclaimed films made by Solás, such as *Lucía* (1968), *Cecilia* (1983), or *Amanda* (1985), its use of various types of art media and Solás's trademark over-the-top and melodramatic representations are key to understanding his interest in employing film as a medium with which to explore history's connection with the present and the overlap between decolonial visual aesthetics and social critique.

Raymundo Gleyzer: *Mexico, the Frozen Revolution*, Cinema of the Base, and Clandestine Documentary Making

Compared to the other filmmakers studied in this chapter, Raymundo Gleyzer has only recently gained some critical attention.[11] Gleyzer was a Jewish Argentine documentary filmmaker whose masterpiece is *México, la revolución congelada* (1971) [*Mexico, the Frozen Revolution*]. Gleyzer's entire body of work engages with social issues in very concrete ways. When compared to other famous documentarians of the period, such as Solanas or Fernando Birri, Gleyzer seems different indeed because of his interest in making documentaries commenting on Argentina's social reality, as well as those of other countries. For instance, in 1964, Gleyzer made

La tierra quema, which deals with impoverished Brazilians living in the northeast of their country (in the *sertãos*), where a small number of elites control the fertile land and the rest of the population is forced to live in barren, drought-stricken areas.

In terms of his film style, Gleyzer was interested in allowing images to speak for themselves and allowing filmed subjects to speak their minds, even if the scenes included in his documentary were lengthy as a result. One could argue that Gleyzer was interested in a more organic and realistic way of filmmaking in which the director's hand and editing job were less prevalent and obvious in the final product. Unlike the other filmmakers studied in this chapter, who had formal film training in film institutes in Rome or elsewhere, Gleyzer studied film in La Plata in the province of Buenos Aires, though he had begun working as a photographer earlier, in 1956. By 1965, however, Gleyzer had left film school and decided to replace it with his own fieldwork and observations. As a product of his early attempts at defining his own style, Gleyzer produced *Pottery Makers Behind the Mountain* (1965), which had been commissioned by the University of Córdoba. During this period, Gleyzer and Jorge Preloran made *It Happened in Hualfin* (1965), though Gleyzer finished the documentary on his own as Preloran did not want to explore fully the root ideological and social causes of poverty in Hualfín, Catamarca, a small village in the northwestern province of Catamarca, Argentina. At this point in Gleyzer's career, his filmmaking style and the topics he chose to document became suspect to the Argentinian government, and were heavily censored by Juan Carlos Onganía's military dictatorship from 1966 to 1970. During Onganía's dictatorship, civil rights were trampled and there was a marked clash among social classes. It should be stressed that it was in this context that *The Hour of the Furnaces* (1966–1968) appeared. In fact, Gleyzer worked as a cameraman on the first part of *The Hour of the Furnaces*. This film would have a profound impact on Gleyzer's filmmaking style, though later there would be ideological differences between Solanas and Gleyzer, which in turn affected their film aesthetics and how they viewed film as a form with which to engage with Peronism (Ardito, *Raymundo*).

Despite the military regime, Gleyzer went on to do a series of interviews for television in the Falkland Islands. Gleyzer asked the English government for a special permit to do so, and was granted it. This was the first time that an Argentine had filmed there. Gleyzer went inside people's homes to see how they lived, which became a signature of his approach to making documentaries, a way to engage people in a more horizontal level of communication. In this sense, this particular type of film aesthetic can be connected to the conversational poetry or the recovery of collective voices of everyday people, including workers, discussed in previous chapters. In 1969, Gleyzer went to Cuba to do a series of interviews. While in Cuba, Gleyzer became very familiar with Santiago Álvarez's documentaries, and these also shaped his film aesthetics (Ardito, *Raymundo*). I draw attention to these developments in Gleyzer's filmography to underscore how his interest in documentaries went beyond Argentina and took on a hemispheric interest in unveiling systemic forms of social inequality. It is in this spirit of engaging documentary filmmaking as an instrument of visual critique that I see Gleyzer's work as contributing to a type of visual archive that resonates with more recent treatment of decolonial film aesthetics in relation to indigenous social movements and to inserting indigenous subjectivities as producers of modes of self-representation.[12]

Read as part of an extended archive of gestures toward decolonizing media representations of indigenous populations, as well as providing a nuanced critique of the Mexican political and social history of the first seven decades of the twentieth century, Gleyzer's *México, la revolución congelada* (1971) is a documentary that takes a historical look at the reasons why the Mexican Revolution failed to materialize and how it neglected workers, indigenous peoples, and other oppressed groups. Through the use of archival images and interviews with survivors of the revolution, Gleyzer offers a critique of the Mexican political system, of the historical domination of one political party (the PRI, Partido Revolucionario Institucional), and of how such factors contributed to the stasis of what could have been an emancipatory project. My interest in this film is related to Gleyzer's personal investment in examining the historical and social foundations of coloniality in other parts of Latin America. In doing so, Gleyzer enables a historical critique of various revolutions' past mistakes, but also seeks to find ways to avoid future failures. It is in this gesture of critiquing coloniality and its embedded history of racialization and the instrumentalization of politics to subjugate the indigenous, the impoverished, and other vast sectors of a disenfranchised Mexican society that decoloniality is enacted. As a tragic figure who suffered the effects of the abuse of power depicted in many of his own documentaries, Gleyzer becomes a pivotal figure in understanding how cinema can become a subversive tool to decolonize viewers' minds and ways of looking at documentary films.

Gleyzer intended *Mexico, the Frozen Revolution* to be screened at universities and workers' unions, and by any group interested in its reception. It was supposedly a Mexican peasant who suggested the title of the film (Gleyzer, *Raymundo Gleyzer* 49). The central argument in *Mexico, the Frozen Revolution* is that land distribution throughout most of Mexico's twentieth century was markedly uneven, particularly when it came to issues related to the long-standing politics of racialization as they intersected with class-based issues. The film makes an explicit critique of the PRI, the political party that had been in power for over five decades at the time the film was made. Although fifty percent of Mexico's people, many of whom were indigenous peoples or peasants, had no land even after the presumed success of the revolution, the PRI neglected to give peasants technical assistance, adequate machinery, or irrigation systems, or to establish agricultural cooperatives to assist the very people who had supported and fought for a redistribution of land alongside Emiliano Zapata and Pancho Villa during the Mexican Revolution in the early decades of the twentieth century. Instead, the documentary shows that many of those who fought believed that their dreams of land distribution and the end of serfdom had actually ended after 1910. Many of these farmers were forced to continue employing primitive and inefficient farming methods, while continuing to live in dire poverty. In light of this grounding, Quijano's words on the entanglement of race and labor are a useful aid to understanding the dynamics against which the Mexican Revolution sought to rebel, but that remained largely undisturbed: "The racist distribution of new social identities was combined . . . with a racist distribution of labor and the forms of exploitation of colonial capitalism. . . . Consequently, the control of a specific form of labor could be, at the same time, the control of a specific group of dominated people. A new technology of domination/exploitation, in this case race/labor, was articulated in such a way that the two elements appeared naturally associated" (Quijano, "Coloniality of Power" 537). In essence, the film makes the argument that the revolution failed those who supported it by leaving unperturbed the mechanisms that imbricated and had rendered normative a racialization of certain sectors of the population in order to justify the type of work they did and thus their standing in the social hierarchy. For instance, and as the film makes it clear, elderly indigenous people even now have to continue working to survive, as there are no mechanisms to ensure their well-being and protection. Such instances in the film, whether viewed on their own or in relation to the long-standing registers of social and political critique that I have been underscoring in this chapter, are reminders that the Fanonian concept of the "wretched of the earth" and Leonardo Boff's more recent articulation of the "dispossessed of the earth" are still very much in place. It is against this naturalization of disenfranchisement that I read Gleyzer's film as a gesture toward decolonizing film aesthetics and turning to the medium of film to critique the coloniality of race and being.

The Frozen Revolution also makes the case that it was the PRI that was responsible for the Tlatelolco massacre in 1968, in which more than 400 people were massacred in one afternoon.[13] Since the film had been able to use archival footage of the revolution of 1910, Gleyzer had hoped also to make use of footage from the Tlatelolco massacre. Instead, Gleyzer was only able to get pictures of the massacre, since all film and most images documenting it had been confiscated by the Mexican government. Needless to say, Gleyzer and his small crew were able to enter Mexico and film only clandestinely, as they did not receive the proper permits from the Mexican government.

The film was screened in Chile within a year of Salvador Allende's rise to power. Chilean audiences were shocked, and in both Argentina and Mexico the film was banned (Ardito, *Raymundo*). In making *Mexico, the Frozen Revolution*, Gleyzer wanted to translate what he had experienced during his visit to Cuba and find ways to materialize a socialist revolution in Argentina and elsewhere in Latin America:

> Uno no puede ser extranjero en América Latina. Hay muchas cosas que unifican nuestra realidad, mas que nada nuestro enemigo común. . . . Llegué a México por la necesidad de mostrar a la Revolución Mexicana de 1911 a 1917 como un ejemplo vinculado con

> algunos movimientos populares frustrados. Cuando un movimiento popular carece de una precisa definición socialista, la burguesía se apropia de las banderas de la revolución. (Ardito, *Raymundo*)
>
> [One cannot be a foreigner in Latin America. There are many things uniting our realities, particularly a common enemy. . . . I went to Mexico to show the Mexican Revolution from 1911 to 1917 as an example connected to failed popular movements. When a popular movement lacks a precise socialist definition, the bourgeoisie appropriates the revolution's flags.]

In 1971 the film was screened at film festivals in Caracas, Berlin, Cannes, Locarno, Venice, Manheim, and Adelaide. It received awards and critical acclaim in Locarno, Manheim, and Adelaide (Gleyzer, *Raymundo Gleyzer* 16).

In 1973, *cine de la base* (cinema of the base) became a social and film movement in Argentina whose founding idea was for people not to go to movies, but for filmmakers to take movies to the people. In this sense, cinema of the base already hinted at a decolonial gesture of making film available to all people by bringing it to them. It also sought to make citizens active participants in witnessing and discussing aspects of social and political reality that deserved a more central place in local communal spaces, rather than film theaters supporting social inequities by censoring what got screened. The intent of the *cine de la base* group was to screen films and have debates and conversations with workers, and this also became an attempt to overcome the problem of distribution. In many ways, cinema of the base shares the initial impulse of Solanas and Getino's third cinema, but takes on a more radical dimension and becomes interested in engaging with societal problems on a smaller scale. For Gleyzer and the cinema of the base, the relationship between the filmmaker and his audience must be more horizontal. Cinema of the base would provide copies of the films and projectors, and find spaces in which to screen the films. By this time, it had become increasingly difficult and dangerous for cinema of the base to show its films in Argentina. Right-wing supporters of Juan Perón's party persecuted Gleyzer and the other members of the group, while all filmmakers making political films were deemed a threat. For instance, in late 1975, the Argentine Anticommunist Association closed down Fernando Birri's Santa Fe Film School. Only three months later, the military coup began, giving rise to a period known as the "dirty war." By late May of 1976, Gleyzer had been kidnapped, tortured, and killed by a paramilitary group.

Gleyzer's tragic life and the circumstances of his death in connection to the rise of a military government bear a resemblance to Víctor Jara's death, which had taken place only three years earlier. After Gleyzer's disappearance, the military dictatorship sought to destroy all the negatives of his films. Nonetheless, some of Gleyzer's friends smuggled his films out of Argentina by cutting them into pieces and piecing them back together once they were safe in exile. Since Gleyzer's death, most of his films have been neglected and have received little critical attention. As one may see from Gleyzer's approach to documentary filmmaking, attention to Gleyzer's works is essential if one seeks to have a better understanding of how film engages with politics and with a critique of the *longue durée* of the various modalities of coloniality, and of how Gleyzer's politically oriented film aesthetics sought to engage in more direct and concrete terms with popular audiences with the ultimate intention of shifting from a colonized film-viewing experience to what today we can call a decolonial option.

Conclusion

Upon reflecting on the filmmaking legacy of the 1960s and 1970s, one inevitably must emphasize the correlation between the spirit that the Cuban Revolution imprinted across Latin America and the ways in which leftist ideologies influenced the development of innovative and combative film aesthetics. Filmmakers such as Solanas, Getino, Gutiérrez Alea, Solás, and Gleyzer aimed to employ film as a medium through which to explore embedded problems as instantiations of coloniality in their respective societies, while also presenting critiques of long-standing histories of oppression. As I have argued, it is in these critiques of social injustice, even if the individual approaches are markedly different, that I have sought to trace decolonial gestures toward an undoing, challenging, and contesting of the coloniality of visual aesthetics, or visuality writ large. In relation to the cinematic experimentations and innovative film approaches arising from this period, Joanna Page has noted, "Interestingly, recourse to documentary modes of filmmaking, or the incursion of 'documentary' techniques into fiction, has accompanied both the rise and the demise of socialism in Latin America" (5). While Solanas and Getino's *The Hour of the Furnaces* paved the way for a new type of politically and socially committed documentary filmmaking praxis, the film also lent itself to subsequent theorization about the new direction that Latin American cinema ought to take in response to Hollywood and European cinema. It was with Solanas and Getino's film manifesto "Toward a Third Cinema" that political cinema in Latin America sought to redefine itself as different from foreign conventions as forms of the coloniality of visuality, while seeking new means of expression and producing new film aesthetics to contest such forms of coloniality.

During the same period, similar film approaches, using fiction films, were being explored in Cuba. Gutiérrez Alea's *Memories of Underdevelopment* fictionalized the internal tensions of its protagonist. To emphasize Sergio's disconnect with the changes under Castro's regime and the political tensions of the Cold War, the film incorporated footage from news broadcasts to resemble the assumed veracity of a documentary. Likewise, the film also made use of still shots to underscore the protagonist's growing alienation from his society. In this attempt to underscore the tensions within a coloniality of knowledge, gender, and race, Gutiérrez Alea introduced subtle decolonial gestures to challenge these modes of coloniality through film aesthetics.

Whereas Solanas and Getino's film was heavily invested in situating what they perceived to be the ripeness of a growing revolutionary spirit in Argentina and Latin America within a historical narrative, Gutiérrez Alea's *Memories of Underdevelopment* employed fiction as a way to mark a contrast between bourgeois sensibilities under Fulgencio Batista's regime and the way in which the elite had no place in revolutionary Cuba. In other words, both films wanted to engage with history, although through different approaches. In the case of Humberto Solás, his filmmaking style reveals a complex relationship among fiction, melodrama, and analysis of historical events as tragedy. In the case of *Lucía*, Solás explores the role and situation of women at three revolutionary moments in Cuba's history. The film conveys a progression in women's consciousness and how women have fought to emancipate themselves from the control of a patriarchal society. As discussed above, I read *Lucía* as a film that very directly engages with the question of coloniality of gender, and through this engagement with melodrama and history produces decolonial gestures to show instances in which patriarchy can be contested. In contrast, *Cantata de Chile* is a more ambitious film project that incorporates sculpture, painting, music, poetry, theater, and deliberate film techniques to present a historical reflection on four moments in Chile's history: colonial times, independence, 1907, and the 1970s. As the bulk of the film's narrative takes place in 1907, Solás employs temporal shifts, and changes in costumes, lighting, and colors to denote the continuity of liberation struggles in Chile. As discussed in the section dedicated to this film, I read *Cantata de Chile* as a film that engages with a multilayered way of producing a critique of various modes of coloniality by tracing a transhistorical arc that connects instances of collective resistance in Chile.

In comparison to Solanas and Getino, Gutiérrez Alea, and Solás, Raymundo Gleyzer's documentary films have until recently been largely neglected as part of an analysis of third cinema or the development of New Latin American Cinema. Given Gleyzer's interest in documenting social realities and historical problems on a smaller scale, rather than creating broad historical narratives as many of his contemporaries have done, it is important to resituate his work within a period of socially committed and politically charged filmmaking that had a profound impact across Latin America, as well as in Africa and Asia. During Gleyzer's time, his work was well-received by popular sectors and by critics, though after his disappearance, and perhaps due to the limited availability of his films, his legacy fell into oblivion. As discussed in the last part of this chapter, Gleyzer's interest in exploring social and historical conditions in Argentina, Brazil, and Mexico is something that also sets him apart from the other three filmmakers discussed here. Whereas Solanas and Getino produced *The Hour of the Furnaces* in Argentina, and Gutiérrez Alea and Solás produced their respective films in Cuba, Gleyzer went to the different locations where he wanted to shoot, regardless of how remote they were or what the political situation was. It is in this context, for instance, that *Mexico, the Frozen Revolution* appears as a documentary and historical document that explores where the Mexican Revolution fell short of materializing redistribution of land and ending social inequities as a way of undoing coloniality, while the film also presents a strong critique of the PRI's control over Mexican politics for most of the twentieth century and discusses the massacre of Tlatelolco at a time when Mexican authorities wanted to avoid further discussions of that event. Screening of the film in various places across Latin America was met with popular support and censorship from the governments of Argentina and Mexico. Furthermore, Gleyzer's approach to filmmaking and exhibiting his works under the principles of cinema of the base—making films for audiences, presenting films in small locations, and engaging viewers in an active discussion—marks a continuity with and an aesthetic-ideological departure from third cinema and New Latin American Cinema.

The four filmmakers discussed in this chapter serve to illustrate some of the major and perhaps most distinct approaches to engaging with the critical and social challenges present in the articulation of New Latin American Cinema in its attempt to distinguish itself from Hollywood and European films (first and second cinemas) and to contest dominant films emulating foreign film language. More importantly, all five filmmakers had divergent aesthetic agendas when producing the films for which they are best-known. Despite their marked differences in film styles, aesthetic innovations, and engagement with historical analysis and critique, they also share common ground in seeking to effect social change and connect in more concrete and direct ways with audiences. In short, Solanas and Getino, Gutiérrez Alea, Solás, and Gleyzer advanced alternative cinematic models to distinguish the social realities and technological means available to Latin America from Hollywood and European conventions, which could no longer be adequately replicated or adapted to suit the needs and aesthetic innovations of New Latin American Cinema filmmakers. It is these modes of contesting the coloniality of visuality that I have traced as decolonial gestures in their respective proposals and approaches to filmmaking.

5

Decolonial Aesthetics in Latin America

Throughout this book, my theorization of decolonial aesthetics has been grounded upon a need to revisit seemingly dissimilar and disjointed so-called "populist" artistic expressions, some of which failed to receive much critical recognition in their time, while others have become part of the canon of cultural texts that get taught and written about in academic circles. Precisely due to their alleged "populist" agenda and presumed alignment with Marxist, communist, or socialist ideologies, the poets, musicians, and filmmakers studied here were often dismissed on the grounds that their works belonged to a low type of art that lacked formal qualities and aesthetic value. Returning to issues related to high and low art is necessary to engage in alternative modes of thinking that dismantle disciplinary boundaries, while questioning what is worth exploring or knowing. In this vein, decolonial aesthetics becomes a type of "*low theory*" that can be at once "a mode of accessibility, but we might also think about it as a kind of theoretical model that flies below the radar, that is assembled from eccentric texts and examples and that refuses to confirm the hierarchies of knowing that maintain the *high* in high theory" (Halberstam 16, emphasis in original). According to a certain sector of the academic establishment, cultural critics, right-wing governments, and apolitical audiences of the time, art forms defined as low did not display artistic merit worthy of critical attention.[1] On the other hand, these artworks also produced a fear among elite sectors and governments across Latin America that if the general public were to consume such popular or ideologically based artworks, communist or socialist values coming from Cuba and the U.S.S.R. would spread like wildfire and ignite cultural and social revolutions. As a result, often, artists such as Roque Dalton, Víctor Jara, Raymundo Gleyzer, Jorge Sanjinés, Mario Benedetti, and others faced political persecution or obstacles that made it difficult for them to produce such art in their respective countries. In extreme instances, as was the case with Jara and Gleyzer, rising political dictatorships (in Chile and Argentina, in their cases) made it a point to "eliminate" contentious voices emerging from the arts. In other instances, artists faced self-exile and often gravitated toward Cuba or other countries with less-repressive governments than those of the mid-1970s in the Southern Cone and Central America.

Given the debates about the nature of culture in Latin America, from the Manichean binaries of civilization vs. barbarism or Ariel vs. Caliban, as succinctly illustrated toward the end of chapter 1, "Sensing Otherwise," I see antipoetry, *nueva canción*, and New Latin American cinema as articulations of the arts seeking to challenge such binaries. While the focus of this book falls upon antipoetry, *nueva canción*, and New Latin American Cinema as particular expressions of art that sought to contest established and accepted notions of what constituted poetry, music, and cinema, I also seek to draw attention to some of the heterogeneous positions and artistic/aesthetic propositions within these movements. Many of their poets, musicians, and filmmakers shared common points in their aesthetic propositions, but there were also divergent approaches to challenge the hegemony of a specific definition of what constituted culture in Latin America, particularly around a canonical or elite perception of culture. What binds these three articulations of art is the desire to decolonize a perception of what constitutes valid art/culture by presenting radical departures from established aesthetic models, inserting a political dimension into artistic production, and seeking to reach and communicate with audiences in more effective and horizontal ways in order to collapse the traditional hierarchical relation of intellectual/artist and audience.

In the case of musicians of *nueva canción*, for instance, it is true that most, if not all, incorporated folk elements into their music. As an example, Violeta Parra renewed an interest in autochthonous Chilean rhythms and incorporated them into a movement that aimed to revive and conserve such traditions, while also making it available to a wider public. While many people identified with such musical innovations, as a musical movement, *nueva canción* became emblematic of connecting working classes from urban centers to the countryside.

While poetry had been dominated by poets of polished poetic language and form (e.g., Octavio Paz, Pablo Neruda, Nicolás Guillén, José Lezama Lima), many of whom were part of the avant-garde poetic movements of the decades preceding World War II and thereafter, one can argue that, notwithstanding their ideological affiliations or poetic innovations, their poetic output remained hermetic and at the vanguard. As the poetic giants of Latin American poetry in the twentieth century, these poets of language and form were the point of reference for younger poets, who sought either to emulate or contest them. Critics and elite circles appreciated, consumed, and found pleasure and aesthetic value in the meaning behind their verses. Instead, and following here Benedetti's suggested concept of an ethics of rebelliousness, some Latin American antipoets (Nicanor Parra, Mario Benedetti, Roque Dalton, Ernesto Cardenal, and others) sought to rebel against these giants by breaking away from poetic forms, while transgressing the genre in the most extreme way by making poetic language readable, colloquial, conversational, and accessible to the everyday reader.

The established poets believed in and became part of the myth of what Angel Rama dubbed the lettered city, while remaining unresponsive to its underside: the unlettered city. The unlettered city, which is to say those who stand at the margins of the power of the letter and who have little use for metaphors or innovations in poetic form, became the antipoets' target audience. The antipoets recognized the need to debunk the conception that poetry was exclusively for a distinct readership able to deal with its impenetrability. As such, the antipoets stood at the gates of the lettered city with a double gaze toward the poetic giants, canonized writers, and star authors, while also looking toward what remained outside. The letter became the wall that separated those within the city from those outside of it.

If the lettered city became a trope useful to understanding the literary culture of Latin America, artists in other cultural forms and genres also understood the mythical implications of such claims. In an effort to appeal to larger audiences often excluded by the power of the letter, filmmakers and musicians turned to popular culture as a way to invite all people to partake of their work, though the primary interest was placed in those often shut out by high art. By aiming to appeal to workers, students, leftist intellectuals, and non-readers (those who are illiterate or who simply choose not to read), popular culture became the most effective medium through which to critique the two dimensions of dominant culture: U.S. and European on the one hand, and elitist and vanguardist creole (*criollo*—culturally, linguistically, and racially mixed with often xenophilic and Eurocentric sensibilities) on the other.

In the case of New Latin American Cinema, its main goal was to generate an alternative way of filmmaking to address the problems of social inequality, political oppression, and the possibility of a new social order. Gutiérrez Alea, Solanas, Solás, and Gleyzer are the focus in this study of the cinematic expression of third cinema, though other filmmakers could also be included in this category (e.g., Patricio Guzmán, Miguel Littín, Glauber Rocha, Jorge Sanjinés, etc.). While each of these filmmakers had proposed his respective cinematic project, they all had also produced modes of artistic execution and theoretical propositions that stood on common ground with each other. Collectively, these filmmakers sought to create national cinemas that contributed to a regional cinema with distinct aesthetics from dominant Hollywood or European models.

The conjoining factor that links antipoets, *nueva canción* musicians, and third cinema filmmakers—although they might seem disparate artistic forms and cultural products—is the way in which the artists have negotiated ideological commitment, aesthetic innovation, and transgression of their respective genres in the service of a wider audience. As Rama suggests, political, social, and artistic movements draw from their own "national traditions" and obey "the historical momentum" that gives rise to such movements (Rama 99). The regional purview of the present study seeks to evince the ways in which a historical momentum manifests itself in countercultural artworks and their place within a national and regional cultural tradition.

In this sense, I see decolonial aesthetics as an approach to understanding different artistic genres, aesthetic propositions, and artistic projects within antipoetry, *nueva canción,* and third cinema. Put differently, I am proposing the concept of decolonial aesthetics as a way to examine and understand these artistic movements both for its ways of questioning established artistic models and for its interest in reinserting into the arts a political dimension and commitment to effecting social change across Latin America. A problem present in the study is the seemingly irreconcilable juxtaposition of "decolonial," suggestive of an undoing of experiential subjugation, and aesthetics, which has been linked to theories about how we come to appreciate art and the value we assign to it. As an initial response to this seeming conundrum, decolonial aesthetics becomes a prism through which we can revisit, reinterpret, and reevaluate a period that gave birth to distinct art forms in poetry, music, film, and other spheres of Latin American popular culture. Rather than treating the multiple aesthetic propositions in poetry, music, and film as irreconcilable and isolated from each other, this project seeks to trace points of convergence and divergence to place them in dialogue. By resituating these art forms in their historical, cultural, and ideological contexts, I seek to unravel the connecting threads that make up these works' aesthetic-political projects with their manifold schisms and linkages.

Before proceeding with a theorization of decolonial aesthetics, I will provide some examples that examine the usage of the decolonial in its practical sense. From examples of decolonial practices, I shift to some of the interventions about aesthetics that inform my theorization. In the fourth section, we come to a more elaborate exposition of what decolonial aesthetics entails, and its implications for the artworks studied here.

Philosophy of Liberation and Decolonial Aesthetics

My conceptualization of decolonial aesthetics is indebted to Enrique Dussel's philosophy of liberation, particularly his aesthetics of liberation. Dussel argues that the project of liberation enables the expression and the exposition of semiotic, poietic, and poetic beauty (Dussel, *Philosophy of Liberation* 124). The expression of such aesthetics is concerned with the past, present, and future of oppression and what a process of liberation can achieve. For Dussel, the value of such liberatory expressions lies in the possibility of what is to come. That is, Dussel is concerned with the potentiality of the aesthetics of liberation. On a different level, however, there is acknowledgment in Dussel's thought of how an appreciation and evaluation of the aesthetics of liberation necessitates a different mindset and a different perspective on aesthetic categories. In reference to the aesthetics of liberation, Dussel notes:

> Its exposition is ugly according to the rules and canons of beauty currently in force; but it is an innovation of the formal coherence of signs and is therefore procreation of the beauty of a new order.
>
> The apparent ugliness of the countenance of the oppressed, the withered face of the farmer, the hardened hand of the laborer, the rough skin of the impoverished woman (who cannot buy cosmetics), is the point of departure of the aesthetics of liberation. It is the entreaty that reveals popular beauty, the non-dominating beauty, the liberator of future beauty. Aestheticism is the dominant ideological imposition of the beauty admired by cultures of the center and of the oligarchical classes (imposed by the mass media). It is the ideology of beauty. (*Philosophy of Liberation* 124–125)

In other words, Dussel suggests quotidian sources from which the aesthetics of liberation draws its expression and points to how these will not always be deemed beautiful according to existing precepts of aesthetics. Instead, the artworks akin to aesthetics of liberation seek to represent and express what would conventionally not be considered beautiful or even worthy of being represented in art. The aesthetics of liberation is concerned with subjects construed as unworthy of representation due to their lack of conformity to what we come to expect when exposed to art. In this sense, the aesthetics of liberation challenges the very concept of what constitutes beauty, how we define, experience, view, and interpret it. Moreover, the aesthetics of liberation challenges the ideological foundations behind existing aesthetic frameworks and offers an alternative to them.

Despite some overlaps between Dussel's conceptualization of the aesthetics of liberation and decolonial aesthetics, there are also some fine differences between them. Among these are terminology, how theory translates into praxis, and the identifiable characteristics that align artworks with either model of aesthetics. In principle, Dussel's aesthetics privileges the final result of liberatory art, in the sense that the emphasis is placed on achieving liberation, with little attention paid to the means of or medium for obtaining it. The potentiality of what liberatory art can achieve becomes the ultimate goal on the horizon of possibilities. The means and precise processes of liberation through aesthetics are merely suggested.

Likewise, in Dussel's philosophical proposition, the shift from theory to praxis is not sufficiently delineated.

Decolonial aesthetics, however, takes a step back from the insistence on liberation as the ultimate goal and assumes that decolonization is only the first step on an arduous road toward a seemingly more distant liberation. The link between decolonization and aesthetics is embedded in the connection between theory (in the form of manifestos and critical writing) and praxis (in the form of artworks). It should be noted here, however, that for artworks to be understood in terms of decolonial aesthetics, an aesthetic manifesto is not always a prerequisite. As we have seen in the preceding chapters, some decolonial artists drafted aesthetic manifestoes and put them into practice in their own art, as in the case of Solanas and Getino. Other decolonial artists, however, refrained from putting into a formal manifesto their aesthetic propositions, though these can be gathered based on modes of artistic production and the art itself. With this in mind, decolonial aesthetics embraces as its primary purpose the need to communicate directly in concrete and discernible language with the oppressed, the dispossessed, the disenfranchised.

Another central difference between the aesthetics of liberation and decolonial aesthetics is how the two models define the role of the intellectual (as a philosopher, public intellectual, or artist), as well as how the intellectual relates to her or his audiences. Dussel makes the assumption that "the most oppressed classes do not always have the most acute critical awareness" (*Philosophy of Liberation* 125). According to Dussel, it is up to another class (that is, intellectuals) to take on the role of materializing or bringing about such an awareness of oppression. This position, of course, reveals Dussel's indebtedness to a Marxist understanding of the role of the intellectual in social struggles. For Dussel, then, the philosopher "as an organic intellectual, as militant, can express the criticism of a people with the maximum of precision even if, by birth, culture, or work, the philosopher does not, from the beginning, belong to the oppressed classes" (*Philosophy of Liberation* 125). Extending Dussel's intervention about the role of the philosopher as organic intellectual to other types of intellectuals, we can observe that the artists who are the focus of *Sensing Decolonial Aesthetics* made it a point to create the "right" medium in which to express the marginalization and subjugation of the oppressed.

I concur with Dussel's assertion that there are inherent contradictions that intellectuals experience in the clash of competing ideological and class-based allegiances. In many cases, the intellectuals in the present study belonged to the middle or upper middle classes, and yet they chose to engage with social problems pertaining to working and impoverished sectors of the population in their respective countries. I differ, however, from Dussel in his understanding of the role of the intellectual. Dussel sees the intellectual as one who speaks for the oppressed, as someone who has the critical tools to express and articulate the various modalities of oppression. In this sense, the role of the intellectual is paternalistic and hierarchical. Dussel suggests that the relationship of the intellectual and the oppressed class for which the former speaks is that of a "teacher-pupil, thinker-people" (*Philosophy of Liberation* 178). This formulation privileges a specific kind of knowledge and thinking, and a specific mode of articulating oppression and subjugation. Following Gramsci, Dussel introduces a pedagogical relationship between the intellectual and the oppressed. Nonetheless, if such a pedagogical relationship remains vertical, the intellectual remains an outsider-insider: an outsider due to his or her own ideological, educational, and class background, but also an insider based on his or her concerns for social justice as issues affecting a social class different from his or her own.

Decolonial aesthetics differs from this hierarchical model by asserting that the intellectual, despite his or her own tensions and outsider status, ought to engage in horizontal and symbiotic pedagogical relationships with the oppressed. As much as the intellectual has the critical tools to articulate social inequities, without the experiential and popular knowledge of the oppressed, the intellectual has little foundation on which to base a critique of oppression. In other words, the relationship between the intellectual and the oppressed is that of mutual learning and mutual need (that is, of mutuality and interdependence). The intellectual learns as much from popular thinking as the oppressed learn from the intellectual. In the case of decolonial aesthetics, the ultimate relationship of pedagogical mutuality is that in which the intellectual as artist does not merely voice or critique oppression, but provides the tools that allow the oppressed to participate actively in the process of critique (as in the works of Raymundo Gleyzer). Of course, not every decolonial artist is able to engage in this level of mutual pedagogical critique, but those who did so in the 1960s became clear symbols with whom the oppressed found it easier to identify and whom they were able to call their own (e.g., Violeta Parra, Víctor Jara, Roque Dalton, Ernesto Cardenal, Raymundo Gleyzer, etc.).

The importance of mutuality and interdependence between the intellectual and the oppressed echoes the positions found in the works of Paolo Freire and Rodolfo Kusch. For instance, in Freire's *Pedagogy of the Oppressed* (1970), he insists that such pedagogy must be created with, and not for, the oppressed. Moreover, the oppressed "must perceive the reality of oppression not as a closed world from which there is no exit, but as a limiting situation which they can transform" (34). The artist as intellectual and teacher has an obligation to express his ideas clearly to his intended audience. Only in this way can decolonial art be effective in raising consciousness among audiences about their oppression and how to challenge it.

In his *Handbook of Inaesthetics*, Alain Badiou introduces three schemata, which he terms didacticism, romanticism, and classicism. Didacticism is related to Plato's views on the arts in relation to society and politics. The romantic schema argues that "art *alone* is capable of truth" (3). Classicism, which Badiou equates with an Aristotelian view of aesthetics, mediates between these two extremes, didacticism and romanticism. Engaging with the intricacies and subtleties of these three schemata is beyond my concerns here. Yet, given the emphasis on aesthetics and education in both Dussel and Freire, it becomes important to reflect briefly on this notion of the didactic dimension of aesthetics. According to Badiou, one of the knots that ties art, philosophy, and education together is the power given to art as a form of control or a didactics of the senses (2–3). By this I understand that art becomes a means by which to instruct a population on how to sense art in specific ways that sustain and uphold values and categories that follow a Eurocentric conception of art and the truths derived from them. It is not that education (or the didactic schema of the arts) in itself necessarily has negative effects. Instead, I am drawing attention to the particular dangers of holding up a given poet (say Mallarmé) or a director (say Truffaut) as a parameter according to which we value and evaluate poetry and films from non-European locations. Simply put, Latin American arts respond to and produce their own sets of truths, which mirror the historically embedded realities and particularities of Latin American social contexts to engage with audiences in a didactic relation in which the arts indeed have something to teach and offer. This didactic relation transfixes or shifts the relationship between art and dominant conceptions of aesthetics. As such, art produced from this didactic perspective (closer to Freire's understanding of didactics and pedagogy than Badiou's) is capable of enacting its own aesthetic categories (antipoetry, third cinema, *nueva canción*, etc.). The aim of this didacticism is limited to seeking to engage audiences in a sensorial confrontation with artworks aimed at producing indignation and to showing Latin America's history of oppression, which in today's categories we call coloniality.

Rodolfo Kusch presents us with similar critical challenges to the importance we give to popular thought. For instance, in his *Indigenous and Popular Thinking in América,* Kusch insists that when we are confronted with the task of distinguishing between European and Latin American thinking, it is not simply a matter of dismissing Western philosophy. Instead, Kusch argues for the need to "look for a formulation closer to our own lives" (1). By this Kusch means that it is not to enough adapt Western philosophy to a Latin American context or merely to emphasize and revalorize indigenous and popular thought. Instead, "it is necessary to think at the margins of the categories of economics, of civilization, or of culture" (Kusch, *Indigenous and Popular Thinking* 7). In this sense, as a way to bring about an awareness of oppression, as Freire argued, Kusch proposes that intellectuals must go beyond established parameters of Western thought, and always work in tandem with those we have been calling throughout this book the oppressed, the wretched, the dispossessed, and the disenfranchised.

Returning to Enrique Dussel's articulation of the aesthetics of liberation, in a more recent text, Dussel rethinks the role of the philosopher of liberation to assert that such a person should neither engage in ventriloquism (speaking for the other) nor "undertake a concrete task in order to overcome or negate some petit-bourgeois sense of guilt" ("Philosophy of Liberation, the Postmodern Debate" 342). The critique I posited before still stands in Dussel's reformulation, particularly as the philosopher of liberation is still constructed as the subject who struggles and critiques oppression for the other. Within the same reformulation, Dussel asserts that the philosophy of liberation

> assumes the responsibility of fighting for the other, the victim, the woman oppressed by patriarchy, and for the future generation which will inherit a ravaged Earth, and so on—that is, it assumes responsibility for all possible sorts of alterity. And it does so with an ethical, "situated" consciousness, that of any human being with an ethical "sensibility" and the capacity to become outraged when recognizing the injustice imposed on the other. ("Philosophy of Liberation, the Postmodern Debate" 342)

There are inherent logical contradictions in Dussel's argument. First, he asserts that the philosopher of liberation does not speak or act on behalf of the other, and then, immediately following this statement, claims that the philosophy itself assumes and accepts the "responsibility" of fighting for the other, the oppressed. My objection to this formulation is the emphasis on the way the relationship between the philosopher and the oppressed is constructed. For Dussel, the philosopher does things *for* the oppressed. In contrast, the decolonial intellectual as artist recognizes her or his ethical duty to critique what is unethical, unjust, that which is embedded in inequity, oppression, and subjugation, and becomes outraged when witnessing injustice, but always *with* or *alongside* the oppressed, the dispossessed. The decolonial artist also has an ethical "sensibility" and a "situated" consciousness, as Dussel suggests. If the decolonial intellectual as artist recognizes and assumes an ethical duty, it is to employ his or her artistic medium to critique injustice, and to inform and educate the oppressed, but also to learn from them, to engage in dialogue with them in a horizontal relationship of mutuality as a decolonial strategy. A complementary part of the artist's duty is the acknowledgment that decolonial artists are also learning from the oppressed, from popular thought, and that the source of inspiration for their decolonial art is the oppression they witness on an everyday basis, as are popular thinking and means of expression, which have been negated and relegated for so long. In sum, the decolonial artist seeks to articulate injustice and oppression with and not only for the oppressed. Achieving such a balance in the relationship between decolonial artist and the oppressed becomes a critical challenge and an ongoing aesthetic-political-ethical project.

Coloniality and Decolonial Aesthetics

Contrary to long-existing perceptions that correlate aesthetics with the idea of beauty or sublime experiences, decolonial aesthetics cannot engage with such concepts, as many of the artists studied here deemed both categories bourgeois and devoid of social concerns. An alternative, however, would be to follow Dussel's and Kusch's critical invitation to view what is popular—the quotidian, a hardened face, portrayals of dire poverty—as beautiful or worthy of artistic representation. However, this would necessitate a reevaluation of the categories of analysis, judgment, taste, and emotional response to aesthetic stimuli. At the foundation of decolonial aesthetics is a convergence of Marxist/socialist ideology with ideas about liberation, decolonization, creating a national identity, promoting national culture, building alliances with regional partners, and turning to different modes of creating works of art to move and engage audiences. Steering away from principles of passivity, complacency, comfort, and enjoyment, decolonial aesthetics turns to social realism (not to be confused with early twentieth century forms of realism) and everyday means of communication as ways to generate in audiences contrasting emotions of pleasure, enjoyment, anger, and frustration. Decolonial aesthetics' intent is to translate the aesthetic experience into a source of social awareness, political engagement, and potential identification with others experiencing deplorable labor conditions, inadequate access to education, selective access to health, uneven distribution of wealth, systemic sexism, and other state practices that make social welfare and equity a reality for an elite few, but only an elusive mirage for the majority. As such, in decolonial art, the images and techniques in a film, the instrumentation or lyrics in a song, or the verses and imagery in a poem are perhaps not enjoyable, beautiful, or sublime if they are studied, understood, and evaluated in terms of established parameters of aesthetics. However, if antipoetry, *nueva canción*, or the films of New Latin American Cinema were to be reevaluated in terms of decolonial aesthetics, the decolonial would be added to existing evaluative aesthetic categories. In turn, these artistic movements draw attention to a need to challenge or go against hegemonic and elitist constructions of culture.

Decolonial aesthetics thus steers away from precepts that determine the value and quality of a given work of art based on its presumed formal accomplishment, technical innovation, or favorable critical reception. Likewise, decolonial aesthetics does not qualify a work of art in terms of binary categories as either good or bad, high or low, pleasant or unpleasant. Instead, decolonial artists are concerned with connecting with audiences for whom "high art" might be irrelevant. In doing so, decolonial artists present audiences with artistic works that problematize the relation between art and audiences. They also question the medium, techniques, language, messages, and purpose of art beyond the principle of entertainment. This is not to say, however, that decolonial artists create art divorced from leisure. Quite the contrary; leisure is constitutive of the decolonial aesthetic, as it becomes a way to awaken audiences to systemic inequities and politicize the aesthetic experience. Decolonial aesthetics injects a political dimension into leisure, so that leisure is no longer simply used for escapism. Instead, decolonial art confronts its audiences with their quotidian realities, while exposing systemic inequities. In doing so, decolonial art reminds audiences of how coloniality shapes their daily existence.

Another foundation for this proposed framework for the study of a constellation of artists at a particular moment in Latin America's cultural history lies in the recent work of Latin Americanist scholars, particularly those who have been working around the concept of coloniality. The basis for such groups finds its seeds in Aníbal Quijano's theorization of coloniality. For Quijano, the categories employed to divide groups along racial and national axes reveal a hierarchical relation of power that traditionally privileged the race and culture of Europeans and other whites over those of mestizos, blacks, or indigenous peoples. In essence, coloniality names the pervasive mechanisms of colonial subjugation and social stratification that gave European elites control over mestizos, indigenous peoples, and blacks during colonial times. Coloniality also underscores the processes of the transfer of power from European elites to mestizo elites with the advent of Latin American republics in the nineteenth century. As such, racial divisions were rearticulated and disguised as class divisions, which maintained the hierarchical structures of subjugation despite the shift in power from one group to another. In other words, coloniality reveals the mechanisms of subjugation and dominance that have pinned similar groups together in colonial and postcolonial (that is, post-independence) times, though the categories and terms of power relations have evolved with time. Coloniality expresses a continuum in the forms of domination, despite the perceived notion that with independence, equality became a reality for all social and racial groups.[2]

The concept of coloniality also points to an uneven relation of post-independence cultures in Latin America with European and U.S. models, particularly with the pervasive dichotomy of inferiority-superiority that Leopoldo Zea and Germán Arciniegas identified during this period.[3] Linked to the conceptualization of coloniality are Raúl Prebisch's concepts of center-periphery, which named the uneven economic relationships among Europe, the United States, and Latin America. This relation left those at the periphery (such as those in Latin America) in a state of dependency on those at the center (the United States and Europe).[4] While this concept is pertinent to economics, it has also been widely used to describe relations of power in postcolonial studies and world-systems analysis, and for decolonial scholars, the concept became a point of departure.

The remnants of colonial hierarchical relations of power continued to facilitate ways for those in control of nation-states to exclude and alienate large sectors of the population via racist, sexist, and classist mechanisms of oppression. Since coloniality names the mechanisms and continuities of oppression from colonial times through post-independence in Latin America, I propose the category of *decolonial* as a way to understand the ways in which antipoetry, *nueva canción,* and New Latin American Cinema artists were addressing such long-standing social inequities.[5] While some artists were preoccupied with exploring issues surrounding economic domination, others were concerned with political and institutionalized authority as another form of domination. Some became preoccupied with addressing issues around gender, while others focused on subjectivity and knowledge. Around the concept of coloniality, these four axes (race, economics, ontology, and knowledge) have been identified as the domains that give birth to a colonial matrix of power.[6] As seen in the preceding chapters, decolonial artists approached these domains of power and sometimes attempted to engage multiple domains within the same artwork.

Coloniality of Knowledge and Decolonial Aesthetics

We should understand coloniality of knowledge as an axis of the coloniality of power that articulates the uneven modalities of production-consumption of cultural capital. This leads to a hierarchical relationship of power that determines who produces and who consumes cultural artifacts and knowledge. This relationship also opens two parallel questions: 1. Who is in a position to judge what type of knowledge gets produced, and how? 2. Who gets to consume that knowledge? For instance, in the mid-1960s, Augusto Salazar Bondy argued for the need for a cohesive and conjoined effort among Latin American nations in superseding a long-standing "culture of dependency" in relation to the West, while also challenging the logic of underdevelopment. For Salazar Bondy, a reaffirmation of the value of national culture cannot hope to challenge the culture of dependency without a transregional consciousness-raising and valorization of Latin American national cultural models.[7] Among Latin American intellectuals there has been a long history of intellectual dependency as they looked toward European models of cultural knowledge. In doing so, Latin American intellectuals assumed (almost unproblematically) a subaltern position in the matrix of knowledge production-consumption. The colonial heritage that denied native knowledge any worth or value, and imposed its own aesthetic values, persisted through the foundation of new republics and remained almost unmodified into the twentieth century.[8]

In relation to an epistemic shift that decenters Eurocentric knowledge, Grosfoguel has argued for the need to make a distinction between "epistemic location" and "social location." Grosfoguel adds the following:

> The fact that one is socially located in the oppressed side of power relations, does not automatically mean that he/she is epistemically thinking from a subaltern epistemic location. Precisely, the success of the modern/colonial world-system consists in making subjects that are socially located in the oppressed side of the colonial difference, to think epistemically like the ones on the dominant positions. (67)

In this distinction there is an implicit call to reevaluate Latin America's intellectual and cultural traditions and how these have perpetuated a non-critical epistemic perspective on the Eurocentric production and consumption of knowledge. There is also an implication that artists as intellectuals ought to situate themselves within these intellectual traditions as a way to determine the effects of the uneven production and consumption of knowledge (including art) and how this has led the oppressed to think and embrace the values of the oppressor.

Following Grosfoguel, then, the situated subject-producer of subaltern knowledge—a type of knowledge seeking to challenge Eurocentric or dominant types of knowledge—needs to establish a relation to ethnic, racial, gender, sexual, political, social, and class-based demands and epistemic locations. In doing so, this situated subject-producer of knowledge refrains from further mythologizing the Western claim to and need for universal truths and absolutist categories, which have led to the West's self-validation and self-justification as the bearer of logic, knowledge, and culture in terms of modes of sensing or aesthetics. Around the sixteenth century the West stratified knowledge into binaries that demarcated the barrier between those with advanced, superior, and valid knowledge, and those without. By extension, this also served to justify oppressors as superior beings and the oppressed as inferiors.[9] As Grosfoguel reminds us, "We went from the sixteenth century characterization of 'people without writing' to the eighteenth and nineteenth century characterization of 'people without history,' to the twentieth century characterization of 'people without development' and more recently, to the early twenty-first century characterization of 'people without democracy'" (68). This critical challenge of inverting the long-standing coloniality of knowledge and the subjugation of non-Western perspectives was taken up by decolonial artists precisely to validate their position as outsiders in the dominant global design. Under such rubrics as antipoetry, *nueva canción*, and New Latin American Cinema, we find examples of how artists sought to distinguish themselves from the dominant forms of making art, while also seeking to challenge the accepted ways of producing and consuming cultural artifacts as sources of knowledge.

Needless to say, the subject-producer of knowledge in relation to decolonial aesthetics seeks to make evident its epistemic location in relation to ethnic, racial, gender, sexual, and class categorizations, while also making political demands and identifying social inequities. The decolonial artist positions her- or himself as a subaltern producer of knowledge. This is not a claim for a populist replacement of one universal paradigm with another. Instead, a Western or Eurocentric perspective on aesthetics has rendered it as concerned either with theories of beauty and the sublime or with categorical judgments on the value and merit of art. The foundation of aesthetics presumed a uniform effect on a universal and homogeneous audience. Simply put, it was assumed that great and beautiful artworks would be viewed and recognized as such regardless of the viewer's geopolitical location or the passage of time. The test of the aesthetic worth of a work of art was its ability to stand the passage of time and still enrapture audiences across the world. Of course, this only became possible through Europe's self-positioning and self-affirmation as the matrix of aesthetics-producing art.

As Western or Eurocentric art has been the benchmark or paradigm for great artworks, it is no wonder that there is a traditional claim for the centrality of the Western tradition. If we return to Prebisch's spatial metaphor of the center-periphery dichotomy, it becomes apparent that Europe's self-positioning at the center of all production-consumption of knowledge often leads to unilateral transactions of knowledge and culture in which what is at the center remains privileged and unchallenged by peripheral and subaltern ways of knowing. Linked to this uneven relationship of production/consumption of knowledge was the way in which creole (*criollo*) groups in Latin America historically upheld the belief that Europe was the location to which emerging republics ought to turn as an authorized producer of culture and knowledge. As new sites of production (in economic, cultural, and political terms), Latin American republics continued validating Europe's claim to power in the center-periphery dyad by merely modeling cultural production on European examples. Prime examples of this can be seen in the ways in which nineteenth-century intellectuals and authors embraced romanticism, realism, Parnassianism, symbolism, etc. Likewise, literary and cultural critics can only examine Latin American cultural productions via European parameters. For instance, if we were to examine an introspective Puerto Rican novel such as Eugenio María de Hostos's *La peregrinación de Bayoán* (1863) in relation to the European realist or psychological novel, what would be the result? As a hypothetical exercise, is it possible to speak of Latin America's influence on the likes of Zola or Dostoyevsky? Clearly, such an exercise would prove unproductive and even irrelevant. This is precisely my argument here, in that most of the cultural production emerging from Latin America from the formation of the republics until well into the twentieth century was at best imitative, adaptive, or parodic, despite some attempts at creating subaltern knowledge/culture. My argument here echoes my opening statements in the introduction to *Sensing Decolonial Aesthetics*, specifically in relation to Fernández Retamar's and Benedetti's positioning of the work produced in the 1960s and how it differed from that of previous generations of authors. Latin American intellectuals have always been well aware of the latest ideas coming from Europe and the United States, but seldom has the exchange of knowledge gone in the opposite direction. In the instances in which there have been attempts at creating artworks of a different sort, such as *modernismo, novelas de la tierra* or Afrocentric poetry (i.e., Luis Palés Matos or Nicolás Guillén), such examples of cultural production were dubbed too context-specific or regionalist (in a derogatory sense), and thus lacking in universality. The claim and quest for the universal in its cosmopolitan dimension is another way of placing cultural production within the accepted framework of a Eurocentered matrix of cultural production, reception, circulation, and consumption.

When considering this critique of coloniality of knowledge, however, one must also be aware of the relative danger in dismissing previous intellectual work due to its debt to European intellectual categories of analysis, or because it operates within a Eurocentric framework of knowledge. Doing this can lead one to seek the origins and permutations of an Anglo-Eurocentrism that has thwarted the emergence of a Latin American subjectivity as a non-subaltern being. In this sense, when conceptualizing decolonial aesthetics, the question of how this form of aesthetics reacts to cultural colonization becomes of prime importance. Following the logic that there is an established order of dominance in which some countries exert power while others endure it (dependency and center-periphery), Sergio Bagú argued that someone living in a country under economic and political subordination is more likely to be convinced that the country is incapable of cultural creation (50). In this sense, Bagú is calling into question the degree to which a country under cultural colonization, or what I have been calling throughout this book the coloniality of aesthetics, is able to engage in innovative and original processes of cultural creation. Implicit in Bagú's formulation is the assumption that cultural colonization closes off the possibility of cultural emancipation, which is a necessary step toward cultural decolonization. Furthermore, Bagú argues that when someone embraces cultural colonization, what is encountered is a dead end at which one realizes that the only possible way to elicit creation is to "importar técnicas y modos de pensar y hacer de países supuestamente superiores en el terreno de la cultura" [import techniques and modes of thinking and doing from supposedly superior countries in the terrain of culture] (50). Prevalent in Bagú's assertion is the hierarchical relation that privileges that which is foreign to Latin America. If modes of thinking, cultural production, and critical apparatuses are produced abroad, usually in Europe or the United States, this preference for what is foreign reveals a xenophilic attitude that places a higher value on foreign ideas and culture over what can be produced in one's own country. As Bagú continues to suggest, it is usually the intellectuals and arbiters of culture who project such xenophilic preferences onto wider sectors of the population in a given country (50). At the root of Bagú's critique is the suggestion that importing foreign cultural models without a critical perspective on what such importation does to one's own culture is to enable the subjugation of autochthonous culture in favor of dominant (foreign) models.

Decolonial aesthetics turns to art as its medium through which to seek a decolonization of the mind. As such, decolonial aesthetics becomes a model that questions accepted conventions of aesthetics and complicates the established categories that demarcate the type of poetry, films, music, novels, and other forms of art and cultural production that are raised to the level of universality and canonicity, based on perceived assumptions of their inherent value and contribution to global culture understood strictly from a Western perspective. In other words, if elites turned to high art to seek distinction and distance from the "plebes," decolonial artists embraced low or popular art forms and conjugated them with established genres to produce art geared toward speaking directly to ordinary people in a given country's population. The archive of decolonial aesthetic gestures to which I have been drawing attention in the preceding chapters sought to put into practice ways of communicating with Latin American audiences to elicit awareness of the extrinsic forces of cultural imperialism and the intrinsic sub-valorization of autochthonous arts. By uncovering embedded preferences for foreign cultural products over native ones, decolonial artists sought to counteract such xenophilic tendencies.

Coloniality of Being and Decolonial Aesthetics

As suggested in the previous section, coloniality of knowledge is linked to the effects of forms of domination at the level of the mind. Nonetheless, it has a more concrete function due to its linkage to uneven modes of production, circulation, and consumption of knowledge, including art. In conjunction with the coloniality of knowledge, the concept of coloniality of being deals with the various modalities of systemic oppression at the level of lived experience and everyday language (Maldonado-Torres 96). The production and consumption of knowledge cannot be separated or abstracted from those beings who are allowed to produce or consume that knowledge. In this sense, the coloniality of being is preoccupied with a re-examination of ontological categories constitutive of a Eurocentric modernity that has validated the existence of beings as thinkers (in a Cartesian sense) and non-beings as incapable of rational thought.[10] If coloniality of knowledge has been used to justify a hierarchical relation of power between the oppressor and the oppressed, between the privileged and the wretched (in the Fanonian sense), it has also been used to negate the validity of popular, indigenous, or Afro-descendant thought, since those are non-aligned with Eurocentric or Western epistemologies.[11]

In the work of Maldonado-Torres we find an approximation of a dimension of coloniality as it relates to subjectivity and knowledge, particularly in connection to the coloniality of being, which is based on the work of Levinas, Dussel, and Fanon. Maldonado-Torres argues that coloniality stratifies Being into beings and non-beings. On the one hand, one can argue that there are those who are considered full beings and therefore fully capable of rational thought, and of creating art and appreciating it. In contrast, for the non-beings or sub-beings, the expressions of their thoughts are dismissed on the grounds of their irrationality. The colonized non-being embraces, consumes, and internalizes such stratification and subjugation. Upon achieving his or her political independence from the colonizer, the colonized non-being reclaims his or her right to full humanity, to create and express thoughts, to have political autonomy and self-determination, and to voice and share previously dismissed (indigenous and/or popular) thought.[12]

In the process of independence throughout Latin America, such rights were reclaimed for some, but negated for others. In an attempt to engage with the question of the Eurocentric ego/subject, what coloniality seeks to do is not merely replace one ego or subject with another; instead, decoloniality seeks to reposition the non-Eurocentric ego without falling into the trap of center-periphery, which would reify a hierarchical relation of power. In so doing, decoloniality confirms the non-Eurocentric ego as an equally valid and important being. This validation comes from the non-Eurocentric ego or the oppressed and their ability to draw from experiential subjugation and silencing as a means to articulate a critique of Eurocentric logic, knowledge, and aesthetics (as related to the realm of the perceptible).[13]

A pivotal component of Maldonado-Torres's ontological critique is the way in which language is used as a means to negate the ability of the non-being (non-Western) subject to employ Western languages in any valid or coherent form, let alone produce high-quality or groundbreaking artwork. In this sense, this critique takes us back to the metaphorical correlation of the barbaric (indigenous, poor, oppressed) with Caliban. In relation to this point, and as a warning of the deep-rootedness of what would decades later be called the coloniality of knowledge and of being, Germán Arciniegas argued the following:

> El complejo del colonialismo asalta a muchas personas a cien y a ciento cincuenta años de ganada, como se dice, la guerra de independencia. Queda aún, como escoria, el espíritu acomplejado de quienes, por huir del imperialismo yanqui, se precipitan a entregar a los rusos su cuerpo y alma. O el de quienes tratan de volver a un planteamiento colonial que coloque bajo cualquier denominación europea al hombre americano. . . . Sólo que si hay algo íntimo, intransferible, es el derecho a expresarse con una voz propia, así sea en el balbuciente iniciarse de un pequeño mundo que nace, y que tiene, como los demás, más que el derecho, la obligación de darle un discurso a su espíritu para mostrar la variedad innumerable de las voces humanas. (*Cosas del pueblo* 78)

> [One hundred and one hundred and fifty years after winning the war of independence, as it is commonly called, the complex of colonialism affects many people. There still remains, like dross, the spirit of those with an inferiority complex who rushed to hand over their body and soul to the Russians in an attempt to escape American

> (Yankee) imperialism. And there are those who want to return to a colonial set-up by subsuming the (Latin) American man under any European influence. . . . But if there is something intimate, non-transferable, it is the right to self-expression in one's own voice, even if it's the stammering beginning of a small world at its birth, and which has, like others, more than the right, the obligation to give its spirit freedom of speech to display the great variety of human voices.]

In this sense, Arciniegas acknowledges the implicit pervasiveness of neocolonial forces, or what Quijano has termed coloniality. More importantly, however, Arciniegas warns Latin Americans against easily taking sides with the Soviets in an attempt to combat American imperialism, while also admonishing those wanting to revert to European or Eurocentric formal colonialism. Implicit in Arciniegas's analysis is the notion that even without the formal and permanent presence of colonial or imperial enterprises in Latin America, there have continued to be uneven relationships of power, particularly in the categorization of wide sectors of the population as non-beings incapable of thought and speech. Arciniegas thus makes it a point to articulate an urgent call for the oppressed and the silenced to come together to begin articulating their demands, even if at first what emerges is nothing other than incoherent or imperfectly formulated utterances. What is important for Arciniegas is that the right to speak no longer be taken away from the oppressed. By underscoring how the right to speak and the right to use language serve as a means by which to make demands and articulate injustices and various modalities of oppression, Arciniegas prefigures what Torres-Maldonado would articulate almost fifty years later as the coloniality of being.

In conjunction with Arciniegas's and Maldonado-Torres's conceptualizations of the centrality of language to the decolonization of the subjugated and oppressed, I should add here the connection I see between coloniality of being and decolonial aesthetics. Whereas the coloniality of being names the processes by which the oppressed have been reduced to non-beings and therefore denied the right to speak, articulate ideas, or produce knowledge, decolonial aesthetics becomes a means by which to challenge Eurocentric categories of the perceptible as a way to meet the demands of the subject in the process of decolonization or undoing coloniality. In a recent volume published in Colombia under the title of *Estéticas y opción decolonial* (2012), Walter D. Mignolo and Pedro Pablo Gómez collected an array of essays that explore the linkages between ways of conceiving of aesthetics and decolonial thinking as an option among the other existing political, theoretical, philosophical, historical, and cultural alternatives available in recent times. The articles in this volume deal with thinking about aesthetics as related to former Soviet locations, the Balkans and the European Union, and various sites in Latin America, including Colombia, Bolivia, and Panama. In the opening article, Mignolo lays out some of the theoretical considerations that enable us to think about aesthetics and the decolonial in relation to each other. Here Mignolo argues that aesthetics has been construed as a Eurocentric philosophical discourse that originated in the eighteenth century and has been historically used to devalue and colonize modes of expressing feeling, sensing, and affect ("Lo nuevo y lo decolonial" 29). As stated earlier in this chapter, the decolonial artist cannot produce artworks that critique Eurocentric aesthetics and ways of knowing without a mutuality that allows the artist both to educate and learn from an audience. The ultimate function of decolonial aesthetics is to alert audiences (the subjugated, the oppressed, non-beings) about the pervasive mechanisms of the coloniality of power. In other words, one of the aims of decolonial aesthetics is to debunk the myth that with independence movements, Latin America freed itself from colonial forces and mechanisms of oppression. A second aim is to valorize popular, indigenous, and Afro-descendant knowledges. In this way, a decolonial process of undoing Eurocentric knowledge and hierarchical ontological categories paves the way for a decolonial subject capable of producing, consuming, and critiquing Eurocentric and non-Eurocentric (decolonial) artworks and their corresponding aesthetics.

Decolonial Aesthetics and Its Challenges

At this juncture I turn to Raymond Williams's seminal essay "Literature and Sociology," in which he warns literary and cultural scholars against the dangers of having "false totalities," which can take the shape of defined literary genres with little or no room for permeation of other ideas or categories that might disrupt such totalities (16). As an analytical concept, decolonial aesthetics does not seek to be totalizing. Quite the contrary—it aims to expand current categorizations of works of art, generate a cross-analysis of overlapping and underlying ideas, and open up possibilities of interpretation. To go beyond such closed and static categorizations that restrict genre-based analyses, Williams employs the term "structures of feelings" as a way to "indicate certain common characteristics in a group of writers but also of others, in a particular historical situation" (22). As such, the concept of structures of feelings enables an analysis of common undercurrents in seemingly dissimilar works of art. It allows for a re-evaluation of an already demarcated group of artists (a movement) and those who might have shared certain of its preoccupations, even if they did not align with such a movement or have not been studied alongside such a group. The structures of feelings also elicit the collapsing and transgression of genres as limiting categories and create the possibility of analyzing sources of critique across forms or modes of art.

In Williams's words, structures of feeling in which we scrutinize structure itself, not merely content, "can show us the organizing principle by which a particular view of the world, and from that the coherence of the social group which maintains it, really operates in consciousness" (23). Put differently, the emphasis in a cross-genre analysis is to explore the underlying and common structure of ideas, feelings, and tendencies that form a common source of critique while also paying attention to the diverse modalities of critique. I diverge, however, from some of Williams's ideas in a number of ways. As a concept, decolonial aesthetics seeks to unearth the "organizing principle" or principles that generate a common approach to viewing and critiquing social problems and inequities. Identifying an organizing principle, however, does not necessarily equate with having a coherent social group or movement uphold or strengthen such principles, leading to critiques. This is why this book has identified heterogeneous examples contributing to an archive of artworks that critique coloniality and that, in so doing, become part of a decolonial ethos. Put differently, the organizing principle or structure reveals disjunctures and fissures among the members of such a group of artists. Moreover, with decolonial aesthetics, the continuation, longevity, and strength of a group's common structure do not rest entirely on its coherence or stability, but rather on the types of critiques and modes in which artworks serve such critiques, while also having an aesthetic value that resonates with the general public and the oppressed.

Following Williams's emphasis on structure, my work on decolonial aesthetics seeks to explore the foundation that grounds a common worldview. When invoking the idea of a common worldview, however, I am cautious about avoiding the trap of false totalities. A common worldview, as used here, recognizes both common ground and points of dispute among artists and intellectuals. It acknowledges discrepancies among artists and their respective projects. For the purposes of decolonial aesthetics, a common worldview from a Latin American vantage point engages with currents of cultural influence, forces of economic dominance, factors of political manipulation, and growing social unrest coming from the United States and Europe. The common worldview as a foundational structure of decolonial aesthetics in Latin America is attuned to the larger picture of a polarized economic and political world. Furthermore, one can argue that the common worldview among decolonial artists studied here elicited the production of decolonial artwork as a response to such global dynamics and the ways in which these affected both their respective countries and the entire region. The structure of feeling (that is, this the common worldview) enables us to identify some artists' common points of contestation and modalities of critique through their art, while we sift through convergent and divergent approaches to deal with the identified problems.

If aesthetics is concerned with a specific type of art and its value, decolonial aesthetics is concerned with what is left outside of that purview. Judgment of taste is different for those not privy to the technical terms or concepts against which one is expected to judge the value of a work of art. For the non-specialist, the decolonial art-object is a democratizing tool through which art moves and affects its non-specialist audience. Due to their refusal to romanticize beauty or reality, decolonial art objects to value judgments made according to existing paradigms or labels. Parallel to the opposition between traditional aesthetics and decolonial aesthetics is the seeming opposition between tradition and revolution.[14] Such an opposition requires a nuanced look at types of tradition and types of revolution, how they become means to specific ends, and who the actors are who embrace either side of the dichotomy. If tradition is passing down an ideology, a belief system, norms, social codes, and established structures, as Fals-Borda has suggested, inevitably revolution stands as its opposite in the sense that it wants to resist, reject, and break away from the fixity and weight of tradition.[15] Yet, revolution has its foundation in tradition (in the dominant culture) as an object against which it reacts. As it seeks to distance itself from tradition, revolution aims to create new (viable) alternatives to supersede that which is dated, wrong, and harmful in a given tradition. Fals-Borda suggests that revolution rejects stagnation and prefers renovation, which presupposes a constant awareness of its foundational reference point. As such, revolution does not aim to destroy tradition in its entirety, but wants to keep what is considered of value in order to generate new paths. Revolution, then, appropriates and reconfigures elements of tradition in a new guise. In this way, revolution's indebtedness to tradition is always present in the new cultural product, though sometimes such a relation may not be readily acknowledged or evident. Revolution's desire for a radical break or departure from tradition is thus not entirely possible, as it marks a triperspectival view of time: revolution is preoccupied with the weight of tradition (past), and self-awareness of its duty (present), while seeking to renovate and prolong its effect (future). In the preceding chapters, I have sought to examine the degree to which antipoetry, *nueva canción*, and New Latin American cinema were "revolutionary" in their attempts at producing a radical break or departure from the types of poetry, music, and cinema that had been produced across Latin America in the decades leading up to the 1960s. The emphasis in my analysis, however, was to pay close attention to what antipoets, *nueva canción* musicians, and New Latin American cinema filmmakers set out to do and the means by which they aimed to accomplish their respective projects as they deployed critiques of coloniality and thus must be read as contributing to a decolonial ethos. Even if terms such as *coloniality* and *decolonial* have relatively recent currency in academic circles, the preceding chapters and the book as a whole have sought to read specific case studies of poets, musicians, and filmmakers as belonging to a heterogeneous archive of decolonial perspectives emerging from the arts, and not just from the academy.

Conclusion

Sensing the Irresolute Past in the Present

In Fanon's seminal study of the modalities of colonial violence, he argues that in a colonized world, it is education, particularly in relation to "aesthetic forms of the status quo," that helps to maintain divisions at all levels of society. Fanon writes, "In capitalist societies, education, whether secular or religious, the teaching of moral reflexes handed down from father to son, the exemplary integrity of workers decorated after fifty years of loyal and faithful service, the fostering of love for harmony and wisdom, those aesthetic forms of respect for the status quo, instill in the exploited a mood of submission and inhibition which considerably eases the task of agents of law and order" (Fanon 3–4). In addition to these insights, which are as relevant and timely today as they were in the early 1960s, I also see Fanon's sense of "the aesthetic forms of the status quo" as related to modes of learning and knowing, which are used to regulate what is learned and how such knowledge is consumed. Put differently, I read Fanon's use of the aesthetic as a way to regulate how forms of knowledge, including art and aesthetics, are sensed.

In this light, *Sensing Decolonial Aesthetics* aims to make an intervention in the ways we understand the cultural historiography of the 1960s and early 1970s in Latin America. To place my book into perspective, in a 1984 volume of *Social Text* dedicated to a re-evaluation of the 1960s, the editors echoed the Gramscian use of hegemony in relation to the neoconservative backlash against the countercultural values of the 1960s. As noted by the editors of this volume, "Gramsci's term of hegemony remains the most convenient shorthand . . . [to understand] a conflict which includes contests over interpretations of history" (Sayres et al. 8). If hegemony names the struggles over historical interpretations and ideological tensions related to the 1960s, a broadening of our understanding of the period is necessary to elicit re-evaluations and reinterpretations of what cultural texts of the sixties have come to mean beyond neoconservative, nostalgic, or apologetic positions that seek either to diminish or magnify the significance of that decade. Moreover, the editors of the same volume note that "visions of history play an enormous—if incalculable—role in people's political practice in the present: and this all the more when the interpretation in question is a matter, not of 'attitudes' towards a bygone age like the era of the Wobblies or of the American Revolution, but rather of people's immediate past" (Sayres et al. 8). While the volume was edited in the mid-1980s, the urgency of the editors' intervention against what they perceived as the "trashing" of or backlash against the legacy of the sixties is still present and much-needed.

Whereas our distance from the 1960s grows with each passing year (obviously this decade is not as immediate now as it was in 1984 when the *Social Text* volume appeared), the call for a more in-depth and nuanced understanding of Latin America's past has recently become quite urgent given the cultural and political developments in the region, its shift toward what political scientists have named the "pink tide" over the last decade, and what might come after that tide. In contemporary Latin America's cultural and political terrains, we have seen similar gradations in the left as in the past. There are those who stand to the more "radical" left (Hugo Chavez, Nicolás Maduro, Evo Morales, Rafael Correa). There are also other leaders (Daniel Ortega, Luiz Inácio "Lula" Da Silva, Dilma Rousseff, José Mujica) who participated in social and political movements during the 1970s and 1980s and still maintain some affinities with the left, while being receptive to the economic demands of Latin America's "post-neoliberalism," the ensuing effects of the global economic crisis, and the maneuvering of strong political opposition emerging from their respective countries.

As Sergio Chejfec reminds us about literary and cultural production of the 1960s and 1970s:

> We live in a time in which socioeconomic conditions have, generally speaking, not gotten better but instead have either deteriorated or been fundamentally altered. These outdated works, therefore, speak to us of an antiquated understanding, obsolete in many ways, yet authentic in its transitory moment: this past offers both a promise and a threat to contemporary literature. It suggests that engagement with the social and the political is possible, but that the realization of this desire is inherently imperfect. (113)

While some of the practical and theoretical positions of the period, such as guerrilla warfare and liberation theology, seem to be of less concern in our days, and thus appear to us as less fashionable or intellectually relevant, the social foundations that sparked those types of struggles remain in place today and have taken on newer dimensions. To mention a few contemporary examples that reveal how works from the long decade of the sixties continue to affect cultural production in Latin America, we could point to Latin American fiction such as Roberto Bolaño's *Los detectives salvajes* (1998) or Elmer Mendoza's *El amante de Janis Joplin* (2003).

The presence and salience of Nicanor Parra's poetry is perhaps more celebrated today than it was in the 1960s, particularly since his longevity has recently been celebrated in terms of his impact as a poet and his age. In terms of critical appraisal, Parra was awarded in 2011 the Premio de Literatura en Lengua Castellana Miguel de Cervantes, and has been nominated several times for the Nobel Prize. Mario Benedetti's legacy is now well-secured given that the Universidad de Alicante has named its Center for Latin American Studies after him and that his works are now housed in the Fundación Mario Benedetti in Montevideo. Violeta Parra's works have a virtual presence, much like those of her brother and Benedetti, due to their availability on a website hosted by a foundation bearing her name. Beyond the Internet, Violeta's impact on younger generations of Chilean (and Latin American) musicians can quickly be gleaned from a performance aired on Televisión Nacional de Chile on November 16, 2011, in which artists such as Inti Illimani, Pedro Aznar, Ana Tijoux, Francisca Valenzuela, and Camila Moreno (the last three being contemporary Chilean singer-songwriters influenced by Violeta's work) covered some of Violeta's most representative songs before a packed stadium. Most recently,

Chilean director Andrés Wood made a biopic entitled *Violeta Went to Heaven* (2011), based on Ángel Parra's biographical account of his mother, which has had significant international circulation and rekindled an interest in Violeta's life and her works. In terms of thinking about the impact of other musicians who were part of *nueva canción,* Francisca Valenzuela also contributed to a tribute album for Inti Illimani when she covered the song "Vuelvo" in 2009 and Natalia Lafourcade did a cover of "Qué he sacado con quererte" in her 2017 album *Musas.* Contemporary musicians and groups such as Kalfu, Gepe, Manuel García, and Camila Moreno continue invoking some of the musical traditions, indigenous instruments, and musical arrangements evocative of the 1960s generation, albeit in an updated fashion for contemporary audiences. Not coincidentally, these people are among the artists gaining greater visibility across Latin America and into the United States among Latino populations. Chilean rapper and singer Ana Tijoux recently released a cover of Víctor Jara's song "Luchín," which is widely available on YouTube or Spotify; this has become perhaps the most recent instance of a sustained interest in what that generation of musicians and artists represents not only in terms of their historical context, but also for what they have come to resignify for contemporary generations of artists and audiences alike. In this gesture by Tijoux of covering Víctor Jara's song, I read an ongoing interest on Tijoux's behalf in employing music as a way to denounce various modes of systemic oppression and various forms of coloniality (see her own songs "Antipatriarca" or "Somos sur"). The song "Luchín," in particular, refers to children who live in dire poverty and disenfranchisement from society.

Before Mercedes Sosa's death in 2009, she recorded two CDs under the title *Cantora,* which featured duets with artists ranging from pop singers such as Shakira and Julieta Venegas, to rock singers such as Gustavo Cerati, Charlie García, and Fito Paez, to urban musicians such as Calle 13. This last collaboration aimed to bridge presumed generation gaps between those practitioners of *nueva canción* and newer trends in pop, rock, and hip-hop music. By bringing together some of the biggest names in Latin American music to cover songs such as Silvio Rodríguez's "La maza" (recorded with Shakira) or overtly socially committed songs such "Canción para un niño de la calle" (recorded with Calle 13) with her, Sosa changed these songs from mere objects of the past to reinscribed pieces of the ongoing social and political struggles facing Latin America. In 2013,

Rodrigo H. Vila released the documentary *Mercedes Sosa: The Voice of Latin America,* which was screened at various film festivals in the United States, Europe, and Latin America. As with the case of Violeta Parra's biopic, the life of this pioneering musician has the potential to reach audiences that may have otherwise not heard of or been aware of her significance to the evolution of music across Latin America. Another recent instance of the renewed relevance the musicians discussed in *Sensing Decolonial Aesthetics* is the case of Chilean rock band Los Bunkers when they made an entire CD entitled *Música libre* (2010). On this CD, they covered songs by Silvio Rodríguez as a way to pay homage to his work and to a spirit of brotherhood between Cuba and Chile, and with Latin America at large. In doing the covers, and updating the songs' sound to meet modern tastes and sensibilities, Los Bunkers were also careful about maintaining the revolutionary and political spirit, as well as the affective weight, of Rodríguez's songs. In fact, in a historical gesture that has a Latin American reach, the photograph on the CD cover was shot in the square of Tlatelolco in Mexico, a site of irresolute memories. I could go on listing the ways in which the work of the musicians, poets, and filmmakers I have discussed in *Sensing Decolonial Aesthetics* continues to have an impact on today's cultural scene in Latin America in both perceptible and subdued ways. My intention in presenting these examples has been to get us thinking about how we deal with cultural texts emerging from the past.

Contemporary generations are temporally and seemingly affectively distant from Latin American artworks of the 1960s. So, in thinking about how these audiences encounter these artworks or how they get to know them, one must think about what Félix Guattari calls "affective contamination," in the sense that specific aesthetic experiences and sensorial encounters with the arts become not a matter "of representation and discursivity, but of existence" (92–93). In Guattari's line of thinking, this encounter with the arts through "affective contamination," as ideas, sounds, and sensorial registers that are out there, coexisting, and not neatly divided or compartmentalized, has the ultimate transformative effect of generating a sensibility for recognizing oneself in another being or in experiences beyond what we know and how we sense. It is in this gesture of moving beyond our restrictive sentient, epistemological subjectivity as linked to specific experiences and affects that an encounter with art—that is, being affectively contaminated by the arts—enables Guattari to write "I am no longer as I was before, I am swept away by a becoming other, carried beyond my familiar existential Territories" (93). Moving beyond experiences and encounters with artworks implies exposing ourselves to other geopolitical and temporal ways of knowing and sensing. Our affective response to these encounters cannot just be to sense as we do, or as we are comfortable sensing, but indeed to sense otherwise.

To understand contemporary social and political movements better—those movements understood by Mignolo and others as a "decolonial turn" in the region—one needs to retrace some of the origins of this sociopolitical and cultural shift, which I place in the 1960s. In relation to many decolonial scholars who place an emphasis on present social and cultural struggles, my work in *Sensing Decolonial Aesthetics* has sought to identify some of the cultural texts and trends that engaged in questioning different modalities of oppression and social inequity by referencing and sensing the irresolute legacy of the decade. While collectively identifying this moment of cultural production as various modalities of cultural resistance (critiquing and delinking from coloniality) emerging from various art forms, and reading them through a decolonial lens, one is fully aware of the problems in aligning poets, film directors, and musicians along a conjoining thread. However, the goal in doing so has been to generate a broader understanding of how artists struggled against dominant and political culture and notions of Western/Eurocentric aesthetics, though their modes of expressing such struggles varied in vision, approach, techniques, goals, and ideological foundations. Nonetheless, in reinterpreting the role of such artists as part of a heterogeneous cultural moment and as contributing to an expanding archive of decolonial gestures emerging from the arts, one can see how ideas are exchanged, contested, and expounded across genres and national borders. Ultimately, as this book has tried to articulate, it is not simply a matter of employing the concept and practices of the decolonial in order to understand contemporary art practices exhibited in either museums or public spaces. To understand truly how the decolonial responds to and seeks to delink from coloniality, it becomes imperative to expand the archive of decolonial works and gestures to include a variety of art practices and a more capacious temporal engagement with the decolonial ethos. As one critic has argued, "Decolonizing aesthetics seeks to recognize open options for liberating the senses" (Rojas-Sotelo, "Decolonizing Aesthetics" 303). To liberate the senses, as I have argued throughout *Sensing Decolonial Aesthetics,* also means to sense artworks from the past as artifacts and texts that create a more expansive register of moments of resistance, from the arts to modes of regulating knowledges and the sensorial. Sensing otherwise such artworks offers us the ability to begin thinking in historical terms about retracing moments and gestures aimed at delinking from coloniality as they emerge from artistic practices such as poetry, music, and film.

As one example of the ways in which the 1960s have been studied, with particular attention to the role of memory, Diana Sorensen's book *A Turbulent Decade Remembered* (2007) seeks to illuminate "scenes" of particular importance to understanding the long decade of the 1960s in Latin America. In her introduction, Sorensen writes that in her view, "Latin America in the sixties encapsulates its [the decade's] predicament: a moment of hope and celebration produced a sense of multiple possibilities, only to reach a closure and despair in its culmination. At the time of present writing, well into the twenty-first century, it is hard to avoid a melancholic sense of loss as one contemplates the aftermath of this utopian decade, as if one had reached the end of a plot with a cheerless outcome. For the sixties were followed by brutal regimes and economic crises whose impact has been profound and long standing" (3). *Sensing Decolonial Aesthetics* seeks to avoid this "melancholic sense of loss" without falling into a naively or historically blindsided utopianism. The melancholic sense of loss will take hold of the present if the cultural and material texts of the 1960s continue to be read exclusively as products of their time, as memorabilia of a utopian decade, or as reminders and remainders of the shortcomings and failures of the decade's euphoria and hope.

Throughout *Sensing Decolonial Aesthetics,* I have employed a decolonial approach, with an emphasis on aesthetics, as a way to reach a more nuanced and relational understanding of Latin America's cultural scene in the 1960s and early 1970s. Contrary to critical positions that may readily dismiss antipoetry, *nueva canción,* and third cinema for their alleged lack of aesthetic value, I have emphasized the need to rethink the ways in which academia and the public shape canon formation. A reason for the relative dismissal or neglect of the above-mentioned forms has been that they have often been placed in similar categories as Marxist, socialist, or leftist art and, on those grounds alone, have been historically given a "negative" connotation and only propagandistic value. Likewise, in framing my project, I became interested in looking at relations among artworks, rather than focusing my book on only one genre—in part because, like Benedetto Croce, I believe that "The so-called arts do not have aesthetic boundaries, since, in order for there to be such boundaries, they would have to have aesthetic existence *qua* particular arts; and we have shown precisely the purely empirical and extrinsic origins of such divisions. It also follows from this that any attempt to give an aesthetic classification of the particular arts is absurd" (Croce 127). Following this line of thinking, *Sensing Decolonial Aesthetics* presents questions and posits the need to discuss what the arts can do in relation to each other and not as separate forms of aesthetic expression.

As such, I looked at key examples of such movements in relation to what I have termed decolonial aesthetics with the purpose of going beyond the claims that such artworks are only important because of their nostalgic aura of a long-gone revolutionary past. In relation to nostalgia for the past, one critic has stated the following:

> Modern nostalgia is a mourning for the impossibility of a mythical return, for the loss of an enchanted world with clear borders and values; it could be a secular expression of a spiritual longing, a nostalgia for an absolute, a home that is both physical and spiritual, the edenic unity of time and space before entry into history. The nostalgic is looking for a spiritual addressee. Encountering silence, he looks for memorable signs, desperately misreading them. (Boym 8)

Without falling into nostalgic traps, my interventions have emphasized the subtleties in the artists' gradations of social and political commitment, levels of leftist tendencies, differences in approaches to combining leftist ideologies and new art, and how these artist-intellectuals contributed to the shaping of heterogeneous decolonial efforts and articulations of decolonial thought in the region. In other words, such art predates and serves as a foundation for the discourses that circulate in academic and intellectual circles today. Surprisingly, however, academia has not given sufficient attention to this period as a cornerstone of postcolonial/decolonial thought.

In the chapters in which I have discussed poetry, music, and films from the 1960s, I have done so with the intent of reading cultural artifacts/texts as artworks through a lens of decolonial aesthetics so as to sense them otherwise. Though these artworks may be deemed populist by some or legacies of historically stagnant time, the decolonial artists studied in *Sensing Decolonial Aesthetics* sought to make their art more accessible to the very public that might not have had access to much of the high-art cultural products of their time. Likewise, as shown earlier in this conclusion, sensing the past requires a rethinking of the presumed fixity of historical time by way of focusing on time's oscillation and the multidirectional temporal arches that can be traced to reconfigure relations and the grounds of comparison. Decolonial artists aimed to draw attention to those groups that were left out of the scope of Western/Eurocentric aesthetics and technical experiments during the 1960s, including the "boom" writers. Of course, some decolonial artists succeeded more than others in staying close to their own aesthetic projects, and some have survived better in the present's recurring return to the past.

In general terms, decolonial artists resisted having to compromise their work for the sake of commercial success, thrived on alternative modes of dissemination (such as grassroots modes of distribution, small presses, and select film festivals), and by extension suffered from the triple-bind of negative/inadequate reception by academic critics, limited exposure to audiences, and state censorship and persecution. Cuba, of course, was an isolated case in that different forces were at work: writers who questioned the revolution were persecuted, while those who embraced it received full government support.

Keeping in mind the historical scope of this book project, which sought to explore cultural texts produced from 1960 until roughly 1975, in this conclusion, I have sought to explore briefly how this irresolute past continues manifesting itself in the twenty-first century. Sensing artworks from the past through decolonial aesthetics implies sensing them as living culture. Clear indications of how these works operate as living culture are the multiple references I offer above that signal the continued presence and emergence of artworks from this decade among contemporary artists and audiences. In this sense, I am thinking of Albert Memmi's notion of living culture as one that "is an ongoing question of traditional beliefs—testing and adapting them to the inevitable transformation all societies undergo. It is thus inherently dangerous, iconoclastic and heretical, because it needs to free itself of all restraints in order to breathe freely" (41–42). For living culture to "breathe freely," it must question the very aesthetic dimensions that circumscribe and determine cultural categories, and particularly those cultural texts used to maintain "the aesthetics of the status quo," to echo Fanon's words at the beginning of this conclusion.

In one of the concluding chapters of *Latinamericanism after 9/11*, John Beverly lauds the cultural production and the reach of 1960s filmmakers, novelist, poets, and musicians in the region. And yet, Beverly is also aware of the difficulties in thinking about and remembering the past, particularly if there is an inclination from the "generation of the sixties," in which Beverly includes himself, "to see where we went wrong [rather] than what we did right" (109). Beverly continues his elucidation of what he calls the "paradigm of disillusion" in relation to armed struggles and the sixties when he argues the following: "But in a way, our disillusion has not been *thorough* enough. It has not worked through the melancholia of defeat. . . . In that way, the paradigm of disillusion has not prepared us to accept that the possibility of radical change has opened up once again in the Americas, North and South" (109, emphasis in original). As I have claimed throughout this book, sensing otherwise, particularly when we are confronted with the task of sensing the irresolute past, implies recognizing the limitations of "the paradigm of disillusion" (to borrow Beverly's term) and its bearing on the pervasiveness of keywords such as "melancholia," "defeat," "disillusion," or "loss" when facing, remembering, and rethinking the past. The logic of dismissiveness through the language of defeat reduces works of the past to mere cultural artifacts emerging from a historically, politically, and theoretically determined epoch, while presupposing that they have little to offer us today. I believe that the opportunities or options for radical change in the present necessitate a reframing of the past so that we may sense it anew and otherwise, lest we fall into the ineluctable traps and weight of cultural and political-economic presentisms.

NOTES

Introduction

1. A few recent studies have engaged with this question of Latin American literature and its place in either cosmopolitan or world literary contexts. For an emphasis on *modernismo* and the boom, see Mariano Siskind's *Cosmopolitan Desires: Global Modernity and Literature in Latin America* (2014). For an emphasis on contemporary Latin American literature, see Héctor Hoyos's *Beyond Bolaño: The Global Latin American Novel* (2015). For a study that triangulates the literary and cultural exchanges across the Atlantic, see Rachel Price's *The Object of the Atlantic: Concrete Aesthetics in Cuba, Brazil, and Spain, 1868–1968* (2014).

2. In this essay, Benedetti is cautious not to undermine the genealogy and development of Latin American literatures. In fact, his essay begins with a brief discussion of El Inca Garcilaso, moving to Andrés Bello and Sarmiento, touching on the *indigenista* and social realist authors of the 1930s, while placing a strong emphasis on the uniqueness of the boom writers and poets of this same period. Among the landmark books of this period, Benedetti mentions Guimarães Rosa's *Grande Sertão* (1956), Juan Rulfo's *Pedro Páramo* (1956), Julio Cortázar's *Rayuela* (1963), and Gabriel García Márquez's *Cien años de soledad* (1967). Furthermore, Benedetti highlights the contributions that Nicanor Parra, Ernesto Cardenal, Roque Dalton, José Donoso, Carlos Fuentes, Claribel Alegría, Jorge Enrique Adoum, and José María Arguedas, among many others, made to the development of "letras de osadía" [letters of audacity or courageousness].

3. Some recent examples of aesthetic models or propositions seeking to recuperate the past from a philosophical perspective are Alain Badiou's *A Handbook of Inaesthetics* (2005) and Jacques Rancière's *Aisthesis: Scenes from the Aesthetic Regime of Art* (2013). From cultural anthropology, some examples are Mark M.

Smith's *Sensing the Past* (2008), and David Howes and Constance Classen's *Ways of Sensing: Understanding the Senses in Society* (2013). For the Latin American case, see Doris Sommer's *The Work of Art in the World* (2014).

4. Some examples include an exhibit entitled "Estéticas Descoloniales" held in Bogotá in November 2010, an issue of *Fuse* magazine (Fall 2013) dedicated to decolonial aesthetics, an article published in a Romanian magazine by Miguel Rojas-Sotelo and Raúl Moarquech Ferrera-Balanquet entitled "Decolonial Aesthetics," and the now-annual Be.Bop Black European Bodies conference and curatorial event held in various locations in Europe, which brings together artists from various locations across the globe.

5. For a more detailed distinction between Mignolo's formulation of the geopolitics of knowledge and geopolitics of knowing, see his book *The Darker Side of Western Modernity* (2011), particularly chapters 3 and 5.

6. On the confrontation between the sensorial and the written, I am thinking about the following statement by Robert Hopkins: "literature, like art, is *about* the sensory. Poetry in any form, drama, short stories, and novels all concern the world as we experience it through our various senses. They are able to do so because the sensory imagination brings that world before us even when our current sensory experience is confined to the sight of words on a page, or—if we silently recite a poem from memory—less" ("Senses and Art" 531).

7. Francisca Valenzuela did several covers of Violeta Parra's songs in the context of a tribute concert held in the Plaza de Armas in Santiago, Chile, in 2011 and then in a series of her own concerts. More detailed reflections on this temporal move of music from the 1960s into the present appear in the conclusion to this book.

8. For a discussion of how coloniality and music intersect, see Carolina Santamaría Delgado's study on the history and reception of bambuco in musicology in her essay "El bambuco, los saberes mestizos y la academia" (2007). Similar claims could be made for the case of Violeta Parra in her reliance on the *cueca* or the mazurca as popular musical styles and forms of accompaniment to her lyrical compositions.

9. Some prime examples of scholarship focusing on this period and that tend to privilege the boom novels are Jean Franco's *The Decline and Fall of the Lettered City* (2002), Diana Sorensen's *A Turbulent Decade Remembered* (2007), and, more recently, Jerónimo Arellano's *Magical Realism and the History of Emotions in Latin America* (2015) and Lucille Kerr and Alejandro Herrero-Olaizola's *Teaching the Latin American Boom* (2015).

10. For a succinct genealogy of decolonial thinking, see Mabel Moraña's "Postscriptum: Decolonial Scenarios and Alternative Thinking: Critical and

Theoretical Explorations" (2016). For an example of non-academic circulation and use of decolonial thinking beyond Latin America, see the website *Decoloniality London.*

11. There is already a growing body of scholarship that seeks to read Latin American authors from a decolonial perspective. See Michael Handelsman's *Género, raza y nación en la literatura ecuatoriana* (2011), Sara Castro-Klarén's *The Narrow Pass of Our Nerves* (2011), Sara Castro-Klarén and Christian Fernández's *Inca Garcilaso and Contemporary World-Making* (2016), Mabel Moraña's *Churata postcolonial* (2015), and Juan G. Ramos and Tara Daly's *Decolonial Approaches to Latin American Literatures* (2016).

12. For ways in which decolonial thinking has moved beyond Latin America, see Madina Tlostanova's "La aesthesis trans-moderna en la zona fronteriza eurasiática y el anti-sublime decolonial" (2011), Tanja Ostojić's "Cruzando fronteras" (2012), and Marina Grzinic's "[Estéticas] decoloniales como/ en/ a la frontera" (2012). Other directions of decolonial aesthetics can be seen in *Social Text's* periscope dossier, edited by Walter D. Mignolo and Rolando Vásquez, primarily Ovidiu Tichindeleanu's "Europe: Potential Paths of Liberation" (2013), Vivian Lee's "Decolonial Moments in Hong Kong Cinema" (2013), and Hong-An Truong, Nayuong Aimee Kwon, and Guo-Jin Hong's "What/Where is 'Decolonial Asia'?" (2013).

Chapter 1. Sensing Otherwise

1. The question of literary canonicity is one that is that has never been altogether out of fashion. Joan L. Brown's *Confronting Our Canons: Spanish and Latin American Studies in the 21st Century* (2010) provides an in-depth assessment of the current formation of the Latin American canon, how it has been formed, and how it is taught at major U.S. universities. For a recent study on the question of canonicity in relation to postcolonial theory, see Ankhi Mukherjee's *What is a Classic? Postcolonial Rewriting and Invention of the Canon* (2013). The question of the literary canon has also been rekindled in relation to theoretical engagements between world literature and comparative literature. For some representative and key studies that have propelled this question, see David Damrosch's *What is World Literature?* (2003); Emily Apter's *Against World Literature* (2013); Pascale Casanova's *The World Republic of Letters* (2004); Franco Moretti's *Modern Epic: The World System from Goethe to García Márquez* (1996) and *Graphs, Maps, Trees: Abstract Models for a Literary History* (2005); and Jonathan Culler's *The Literary in Theory* (2007).

2. For an eloquent discussion of the role of revolutionary intellectuals during this decade, see Claudia Gilman's *Entre la pluma y el fusil* (2003), particularly

for a detailed historical context of the involvement of intellectuals pertinent to the present study such as Fernández Retamar, Benedetti, or Dalton in the journal *Casa de las Américas*. In contrast, a study that seeks to trace key moments in Latin American popular culture from the nineteenth century until now, but fails to acknowledge fully the centrality of the 1960s to an understanding of the evolution of popular culture, is Geoffrey Kantaris and Rory O'Brien's edited volume *Latin American Popular Culture* (2013), particularly their introduction to the volume. Stephan Hart's chapter in this volume focuses on Cuba's engagement with popular culture through the ICAIC.

3. See Diana Sorensen's *A Turbulent Decade Remembered: Scenes from the Latin American Sixties* (2007) and Jean Franco's *The Decline and Fall of the Lettered City: Latin America in the Cold War* (2002).

4. See Walter Mignolo's *The Darker Side of Western Modernity* (2011), particularly chapter 3, in which he talks at length about delinking as both a conceptual tool and also a set of actions necessary for decoloniality to have its effect on an experiential and not simply a theoretical level.

5. See Patricio Rodríguez-Plaza's "Crítica, estética y mayorías latinoamericanas" (2005) for further elaboration of these questions.

6. As suggested earlier, a return to aesthetics as a mode of sensing opens up the possibility of discussing how sounds, foods, and textures are linked to aesthetic sensibilities. For a discussion of how decolonial aesthetics is linked to questions of memory, the nation, ancestral memories, coloniality, and taste/food, see Adolfo Albán Achinte's essay "Comida y colonialidad: tensiones entre el proyecto hegemónico moderno y las memorias del paladar" (2010).

7. For a study that critiques both globalization and a return to cosmopolitanism, see Walter Mignolo's "Cosmopolitanism and the De-colonial Option" (2009), particularly on Mignolo's proposal for a decolonial cosmopolitanism.

8. For a prime example of how coloniality of aesthetics operated throughout the nineteenth century in Latin America, see the variety of studies in a variety of art forms present in Paul B. Niell and Stacie G. Widdfield's *Buen Gusto and Classicism in the Visual Cultures of Latin America, 1780–1910* (2013). While the authors in this volume do not necessarily engage with concepts such as coloniality or decoloniality, the studies certainly argue in eloquent ways that the coloniality of aesthetics operates on two levels: that of colonial/state powers, and that of the ingrained coloniality among elite and popular sectors of Latin American populations.

9. My emphasis on the singularity of the 1960s in Latin America as an unprecedented moment of explosion in the arts, and not exclusively in fiction—as the term "the boom" might indicate—is grounded in essays by Benedetti and

Fernández Retamar, which I point out in my introduction, and, more recently, in Claudia Gilman's *Entre la pluma y el fusil* (2003), Hector Amaya's *Screening Cuba* (2010), and Pablo Vila's *The Military Song Movement in Latin America* (2014).

Chapter 2. The Poetics of Sensing: Decolonial Verses in Antipoetry and Conversational Poetry

Author's note: Esta es la reedición de un artículo publicado en *Hispanófila* "Utopian Thinking in Verse: Temporality and Poetic Imaginary in the Poetry of Nicanor Parra, Mario Benedetti, and Roque Dalton" (vol 178, Diciembre 2016). Se puede ingresar a Hispanofila en la red en: http://muse.jhu.edu/ [https://muse.jhu.edu/article/656803.

This is a reprint of parts of an article, "Utopian Thinking in Verse: Temporality and Poetic Imaginary in the Poetry of Nicanor Parra, Mario Benedetti, and Roque Dalton," published in *Hispanófila* (vol 178, December 2016). The article can be accessed electronically through Hispanófila: http://muse.jhu.edu/ [https://muse.jhu.edu/article/656803.

1. As much as I appreciate the efforts in contemporary scholarship to critique a coloniality of aesthetics by proposing decolonial aesthetics as a critical concept, I feel it is important to note that there are two distinct, though complementary, emphases on the decolonial. On the one hand, some efforts primarily focus on alternative spaces of exhibition for performance-based or visual artifacts striving toward a critique of various modalities of coloniality. Prime examples are the *Social Text* periscope dedicated to decolonial aesthetics, or Joaquín Barriendo's essay "Geopolitics as Global Art" (2009). A second point of emphasis deals with popular art forms or food as aesthetic (sensorial) experience, as in the case of Carolina Santamaría Delgado's "El bambuco, los saberes mestizos, y la academia" (2007) or Adolfo Albán Achinte's "Comida y colonialidad" (2010). Yet, only recently have Latin Americanists begun engaging decolonial thinking in relation to literary and cultural analysis, particularly in the case of scholarship produced in English. For some examples of recent scholarship in English seeking to trace an archive of decolonial thinking in relation to literary and cultural practices in the Americas, see Sara Castro Klarén's edited volume *A Companion to Latin American Literatures and Cultures* (2008), Javier Sanjinés's *Embers of the Past* (2013), Yolanda Martínez-San Miguel's *Coloniality of Diasporas* (2014), and Juan G. Ramos and Tara Daly's *Decolonial Approaches to Latin American Literatures and Cultures* (2016).

2. For instance, see Alemany Bay, *Poética coloquial hispanoamericana* (1997); Brotherston, *Latin American Poetry: Origins and Presence* (1975); Fernández Re-

tamar, "Antipoesía y poesía conversacional en Hispanoamérica" (1995); Grossman, *The Antipoetry of Nicanor Parra* (1975); Rowe, *Poets of Contemporary Latin America: History and Inner Life* (2000); Sarabia, *Poetas de la palabra hablada: un estudio de la poesía hispanoamericana contemporánea* (1997).

3. "Roller Coaster" By Nicanor Parra, translated by Miller Williams, from *Poems and Antipoems*, copyright 1967 by Nicanor Parra. Reprinted by permission of New Directions Publishing Corp.

4. A discussion about the relationship between antipoetry and visual art is beyond the scope of this chapter and study.

5. "Changes of Name" By Nicanor Parra, translated by Miller Williams, from *Poems and Antipoems*, copyright 1967 by Nicanor Parra. Reprinted by permission of New Directions Publishing Corp.

6. "Litany of the Little Bourgeois" By Nicanor Parra, translated by James Laughlin, from *Poems and Antipoems*, copyright 1967 by Nicanor Parra. Reprinted by permission of New Directions Publishing Corp.

7. "Test" By Nicanor Parra, translated by Miller Williams, from *Poems and Antipoems*, copyright 1967 by Nicanor Parra. Reprinted by permission of New Directions Publishing Corp.

8. Another instance of Parra's decolonial gestures in his antipoetry is the use of the *cueca* as a musical and poetic form that is quintessential to Chilean identity, but that can be used in anti-traditional ways. An in-depth critique or study of this connection is beyond the scope of this chapter. A clear distinction between musical styles and poetic propositions in relation to Neruda and Parra is present in Mario Rodríguez's "Dos metonimias de Neruda y Parra" (2011).

9. "Porque no debemos olvidar que, a lo largo del proceso hispano-americanizante de nuestro pensamiento, palpita y vive y corre, de manera intermitente pero indestructible, el hilo de sangre indígena, como cifra dominante de nuestro porvenir" (Vallejo, "Una gran reunión latino-americana" 31–32).

10. See Benedetti, "Ernesto Cardenal: Evangelio y revolución" (1972); Fernández Retamar, "Antipoesía y poesía conversacional en Hispanoamérica" (1995); Alemany Bay, *Poética coloquial hispanoamericana* (1997).

11. For some recent reassessments of Dalton's poetry in relation to Salvadorian history and politics, see Adriana P. Álvarez Cruz et al.'s "Por la vía de la poesía" (2015), Leonel Delgado Aburto's "Ironías materiales" (2009), Juana M. Ramos's "La construcción de una po(ética)" (2011), and Mario Vázquez Olivera's "'País mío no existes'" (2005).

12. "Sobre Nuestra Moral Poética"/ "On Our Poetic Moral." In *Poemas Clandestinos/ Clandestine Poems*. Translated by Jack Hirschman. Edited by Barbara Paschke and Eric Weaver. Introduction by Margaret Randall. Willimantic, CT:

Curbstone Press, 1990. Originally published in San Francisco by Solidarity Publications, 1984. Copyright 1986. (82)

13. See María Lugones's "Interseccionalidad y feminismo decolonial" (2012) and "The Coloniality of Gender" (2010) and Rita Segato's "Género y colonialidad" (2011).

14. "Arte Poética 1974"/ "Poetic Art 1974." In *Poemas Clandestinos/ Clandestine Poems.* Translated by Jack Hirschman. Edited by Barbara Paschke and Eric Weaver. Introduction by Margaret Randall. Willimantic, CT: Curbstone Press, 1990. Originally published in San Francisco by Solidarity Publications, 1984. Copyright 1986.

15. For a more in-depth discussion of how these poets saw themselves as descending from Vallejo's poetic lineage perhaps more in spirit than in form or language, see Mario Benedetti's interviews with Roque Dalton and Nicanor Parra in *Los Poetas comunicantes* (1972).

16. See Fernández Retamar, "Antipoesía y poesía conversacional en Hispanoamérica" (1995); Rowe, *Poets of Contemporary Latin America: History and Inner Life* (2000); Brotherston, *Latin American Poetry: Origins and Presence* (1975); Sarabia, *Poetas de la palabra hablada: un estudio de la poesía hispanoamericana contemporánea* (1997); and Alemany Bay, *Poética coloquial hispanoamericana* (1997).

Chapter 3. Decolonial Sounds: Redolent Echoes of *Nueva Canción*

1. For a more detailed assessment of commercial pop music of the period in Chile, see Osvaldo Rodríguez Musso's *La nueva canción chilena* (1988) and Patricia Vilches's "De Violeta Parra a Víctor Jara y Los Prisioneros" (2004).

2. For the usage of "countersong," see Fernando Reyes Matta's "The 'New Song' and Its Confrontation in Latin America" 448.

3. For an article that explores the communal function of *arpilleras* as a modality of feminist resistance and preservation of memory, see Eliana Moya-Raggio's "'Arpilleras'" (1984).

4. The wealth of popular songs, musical styles, notes on instrumentation, and musical arrangements were collected and published after Violeta's death. For a broader account of popular music Violeta collected, see Violeta Parra's *Cantos folklóricos chilenos* (1979).

5. In addition to a renewed interest in exploring musical traditions in Latin America, there is also a growing body of scholarship that also looks at the role of media and modes of dissemination of sound across the region. For a recent exploration of the role of media and sound studies in Latin America, see Ale-

jandra Bronfman and Andrew Grant Wood's *Media, Sound, and Culture in Latin America and the Caribbean* (2012).

6. According to Juan Pablo González (2005), the *tonada* has a 6/8 meter and the *cueca* has a 3/4 meter.

7. For additional information on this period of Violeta's artistic career, see Ericka Kim Verba's "To Paris and Back" (2013). Permission granted by the Fundación Violeta Parra to reprint lyrics from "Cantores que Reflexionan" and "Mazúrquica Modérnica."

8. Hereafter the translations of Violeta Parra's lyrics are mine.

9. For a representation of the political turmoil and factions in Chilean society, please refer to Patricio Guzmán's film trilogy *The Battle of Chile* (1975–1979).

10. The information on Mercedes Sosa's albums was gathered from her official webpage.

11. According to Moore (2006), *Días y flores* was the "first widely disseminated *nueva trova* LP" (156).

12. For particular philosophical inquiries that explore the relationship among listening, music, and history, see Peter Szendy (2007), Jean-Luc Nancy (2007), and Lawrence M. Zbikowski (2013).

Chapter 4. Decolonial Visuality and New Latin American Cinema

1. For in-depth studies that examine the appearance of cinema in Latin America and its relationship to early film aesthetics, see Ana M. López's "'A Train of Shadows': Early Cinema and Modernity in Latin America" (2000); Ana M. López's "The State of Things: New Directions in Latin American Film History (2006); Jorge Finkielman's *The Film Industry in Argentina* (2004); and Flora Süsekind's *Cinematograph of Words: Literature, Technique, and Modernization in Brazil* (1997).

2. Here I am following Nicholas Mirzoeff's *The Right to Look: A Counterhistory of Visuality* (2011), particularly when he writes in the Preface that "visuality and its visualizing history are part of how the 'West' historicizes and distinguishes itself from others" (xiv). Later in the Preface, Mirzoeff adds that he considers visuality "to be both a medium for transmission and dissemination of authority, and a means for the mediation of those subject to that authority" (xv).

3. Unless otherwise noted, translations from Spanish into English are mine.

4. For critical work linking Fanon's work with coloniality, see Catherine Walsh, "Fanon y la pedagogía de-colonial" (2009) and Nelson Maldonado Torres's "On the Coloniality of Being" (2007).

5. For a more updated account of New Latin American Cinema, see Paul A. Schroeder Rodríguez's "After New Latin American Cinema" (2012).

6. In "Estética y ser," Enrique Dussel (1994) points to the ways in which aesthetics has been employed to privilege certain forms of (Eurocentric/Western) knowledge. In a different and more updated articulation of this linkage, Mignolo (2012) also argues for this connection, but goes a step farther by arguing for certain ways in which art can produce and be seen from the perspective of decolonial aesthetics as an option to other existing aesthetic projects.

7. In his work *The Emancipated Spectator* (2011), Rancière argues for the need to emancipate the spectator from ulterior responsibilities or duties. Instead, Rancière argues, "Being a spectator is not some passive condition that we should transform into activity. It is our normal situation. We also learn and teach, act and know, as spectators who all the time link what we see to what we have seen and said, done and dreamed. . . . We do not have to transform spectators into actors, and ignoramuses into scholars. We have to recognize the knowledge at work in the ignoramus and the activity peculiar to the spectator. Every spectator is already an actor in her story; every actor, every man of action, is the spectator of the same story" (17). While I do not agree with the distinction made between a so-called ignoramus and the spectator, Rancière's notion that the spectator is always an active participant and constructs knowledge by making associations or establishing relations between what she or he sees/experiences/senses and her or his prior knowledge is a thought-provoking suggestion to explore more fully elsewhere. For the sake of my overall argument, I cannot engage more fully with this proposition here.

8. For a detailed account of the reception of *Memories of Underdevelopment* in both Cuba and the United States, see Hector Amaya's *Screening Cuba: Film Criticism as Political Performance During the Cold War* 107–124.

9. For a detailed account of the reception of *Lucía* in both Cuba and the United States, see Hector Amaya's *Screening Cuba: Film Criticism as Political Performance During the Cold War* 125–143.

10. For an account of Chilean cinema surrounding Salvador Allende's government, see Camilo D. Trumper's "Social Violence, Political Conflict, and Latin American Film: The Politics of Place in the 'Cinema of Allende'" (2010).

11. For recent critical work on Gleyzer's films, see David William Foster's "Contestando una revolución" (2011), Fernando Martín Peña's "Raymundo Gleyzer (1941–1976): El otro cine militante" (2002), Valeria Manzano's "Combates por la historia" (2004), David M. J. Wood's "Raiding the Archive" (2011), and Mariano Mestman's "Third Cinema/Militant Cinema" (2011).

12. For a more in-depth discussion of decolonial approaches to indigenous filmmaking and media production, see Freya Schiwy's *Indianizing Film: Decolonization, the Andes, and the Question of Technology* (2009).

13. For a recent discussion of the Tlatelolco massacre as a key moment in the long decade of the 1960s, see Diana Sorensen, *A Turbulent Decade Remembered: Scenes from the Latin American Sixties* (2007), Samuel Steinberg's *Photopoetics at Tlatelolco* (2016), and Juan J. Rojo's *Revisiting the Mexican Student Movement of 1968* (2016). In Sorensen's treatment of this tragic episode in Mexican history, and in other instances in her book, she does not engage with Gleyzer's documentary film as a text that provides an almost immediate outsider's perspective on the event.

Chapter 5. Decolonial Aesthetics in Latin America

1. For an example of early reception of the music and poetry of the 1960s, particularly in relation to Nicanor Parra and the poets of his generation, see Roberto Falabella's "Problemas estilísticos del joven compositor en América y en Chile" (1958). For an early American review of Otto Rene Castillo, one of Roque Dalton's contemporaries, and a discussion of whether Castillo's poetry belongs to history rather literature, see Guy Davenport's review "Distant Voices" (1971–1972), particularly his contrast of *low* poetry and *belles lettres* in the case of his high opinion of Octavio Paz. These are just two instances that illustrate my point.

2. For a more detailed articulation of coloniality of power, see Quijano's "Coloniality of Power, Eurocentrism, and Latin America" (2000), Quijano's "Colonialidad del poder y clasificación social" (2007), and Walter D. Mignolo's *Local Histories/Global Designs* (2012 [2000]).

3. Key arguments are presented in Leopoldo Zea's *Colonización y descolonización de la cultura latinoamericana* (1970) and Germán Arciniégas's *Cosas del pueblo: crónicas de la historia vulgar* (1962).

4. See Prebisch's *The Economic Development of Latin America and Its Principal Problems* (1950).

5. Mignolo has employed the term decolonial in a variety of theoretical writings. For his use of the concept, see, for example, his coedited volume with Arturo Escobar, *Globalization and the Decolonial Option* (2010), or his most recent book, *The Darker Side of Western Modernity* (2011). For Mignolo's use of decolonial aesthetics, see his article "Lo nuevo y lo decolonial" (2012). For different perspectives on the concept of the decolonial, see Ramón Grosfoguel's "The Epistemic Decolonial Turn: Beyond Political-Economy Paradigms" (2010) and

Arturo Escobar's "Worlds and Knowledges Otherwise: The Latin American Modernity/Coloniality Research Program" (2010).

6. For a discussion of the domains in the matrix of the coloniality of power, see Quijano (2000).

7. See Salazar Bondy's *La cultura de la dependencia* (1966).

8. See Escobar (2010), Grosfoguel (2010), and Mignolo's "Epistemic Disobedience, Independent Thoughts and Decolonial Freedom" (2009).

9. See Grosfoguel (2010), Quijano (2000), Kusch (1975), Arciniegas (1962), and O'Gorman's *La invención de América* (1986) [1958].

10. For a more detailed analysis of the ontological critique that coloniality of being posits, see Maldonado-Torres's "On the Coloniality of Being: Contributions to the Development of a Concept" (2010).

11. See Maldonado-Torres (2010), Kusch (2010), Kusch (1975), and Lao-Montes's "Decolonial Moves: Trans-locating African Diaspora Spaces" (2007).

12. See Maldonado-Torres (2010), Kusch (2010), and Kusch's *La negación en el pensamiento popular* (1975).

13. See Maldonado-Torres (2010) and Rancière's "The Rationality of Disagreement" (1999).

14. See Fals-Borda's "Casos de imitación intelectual colonialista." (1970) and *Las revoluciones inconclusas en América Latina (1809–1968).* (1970).

15. See Fals-Borda's *Las revoluciones inconclusas en América Latina (1809–1968).* (1970).

WORKS CITED

Achugar, Hugo. "The Book of Poems as a Social Act: Notes toward an Interpretation of Contemporary Hispanic American Poetry." *Marxism and the Interpretation of Culture,* edited by Car Nelson and Lawrence Grossberg, translated by George Yúdice and María Díaz de Achugar, University of Illinois Press, 1988, pp. 651–662.

Albán Achinte, Adolfo. "Comida y colonialidad: tensiones entre el proyecto hegemónico moderno y las memorias del paladar." *Calle 14: Revista de investigación en el campo del arte,* vol. 4, no. 5, 2010, pp. 10–23.

Albright, Daniel. *Panaesthetics: On the Unity and Diversity of the Arts.* Yale University Press, 2014.

Alemany Bay, Carmen. *Poética coloquial hispanoamericana.* Universidad de Alicante, 1997.

Álvarez Cruz, Adriana P., Adam A. Álvarez Calderón, and J. Larissa Soto Villalobos. "'Por la vía de la poesía': La poesía de Roque Dalton y Otto René Castillo en el marco de la segunda mitad del siglo XX en Centroamérica." *Istmo: Revista virtual de estudios literarios y culturales centroamericanos,* no. 29–30, 2015, pp. 1–17.

Amaya, Hector. *Screening Cuba: Film Criticism as Political Performance During the Cold War.* University of Illinois Press, 2010.

Anonymous. "Constitución del Comité de Cineastas de América Latina: 1967–1985." *Hojas de cine: Testimonios y documentos del nuevo cine latinoamericano,* vol. I, edited by Fundación Mexicana de Cineastas, Dirección General de Publicaciones y Medios, Secretaría de Educación Pública, Fundación Mexicana de Cineastas, Universidad Autónoma Metropolitana, 1988, pp. 545–548.

Apter, Emily. *Against World Literature: On the Politics of Untranslatability.* Verso, 2013.

Arciniegas, Germán. *Cosas del pueblo: Crónicas de la historia vulgar*. Editorial Hermes, 1962.

Arellano, Jerónimo. *Magical Realism and the History of Emotions in Latin America*. Bucknell University Press, 2015.

Badiou, Alain. *Handbook of Inaesthetics*. Translated by Alberto Toscano, Stanford University Press, 2005.

Balibar, Étienne. "Toward a Diasporic Citizen? From Nationalism to Cosmopolitics." *The Creolization of Theory*, edited by Françoise Lionnet and Shu-mei Shih, Duke University Press, 2011, pp. 207–225.

Bagú, Sergio, and Humberto Gussoni. *El desarrollo cultural en la liberación de América Latina*. Biblioteca de la Cultura Universitaria, 1967.

Barriendos, Joaquín. "Geopolitics of Global Art: The Reinvention of Latin America as Geo-Aesthetic Region." *The Global Art World: Audiences, Markets, and Museums*, edited by Hans Belting and Andrea Buddensieg, Hatje Cantz, 2009, pp. 98–115.

Barzuna, Guillermo. "Poesía y canto en Hispanoamerica." *Canción hispanoamericana: Entre literatura y folclore*, edited by Guillermo Barzuna, Editorial Nueva Década, 1988, pp. 32–34.

Béhague, Gérard. "Música folklórica de Latinoamérica." *Música foklórica y tradicional de los continentes occcidentales*, edited by Bruno Nettl, translated by Miren Rahm, Alianza Editorial, 1973, pp. 203–228.

Benedetti, Mario. "La canción como instrumento." *Canción hispanoamericana: Entre literatura y folclore*, edited by Guillermo Barzuna, Editorial Nueva Década, 1988, pp. 32–34.

———. "Ernesto Cardenal: Evangelio y revolución." *Los poetas comunicantes*. Biblioteca de Marcha, 1972, pp. 97–124.

———. *Inventario I*. Punto de Lectura, 1999.

———. "Nicanor Parra o el artefacto con laureles." *Los poetas comunicantes*, 1972, pp. 41–64.

———. "Prólogo." *Los poetas comunicantes*, 1972, pp. 7–17.

———. "Subdesarrollo y letras de osadía." *Subdesarrollo y letras de osadía*, Alianza Editorial, 2002, pp. 30–57.

———. "Una hora con Roque Dalton." *Los poetas comunicantes*, 1972, pp. 19–40.

Benmayor, Rina. "La 'Nueva Trova': New Cuban Song." *Latin American Music Review / Revista de Música Latinoamericana*, vol. 2, no. 1, 1981, pp. 11–44.

Bernstein, Jane A. "'Thanks for My Weapons in Battle—My Voice and the Desire to Use It': Women and Protest Music in the Americas." *Women's Voices across Musical Worlds*, edited by Jane A. Bernstein, Northeastern University Press, 2004, pp. 166–186.

Beverly, John. *Latinamericanism after 9/11*. Duke University Press, 2011.

Boff, Leonardo. *Essential Care: An Ethics of Human Care*, translated by Alexandre Guilherme, Baylor University Press, 2008.

Bosteels, Bruno. "Global Aesthetics and its Discontents." *Parallax*, vol. 20, no. 4, 2014, pp. 384–395.

Boym, Svetlana. *The Future of Nostalgia*. Basic Books, 2001.

Bronfman, Alejandra, and Andrew Grant Wood, editors. *Media, Sound, and Culture in Latin America and the Caribbean*. University of Pittsburgh Press, 2012.

Brown, Marshall. *The Tooth That Nibbles at the Soul: Essays on Music and Poetry*. University of Washington Press, 2010.

Brotherston, Gordon. *Latin American Poetry: Origins and Presence*. Cambridge UP, 1975.

Brown, Joan L. *Confronting Our Canons: Spanish and Latin American Studies in the 21st Century*. Bucknell UP, 2010.

Burton, Julianne, and Marta Alvear. "Interview with Humberto Solás: 'Every Point of Arrival is a Point of Departure.'" *Jump Cut: A Review of Contemporary Media*, no. 19, 1978, pp. 32–33.

Caballero, Rufo, editor. *A solas con Solás*. Editorial Letras Cubanas, 1999.

Caetano, Maria do Rosário. *Cineastas Latino-americanos: Entrevistas e filmes*. Estação Libertade, 1997.

Cantata de Chile. Directed by Humberto Solás, ICAIC, 1975.

Cardenal, Ernesto. *Este mundo y otro*. Minima Trotta, 2011.

———. *The Psalms of Struggle and Liberation*. Herder and Herder, 1971.

———. *Salmos*. Ediciones Lohlé, 1969.

Carrasco, Eduardo. "Eduardo Carrasco: Miembro y fundador de Quilapayún y profesor de filosofía en la Universidad." *El Chile de Víctor Jara*, edited by Omar Jurado and Juan Miguel Morales, LOM Ediciones, 2003, pp. 53–55.

Casanova, Pascale. *The World Republic of Letters*, translated by M. B. Debevoise. Harvard University Press, 2004.

Castillo, Patricio. "Patricio Castillo: Miembro y fundador de Quilapayún y colaborador musical de Víctor Jara." *El Chile de Víctor Jara*, edited by Omar Jurado and Juan Miguel Morales, LOM Ediciones, 2003, pp. 56–58.

Castro-Klarén, Sara. *The Narrow Pass of Our Nerves: Writing, Coloniality and Postcolonial Theory*. Iberoamericana, 2011.

Castro-Klarén, Sara, and Christian Fernández. *Inca Garcilaso and Contemporary World-Making*. University of Pittsburgh Press, 2016.

Chanan, Michael. Introduction. *Twenty-Five Years of the New Latin American Cinema*, edited by Michael Chanan, British Film Institute, 1983, pp. 2–8.

Cheah, Pheng. *Spectrality of Nationality: Passages of Freedom from Kant to Postcolonial Literatures of Liberation*. Columbia University Press, 2003.

Chejfec, Sergio. "A Few Notes on Constructed Worlds: The Contradictory Legacy of Past Decades." *The Ethics of Latin American Literary Criticism: Reading Otherwise*, edited by Erin Graff Zivin, translated by Heather Cleary, Palgrave MacMillan, 2007, pp. 105–114.

Clayton, Michelle. *Poetry in Pieces: César Vallejo and Lyric Modernity*. University of California Press, 2011.

Coleman, Alexander. Introduction. *The Antipoetry of Nicanor Parra*, by Edith Grossman, New York University Press, 1975, pp. xiii–xvi.

Croce, Benedetto. *The Aesthetic as the Science of Expression and of the Linguistic in General*. Translated by Colin Lyas, Cambridge University Press, 1992.

———. *Breviary of Aesthetics*. Introduction by Remo Bodei, translated by Hiroko Fudemoto, University of Toronto Press, 2007.

Culler, Jonathan. *The Literary in Theory*. Stanford University Press, 2007.

Dalton, Roque. *Poemas Clandestinos / Clandestine Poems*. Introduction by Margaret Randall, translation by Jack Hirschman, Solidarity Publications, 1984.

———. *Poetry and Militancy in Latin America*. Curbstone Press, 1981.

———. *Taberna y otros lugares*. Ocean Sur, 2007.

Damrosch, David. *What is World Literature?* Princeton University Press, 2003.

Davenport, Guy. "Distant Voices." *The Hudson Review*, vol. 24, no. 4, 1971–1972, pp. 696–701.

Decoloniality London. https://www.decolonialitylondon.org/. Accessed 15 April 2016.

DeHay, Terry. "The Kingdom of God on Earth: Ernesto Cardenal's *Salmos*." *Postcolonial Literature and the Biblical Call for Justice*, edited by Susan VanZanten Gallagher, University of Mississippi Press, 1994, pp. 48–59.

Delgado Aburto, Leonel. "Ironías materiales: La cultura centroamericana a partir de las poeticas postvanguardistas de Paz, Coronel y Dalton." *Hipertexto* vol. 9, 2009, pp. 106–114.

Delgado Linares, Carlos. *El movimiento de la nueva trova cubana y la trova tradicional*. Ediciones Namar, 1996.

Díaz Pérez, Clara. *Hay quien precisa . . . Silvio Rodríguez*. Editorial Música Mundana, 1995.

Dussel, Enrique. "Estética y ser." *Historia de la filosofía y filosofía de la liberación*, Editorial Nueva América, 1994, pp. 289–296.

———. *Philosophy of Liberation*. Translated by Aquilina Martinez and Christine Morkovsky, Orbis Books, 1985.

———. "Philosophy of Liberation, the Postmodern Debate, and Latin American Studies." *Coloniality at Large: Latin America and the Postcolonial Debate*, edited by Mabel Moraña, Enrique Dussel, and Carlos Jáuregui, translated by Rosalía Bermúdez, Duke University Press, 2008, pp. 335–349.

Eidsheim, Nina Sun. *Sensing Sound: Signing and Listening as Vibrational Practice.* Duke University Press, 2015.

Escobar, Arturo. "Worlds and Knowledges Otherwise: The Latin American Modernity/Coloniality Research Program." *Globalization and the Decolonial Option*, edited by Walter D. Mignolo and Arturo Escobar, Routledge, 2010, pp. 33–64.

Espada, Martín. "Poetry Like Bread: Poetry of the Political Imagination." *Zapata's Disciple: Essays*. South End Press, 1998, pp. 99–106.

Falabella, Roberto. "Problema estilístico del joven compositor en América y en Chile. Segunda Parte." *Revista Musical Chilena*, vol. 12, no. 58, 1958, pp. 77–93.

Fals-Borda, Orlando. "Casos de imitación intelectual colonialista." *Ciencia propia y colonialismo intelectual*. Editorial Nuestro Tiempo, 1970.

———. *Las revoluciones inconclusas en América Latina (1809–1968)*. Siglo XXI, 1970.

Fanon, Frantz. *The Wretched of the Earth*. Translated by Richard Philcox, Grove Press, 2004.

Fernández Retamar, Roberto. "Antipoesía y poesía conversacional en Hispanoamérica." *Para una teoría de la literatura hispanoamericana*, Instituto Caro y Cuervo, 1995, pp. 159–176.

———. "Caliban: Notes Toward a Discussion of Culture in Our America." *Caliban and Other Essays*, translated by Edward Baker, University of Minnesota Press, 1989, pp. 3–45.

———. "La contribución de las literaturas de la América Latina a la literatura universal del siglo XX." *Revista de crítica literaria latinoamericana*, vol. 2, no. 4, 1976, pp. 17–29.

———. "Prologue to Ernesto Cardenal." *Caliban and Other Essays*, pp. 100–110.

Finkielman, Jorge. *The Film Industry in Argentina: An Illustrated Cultural History*. McFarland & Co., Inc., 2004.

Franco, Jean. *The Decline and Fall of the Lettered City: Latin America in the Cold War*. Harvard University Press, 2002.

Foley, Helene P. *Reimagining Greek Tragedy on the American Stage*. University of California Press, 2012.

Foster, David William. "Contestando una revolución: La revolución congelada de Raymundo Gleyzer." *Revista de crítica literaria latinoamericana*, vol. 37, no. 73, 2011, pp. 173–181.

Freire, Paolo. *Pedagogy of the Oppressed.* Translated by Myra Bergman Ramos, Herder and Herder, 1970.

Fuse Magazine. Special Issue: States of Coloniality, 36–4 Fall 2013, e-artexte.ca/25209/1/FUSE_36–4.pdf. Accessed 15 April 2016.

Gabriel, Teshome H. *Third Cinema in the Third World.* UMI Research Press, 1982.

Gaztambide-Fernández, Rubén. "Decolonial Options and Artistic/AestheSic Entanglements: An Interview with Walter Mignolo." *Decolonization: Indigeneity, Education & Society,* vol. 3, no. 1, 2014, pp. 196–212.

Gilman, Claudia. *Entre la pluma y el fusil: Debates y dilemas del escritor revolucionario en América Latina.* Siglo Veintiuno Editores, 2003.

Gleyzer, Rayumundo. *Raymundo Gleyzer: Documentos/testimonios.* Cinemateca Uruguaya, 1985.

Glissant, Édouard. *Poetic Intention.* Translated by Nathalie Stephens, Nightboat Books, 2010.

———. *Poetics of Relation.* Translated by Betsy Wing, The University of Michigan Press, 1997.

González, Juan Pablo. "The Making of a Social History of Popular Music in Chile: Problems, Methods, and Results." *Latin American Music Review / Revista de Música Latinoamericana,* vol. 26, no. 2, 2005, pp. 248–272.

González, Ruben E., and Delilah Dotremon. "Nicanor Parra: The Physicist Who Made a Significant Contribution to the Literary World." *Hipertexto,* no. 19, 2014, pp. 63–82.

Grosfoguel, Ramón. "The Epistemic Decolonial Turn: Beyond Political-Economy Paradigms." *Globalization and the Decolonial Option,* edited by Walter D. Mignolo and Arturo Escobar, Routledge, 2010, pp. 65–77.

Grossman, Edith. *The Antipoetry of Nicanor Parra.* New York University Press, 1975.

Grzinic, Marina. "[Estéticas] decoloniales como / en / a la frontera." *Estéticas y opción decolonial,* edited by Walter Mignolo and Pedro Pablo Gómez, Universidad Distrital Francisco José de Caldas, 2012, pp. 115–126.

Guattari, Félix. *Chaosmosis: An Ethico-Aesthetic Paradigm,* Translated by Paul Bains and Julian Pefanis, Indiana University Press, 1995.

Halberstam, Judith. *The Queer Art of Failure.* Duke University Press, 2011.

Handelsman, Michael. "Género, raza y nación en la literature ecuatoriana: Hacia una lectura decolonial." *Guaraguao: Revista de Cultura Latinoamericana,* no. 38, 2011.

Hart, Stephen M. "Latin American Poetry." *A Companion to Latin American Literature and Culture,* edited by Sara Castro-Klarén, Blackwell, 2008, pp. 426–441.

Hegel, Georg W. F. *Introductory Lectures on Aesthetics.* Translated by Bernard Bosanquet, edited and introduction by Michael Inwood, Penguin, 2004.

Heidegger, Martin. "Language." *Poetry, Language, Thought,* translated and introduction by Albert Hofstadter, Harper Perennial, 2001, pp. 185–208.

Hopkins, Robert. "Senses and Art." *A Companion to Aesthetics,* 2nd ed., edited by Stephen Davies et al., Wiley-Blackwell, 2009, pp. 530–534.

Howes, David, and Constance Classen. *Ways of Sensing: Understanding the Senses in Society,* Routledge, 2013.

Hoyos, Héctor. *Beyond Bolaño: The Global Latin American Novel.* Columbia University Press, 2015.

Ibáñez Langlois, José Miguel. *Poesía chilena y latinoamericana actual.* Editorial Nascimento, 1975.

Kerr, Lucille, and Alejandro Herrero-Olaizola, editors. *Teaching the Latin American Boom.* The Modern Language Association of America, 2015.

Jara, Joan. *An Unfinished Song: The Life of Victor Jara.* Ticknor and Fields, 1984.

Jara, Víctor. *Manifiesto.* Warner Music Argentina, 2001.

Jay, Martin. "Conclusion: A Parting Glance: Empire and Visuality." *Empires of Vision: A Reader,* edited by Martin Jay and Sumathi Ramaswamy, Duke University Press, 2014, pp. 609–620.

Joncus, Berta. "Private Music in Public Spheres: Chamber Cantata and Song." *The Cambridge History of Eighteenth-Century Music,* edited by Simon P. Keefe, Cambridge University Press, 2009, pp. 513–540.

Kantaris, Geoffrey and Rory O'Brien, editors. *Latin American Popular Culture: Politics, Media, Affect.* Tamesis, 2013.

Kramer, Lawrence. *Interpreting Music.* University of California Press, 2011.

Kunheim, Jill S. *Beyond the Page: Poetry and Performance in Spanish America.* The University of Arizona Press, 2014.

Kusch, Rodolfo. *Indigenous and Popular Thinking in América.* Introduction by Walter D. Mignolo, translated by María Lugones and Joshua M. Price, Duke University Press, 2010.

———. *La negación en el pensamiento popular.* Editorial Cimarrón, 1975.

———. "Planteo de un arte americano." *Obras Completas,* vol. 4, Editorial Fundación Ross, 1998, pp. 775–778.

La hora de los hornos: Notas y testimonios sobre el neocolonialismo, la violencia y la liberación. Directed by Fernando Solanas, written by Octavio Getino and Fernando Solanas, Cinema Tercio Mundo; Grupo Cine Liberación, 1968.

Lambuley Alférez, Edgar Ricardo. "Sonoridades otras: Músicas de resistencia." *Estéticas y opción decolonial,* edited by Walter Mignolo and Pedro Pablo Gómez, Universidad Distrital Francisco José de Caldas, 2012, pp. 263–278.

Lao-Montes, Agustín. "Decolonial Moves: Trans-locating African Diaspora Spaces." *Cultural Studies,* vol. 21, nos. 2–3, 2007, pp. 309–338.

Lee, Vivian. "Decolonial Moments in Hong Kong Cinema." *Social Text: Periscope,* July 15, 2013, https://socialtextjournal.org/periscope_article/decolonial-moments-in-hong-kong-cinema/. Accessed 15 Feb. 2014.

Legrás, Horacio. "The Rule of Impurity: Decolonial Theory and the Question of Literature." *Decolonial Approaches to Latin American Literatures and Cultures,* edited by Juan G. Ramos and Tara Daly, Palgrave, 2016, pp. 19–36.

Lerzundi, Patricio. "From *In Defense of Antipoetry: An Interview with Nicanor Parra.*" Translated by Tom J. Lewis, *Review,* vol. 38, no. 2, 2005, pp. 151–155.

Lindstrom, Naomi. "Las décimas de Violeta Parra: Versos autobiográficos y crítica cultural." *Discurso femenino actual,* edited by Adelaida López de Martínez, Editorial de la Universidad de Puerto Rico, 1995, pp. 323–338.

Lionnet, Françoise, and Shu-mei Shih. Introduction: The Creolization of Theory. *The Creolization of Theory,* edited by Françoise Lionnet and Shu-mei Shih, Duke University Press, 2011, pp. 1–33.

Lippman, Edward. *A History of Western Musical Aesthetics.* University of Nebraska Press, 1992.

López, Ana M. "'A Train of Shadows': Early Cinema and Modernity in Latin America." *Through the Kaleidoscope: The Experience of Modernity in Latin America,* introduced and edited by Vivian Schelling, Verso, 2000, pp. 148–76.

———. "The State of Things: New Directions in Latin American Film History." *The Americas,* vol. 63, no. 2, 2006, pp. 197–203.

López, Silvia L. "Beyond the Visible, the Audible and the Sayable: Rethinking Aesthetic Modernity in Latin America." *Parallax,* vol. 20, no. 4, 2014, pp. 293–302.

Lucía. Directed by Humberto Solás. ICAIC, 1968; Mr. Bongo Films, 2010.

Lugones, María. "The Coloniality of Gender." *Globalization and the Decolonial Option,* edited by Walter D. Mignolo and Arturo Escobar, Routledge, 2010, pp. 369–390.

———. "Interseccionalidad y feminismo decolonial." *Lugares descoloniales: Espacios de intervención en las Américas,* edited by Ramón Grosfoguel y Roberto Almanza Hernández, Pontificia Universidad Javeriana, 2012, pp. 119–124.

Maldonado-Torres, Nelson. "On the Coloniality of Being." *Cultural Studies,* vol. 21, no. 2, 2007, pp. 240–270.

———. "On the Coloniality of Being: Contributions to the Development of a Concept." *Globalization and the Decolonial Option,* edited by Walter D. Mignolo and Arturo Escobar, Routledge, 2010, pp. 94–124.

Manns, Patricio. "The Problems of the Text in Nueva Cancion." Translated by

Catherine Boyle and Mike Gonzalez, *Popular Music,* vol. 6, no. 2, 1987, pp. 191–195.

Manzano, Valeria. "Combates por la historia: Interpretaciones de la historia del movimiento obrero en el cine militante argentino de los 1970s." *Film & History,* vol. 34, no. 2, 2004, pp. 46–57.

Mara, Oscar C., and Vicente Zito Lema, editors. *Homenaje a Víctor Jara.* Comisión de Homenaje a Víctor Jara, 1974.

Martínez Andrade, Luis. *Social Contradictions and Awakened Dreams in Latin America.* Translated by Antonio Carmona Báez, foreword by Michael Löwy, Pluto Press, 2015.

Martínez-San Miguel, Yolanda. *Coloniality of Diasporas: Rethinking Intra-Colonial Migrations in a Pan-Caribbean Context.* Palgrave, 2014.

Memmi, Albert. *Decolonization and the Decolonized.* Translated by Robert Bononno, University of Minnesota Press, 2006.

Memorias del subdesarrollo. Directed by Tomás Gutiérrez Alea, ICAIC, 1968; Mr. Bongo Films, 2008.

Mercedes Sosa: Sitio no oficial. www.mercedessosa.com.ar/marcosmasterm.htm. Accessed 13 Aug. 2014.

Mestman, Mariano. "Third Cinema/Militant Cinema: At the Origins of the Argentinian Experience (1968–1971)." *Third Text,* vol. 25, no. 1, 2011, pp. 29–40.

Mexico, the Frozen Revolution. Directed by Raymundo Gleyzer. 1971. Macondo Cine, Gleyzer Films, Facets Video, 2007.

Mignolo, Walter D. "Aisthesis decolonial." *Calle 14,* vol. 4, no. 4, 2010, pp. 10–25.

———. "Cosmopolitanism and the De-Colonial Option." *Studies in Philosophy and Education,* vol. 29, no. 2, 2009, pp. 111–127.

———. *The Darker Side of Western Modernity: Global Futures, Decolonial Options.* Durham: Duke University Press, 2011.

———. "Epistemic Disobedience, Independent Thought and Decolonial Freedom." *Theory, Culture, and Society,* vol. 26, nos. 7–8, 2009, pp. 159–181.

———. "Introduction: Coloniality of Power and De-colonial Thinking." *Globalization and the Decolonial Option,* edited by Walter D. Mignolo and Arturo Escobar, Routledge, 2010, pp. 1–21.

———. *Local Histories/Global Designs: Coloniality, Subaltern Knowledges, and Border Thinking,* 2nd ed. Princeton University Press, 2012.

———. "Lo nuevo y lo decolonial." *Estéticas y opción decolonial,* edited by Walter Mignolo and Pedro Pablo Gómez, Universidad Distrital Francisco José de Caldas, 2012, pp. 21–48.

Mignolo, Walter and Roland Vázquez. "Decolonial AestheSis: Colonial Wounds/ Decolonial Healings." *Social Text: Periscope,* July 15, 2013. https://socialtextjournal.org/periscope_article/decolonial-aesthesis-colonial-woundsdecolonial-healings/. Accessed 15 April 2016.

Mirzoeff, Nicholas. *The Right to Look: A Counterhistory of Visuality*. Duke University Press, 2011.

Moore, Robyn D. "Transformations in *Nueva Trova*." *Music and Revolution: Cultural Change in Socialist Cuba*. University of California Press, 2006, pp. 135–169.

Moraña, Mabel. *Churata postcolonial*. CELAP/Latinoamericana Editores, 2015.

———. "Postscriptum: Decolonial Scenarios and Alternative Thinking: Critical and Theoretical Explorations." *Decolonial Approaches to Latin American Literatures and Cultures,* edited by Juan G. Ramos and Tara Daly, Palgrave, 2016, pp. 215–224.

Moretti, Franco. *Graphs, Maps, Trees: Abstract Models for a Literary History*. Verso, 2005.

———. *Modern Epic: The World System from Goethe to García Márquez*. Verso, 1996.

Morris, Nancy. "Canto porque es necesario cantar: The New Song Movement in Chile, 1973–1983." *Latin American Research Review,* vol. 21, no. 2, 1986, pp. 117–136.

Moya-Raggio, Eliana. "'Arpilleras': Chilean Culture of Resistance." *Feminist Studies,* vol. 10, no. 2, 1984, pp. 277–290.

Mukherjee, Ankhi. *What is a Classic? Postcolonial Rewriting and Invention of the Canon*. Stanford University Press, 2014.

Nancy, Jean-Luc. "Art, a Fragment." *The Sense of the World,* translated by Jeffrey S. Librett, University of Minnesota Press, 1997, pp. 123–139.

———. *Listening.* Translated by Charlotte Mandell, Fordham University Press, 2007.

———. *The Muses*. Translated by Peggy Kamuf, Stanford University Press, 1996.

Nandorfy, Martha. "The Right to Live in Peace: Freedom and Social Justice in the Songs of Violeta Parra and Víctor Jara." *Rebel Musics: Human Rights, Resistant Sounds, and the Politics of Music Making,* edited by Daniel Fischlin and Ajay Heble, Black Rose Books, 2003, pp. 172–209.

Nettl, Bruno. "Músicas folklóricas y tribales en su entorno cultural." *Música foklórica y tradicional de los continentes occcidentales,* edited by Bruno Nettl, translated by Miren Rahm, Alianza Editorial, 1973, pp. 11–24.

Niell, Paul B., and Stacie G. Widdfield, editors. *Buen Gusto and Classicism in the Visual Cultures of Latin America, 1780–1910*. University of New Mexico Press, 2013.

O'Gorman, Edmundo. *La invención de América: Investigación acerca de la es-*

tructura histórica del nuevo mundo y del sentido del devenir. Fondo de Cultura Económica, 1986.

Osorio Fernández, Javier. "Canto para una semilla: Luis Advis, Violeta Parra y la modernización de la música popular chilena." *Revista musical chilena,* vol. 60, no. 25, 2006, pp. 34–43.

Ostojić, Tanja. "Cruzando fronteras." *Estéticas y opción decolonial,* edited by Walter Mignolo and Pedro Pablo Gómez, Universidad Distrital Francisco José de Caldas, 2012, pp. 103–114.

Page, Joanna. "Introduction: Fiction, Documentary, and Cultural Change in Latin America." *Visual Synergies in Fiction and Documentary Film from Latin America,* edited by Miriam Haddu and Joanna Page, Palgrave MacMillan, 2009, pp. 3–13.

Parra, Isabel. "Isabel Parra: Cantautora, hija de Violeta Parra." *El Chile de Víctor Jara,* edited by Omar Jurado and Juan Miguel Morales, LOM Ediciones, 2003, pp. 47–50.

Parra, Nicanor. *Obra gruesa.* Editorial Universitaria, 1969.

———. *Poems and Antipoems.* Edited by Miller Williams, New Directions, 1967.

Parra, Violeta. *Cantos folklóricos chilenos.* Editorial Nascimento, 1979.

———. *Gracias a la vida y otras canciones.* Edited by Mario Benedetti, Editora Espasa Calpe, 1996.

———. *Las últimas composiciones de. . . .* Warner, 2011.

Party, Daniel. "Beyond 'Protest Song': Popular Music in Pinochet's Chile (1973–1990)." *Music and Dictatorship in Europe and Latin America,* edited by Roberto Illiano and Massimiliano Sala Turnhout, Brepols, 2009, pp. 671–684.

Peña, Fernando Martín. "Raymundo Gleyzer (1941–1976): El otro cine militante." *Studies in Latin American Popular Culture,* no. 21, 2002, pp. 105–118.

Pérez, Alberto Julián. *Revolución poética y modernidad periférica: Ensayos de poesía hispanoamericana.* Corregidor, 2009.

Prebisch, Raul. *The Economic Development of Latin America and Its Principal Problems.* United Nations, Department of Economic Affairs, Economic Commission for Latin America, 1950.

Price, Rachel. *The Object of the Atlantic: Concrete Aesthetics in Cuba, Brazil, and Spain, 1868–1968.* Northwestern University Press, 2014.

Quijano, Anibal. "Colonialidad del poder y clasificación social." *El giro decolonial: Reflexiones para una diversidad epistémica más allá del capitalismo global,* Siglo del Hombre Editores, Universidad Central, Pontificia Universidad Javeriana, 2007, pp. 93–126.

———. "Coloniality of Power, Eurocentrism, and Latin America." *Nepantla: Views from the South,* vol. 1, no. 3, 2000, pp. 533–580.

Rama, Angel. *The Lettered City.* Edited and translated by John Charles Chasteen, Duke University Press, 1996.

Ramírez, Mario Teodoro. "La estética." *El pensamiento filosófico latinoamericano, del Caribe y "latino" (1300–2000): Historia, corrientes, temas, filósofos,* edited by Enrique Dussel, Eduardo Mendieta, and Carmen Bohórquez, Siglo XXI Editores, 2011, pp. 542–552.

Ramos, Juan G., and Tara Daly, editors. *Decolonial Approaches to Latin American Literatures and Cultures.* Palgrave, 2016.

Ramos, Juana M. "La construcción de una po(ética): Desterritorialización, colectivización y politización del discurso daltoniano." *Revista Surco Sur,* vol. 2, no. 4, 2011, pp. 61–65.

Rancière, Jacques. *Aesthetics and Its Discontents.* Translated by Steve Corcoran, Polity, 2009.

———. "Aesthetics, Inaesethetics, Anti-aesthetics." *Think Again: Alain Badiou and the Future of Philosophy,* edited by Peter Hallward, Continuum, 2004, pp. 219–231.

———. *Aisthesis: Scenes from the Aesthetic Regime of Art.* Translated by Zakir Paul, Verso, 2013.

———. *The Emancipated Spectator.* Translated by Gregory Elliott, Verso, 2011.

———. "The Future of the Image." *The Future of the Image.* Translated by Gregory Elliott, Verso, 2009, pp. 1–31.

———. "The Rationality of Disagreement." *Disagreement: Politics and Philosophy.* Translated by Julie Rose, University of Minnesota Press, 1999, pp. 43–60.

———. *The Politics of Aesthetics.* Translated by Gabriel Rockhill, Bloomsbury, 2013.

Randall, Margaret. "Pensando en Roque/ Thinking about Roque." *Poemas Clandestinos/ Clandestine Poems.* By Roque Dalton. Translated by Jack Hirschman, Solidarity Publications, 1984, pp. I–xii.

Raul Encina, T., and H. Rodrigo Fuenzalida, editors. *Víctor Jara: Testimonio de un artista.* CERET (Centro de Recopilación y Testimonio), 1987.

Raymundo: La lucha de toda una generación de cineastas revolucionarios. Directed by Ernesto Ardito, Virna Molina, et al., Filmraymundo, 2004.

Reyes Matta, Fernando. "The 'New Song' and Its Confrontation in Latin America." *Marxism and the Interpretation of Culture,* edited by Car Nelson and Lawrence Grossberg, translated by George Yúdice and María Díaz de Achugar, University of Illinois Press, 1988, pp. 447–460.

Rodó, José Enrique. *Ariel.* Translated by Margaret Sayers Paden, University of Texas Press, 1988.

Rodríguez, Mario. "Dos metonimias de Neruda y Parra: El bolero y la cueca." *Revista chilena de literature*, no. 79, 2011, pp. 145–154.

Rodríguez, Silvio. *Días y flores*. Sony/BMG International, 1999 [1975].

Rodríguez Musso, Osvaldo. *La nueva canción chilena: Continuidad y reflejo*. Ediciones Casa de las Américas, 1988.

Rodríguez-Plaza, Patricio. "Crítica, estética y mayorías latinoamericanas." *Aisthesis: Revista Chilena de Investigaciones Estéticas*, no. 38, 2005, pp. 99–102.

Rojas-Sotelo, Miguel. "Decolonizing Aesthetics." *Encyclopedia of Aesthetics*, vol. 2, edited by Michael Kelly, Oxford University Press, 2014, pp. 301–304.

Rojas-Sotelo, Miguel, and Raúl Moarquech Ferrera-Balanquet. "Decolonial Aesthetics: Collective Creative Practice in Process." *Idea: Artă + societate*, vol. 39, 2011. http://idea.ro/revista/?q=en/node/41&articol=718. Accessed 15 April 2016.

Rojo, Juan J. *Revisiting the Mexican Student Movement of 1968: Shifting Perspectives in Literature and Culture since Tlatelolco*. Palgrave, 2016.

Rostagno, Irene. "*The Plumed Horn/El Corno Emplumado*: The Spell of Cuba in the 1960s." *Searching for Recognition: The Promotion of Literature in the United States*, by Irene Rostagno, Greenwood Press, 1997, pp. 59–87.

Rowe, William. *Poets of Contemporary Latin America: History and Inner Life*. Oxford University Press, 2000.

Sadlier, Darlene J. "Introduction: A Short History of Film Melodrama in Latin America." *Latin American Melodrama: Passion, Pathos, and Entertainment*, edited by Darlene J. Sadlier, University of Illinois Press, 2009, pp. 1–18.

Salazar Bondy, Augusto. *La cultura de la dependencia*. Instituto de Estudios Peruanos, 1966.

Saldívar, José David. *Trans-Americanity: Subaltern Modernities, Global Coloniality, and the Cultures of Greater Mexico*. Duke University Press, 2012.

Sanjinés C., Javier. *Embers of the Past: Essays in Times of Decolonization*. Duke University Press, 2013.

Santamaría Delgado, Carolina. "El bambuco, los saberes mestizos y la academia: Un análisis histórico de la persistencia de la colonialidad en los estudios musicales latinoamericanos." *Latin American Music Review*, vol. 28, no. 1, 2007, pp. 1–23.

Santana de Kiguel, Delia Elena. *Latinoamérica: Singular aventura de sus danzas*. Lumen, 2007.

Sarabia, Rosa. *Poetas de la palabra hablada: Un estudio de la poesía hispanoamericana contemporánea*. Tamesis, 1997.

Sarmiento, Domingo Faustino. *Facundo, or, Civilization and Barbarism*. Translated by Mary Mann, Penguin, 1998.

Sayres, Sohnya, et al. Introduction. *The 60s Without Apology*, edited by Sohnya Sayres, Anders Stephanson, Stanley Aronowitz, and Fredric Jameson, University of Minnesota Press, 1984, pp. 1–9.

Schiwy, Freya. *Indianizing Film: Decolonization, the Andes, and the Question of Technology*. Rutgers University Press, 2009.

Schnabel, Tom. "Mercedes Sosa." *Rhythm Planet: The Great World Music Makers*, by Tom Schnabel, Universe Publishing, 1998, pp. 130–133.

Schroeder Rodríguez, Paul A. "After New Latin American Cinema." *Cinema Journal*, vol. 51, no. 2, 2012, pp. 87–112.

Segato, Rita Laura. "Género y colonialidad: En busca de claves de lectura y de un vocabulario estratégioc descolonial." *Feminismos y postcolonialidad: Descolonizando el feminism de y en América Latina*, edited by Karina Bidaseca and Laura Vazquez Laba, Ediciones Godot, 2011, pp. 17–47.

Shih, Shu-mei. "Relation as Comparison." *Comparison: Theories, Approaches, Uses*, edited by Rita Felski and Susan Stanford Friedman, The Johns Hopkins University Press, 2013, pp. 79–98.

Siskind, Mariano. *Cosmopolitan Desires: Global Modernity and Literature in Latin America*. Northwestern University Press, 2014.

Smith, Mark M. *Sensing the Past: Seeing, Hearing, Smelling, Tasting, and Touching in History*. University of California Press, 2008.

Solanas, Fernando, and Octavio Getino. "Primera declaración del grupo cine liberación." *Cine, cultura y descolonización*, by Fernando Solanas and Octavio Getino. Siglo veintiuno, 1973, pp. 9–10.

———. "Toward a Third Cinema." *Twenty-Five Years of the New Latin American Cinema*, edited by Michael Chanan, British Film Institute, 1983, pp. 17–27.

Sommer, Doris. *The Work of Art in the World: Civic Agency and Public Humanities*. Duke University Press, 2014.

Sorensen, Diana. *A Turbulent Decade Remembered: Scenes from the Latin American Sixties*. Stanford University Press, 2007.

Sosa, Mercedes. *Cantata sudamericana*. Polygram, 1996 [1972].

Steinberg, Samuel. *Photopoetics at Tlatelolco: Afterimages of Mexico, 1968*. The University of Texas Press, 2016.

Süsekind, Flora. *Cinematograph of Words: Literature, Technique, and Modernization in Brazil*. Stanford University Press, 1997.

Szendy, Peter. *Listen: A History of Our Ears*. Translated by Charlotte Mandell, Fordham University Press, 2007.

Tichindeleanu, Ovidiu. "Europe: Potential Paths of Liberation." *Social Text: Periscope*, July 15, 2013. https://socialtextjournal.org/periscope_article/decolonial-aesthesis-in-eastern-europe-potential-paths-of-liberation/. Accessed 15 Feb. 2014

Tlostanova, Madina. "La aesthesis trans-moderna en la zona fronteriza eurasiática y el anti-sublime decolonial." *Calle 14: Revista de Investigación en el Campo del Arte,* vol. 5, no. 6, 2011, pp. 10–31.

Tlostanova, Madina V., and Walter D. Mignolo. *Learning to Unlearn: Decolonial Reflections from Eurasia and the Americas.* Ohio State University Press, 2012.

Torres Alvarado, Rodrigo. "Singing Difference: Violeta Parra and Chilean Song." *A Latin America Music Reader: Views from the South,* edited by Javier F. León and Helena Simonett, University of Illinois Press, 2016, pp. 258–278.

Trumper, Camilo D. "Social Violence, Political Conflict, and Latin American Film: The Politics of Place in the 'Cinema of Allende.'" *Radical History Review,* no. 106, 2010, pp. 109–136.

Truong, Hong-An, Nayuong Aimee Kwon, and Guo-Jin Hong. "What/Where is 'Decolonial Asia'?" *Social Text: Periscope,* July 15, 2013. https://socialtextjournal.org/periscope_article/whatwhere-is-decolonial-asia/. Accessed 15 Feb. 2014.

Vallejo, César. "Una gran reunión latino-americana." *Literatura y arte: Textos escogidos,* by César Vallejo, Ediciones del Mediodía, 1966, 29–32.

———. "Poesía nueva." *Literatura y arte,* pp. 11–13.

Vallegas, Alejandro A. "Fecund Undercurrents: On the Aesthetic Dimension of Latin American and Decolonial Thought." *Latin American Philosophy: From Identity to Radical Exteriority,* by Alejandro A. Vallegas, Indiana University Press, 2014, pp. 196–217.

Vázquez Olivera, Mario. "'País mío no existes': Apuntes sobre Roque Dalton y la historiografía contemporánea de El Salvador." *Istmo: Revista Virtual de Estudios Literarios y Culturales Centroamericanos,* no. 11, 2005, n.p.

Verba, Ericka Kim. "To Paris and Back: Violeta Parra's Transnational Performance of Authenticity. *The Americas,* vol. 70, no. 2, 2013, pp. 269–302.

Vila, Pablo. Introduction." *The Militant Song Movement in Latin America: Chile, Uruguay, and Argentina,* edited by Pablo Vila, Lexington Books, 2014, pp. 1–17.

Vilches, Patricia. "De Violeta Parra a Víctor Jara y Los Prisioneros: Recuperación de la memoria colectiva e identidad cultural a través de la música comprometida." *Latin American Music Review/ Revista de Música Latinoamericana,* vol. 25, no. 2, 2004, pp. 195–215.

Viola chilensis. Directed by Luis R. Vera. Alerce, La Otra Música, 2006.

Wald, Elijah. "Mercedes Sosa." *Global Minstrels: Voices of World Music,* by Elijah Wald, Routledge, 2007, pp. 101–103.

Walsh, Catherine. "Fanon y la pedagogía de-colonial," *Revista Nuevamérica/Novamérica*, no. 122, 2009. http://www.novamerica.org.br/Revista_digital/L0122/rev_opiniao.asp. Accessed 15 Sept. 2014.

Welsch, Wolfgang. "Aesthetics Beyond Aesthetics." *Rediscovering Aesthetics: Transdisciplinary Voices from Art History, Philosophy, and Art Practice*, edited by Francis Halsall, Julia Jansen, and Tony O'Connor, Stanford University Press, 2009, pp. 178–192.

Williams, Miller. Introduction. *Poems and Antipoems*, by Nicanor Parra, edited by Miller Williams, New Directions, 1967, pp. vii–ix.

Williams, Raymond. "Literature and Sociology." *Culture and Materialism*, by Raymond Williams. Verso, 2005, pp. 11–30.

Wood, David M. J. "Raiding the Archive: Documentary Appropriations of Mexican Revolution Footage." *Quarterly Review of Film and Video*, vol. 28, no. 4, 2011, pp. 275–291.

Zbikowski, Lawrence M. "Listening to Music." *Speaking of Music: Addressing the Sonorous*, edited by Keith Chapin and Andrew H. Clark, Fordham University Press, 2013, pp. 101–119.

Zea, Leopoldo. *Colonización y descolonización de la cultura latinoamericana*. Universidad Católica Andrés Bello, Ministerio de Educación, 1970.

INDEX

JUAN G. RAMOS is associate professor of Spanish at the College of the Holy Cross. He is coeditor of *Decolonial Approaches to Latin American Literatures and Cultures.*

www.ingramcontent.com/pod-product-compliance
Lightning Source LLC
Chambersburg PA
CBHW060806310726
48980CB00002B/255

* 9 7 8 1 6 8 3 4 0 0 2 4 0 *